## The Delaney Kids~
# Bought and Paid For

John Standridge

© 2009 Motherless Child Press

ISBN# 978-0-9842721-0-5

LCCN# 2009910221

All Rights Reserved Under
International and Pan-American Copyright Conventions.
No part of this book may be used or reproduced in any manner whatsoever without written permission except in the case of brief quotations embodied in critical articles or reviews.

To Paula Crippen Cope,
née Mary Elizabeth Delaney,
and
Jeffrey Dean Boyar,
né Marion Richard Delaney,
who found me and taught me.

# Table of Contents

Chapter 1
In the Beginning ............................................................. 1

Chapter 2
Stolen Babies ................................................................ 13

Chapter 3
Tennessee in the 1940s ................................................ 31

Chapter 4
Tennessee's Right to Know .......................................... 45

Chapter 5
The First Delaney Kids Reunion ................................. 53

Chapter 6
Mary Elizabeth Delaney .............................................. 65

Chapter 7
The Second Delaney Kids Reunion ............................. 75

Chapter 8
Marion Richard Delaney ............................................. 81

Chapter 9
Jerri Wayne Delaney ................................................. 100

Chapter 10
Our Time Together ................................................... 120

Chapter 11
The Events of September and October, 2006 ........... 127

CHAPTER 12
God and Job (Making Sense of Fate) ............................ 148

CHAPTER 13
I Am Becoming *Hibernicis Ipsis Hiberniores* ..................... 155

CHAPTER 14
Thoughts on God, Art, Music, and Enlightenment ...... 170

CHAPTER 15
Closure ........................................................................ 180

APPENDIX A –
First Contact: Letter and Emails ..................................... 187

APPENDIX B –
The Adoption Records and Other Documents ............. 213

APPENDIX C –
Photograph Album ...................................................... 263

APPENDIX D –
Genealogy ................................................................... 277

APPENDIX E –
Bibliography ................................................................ 325

## Acknowledgements

I would especially like to thank dear friends who read earlier versions of the manuscript and encouraged me – Paula and Carl Henderson, Susan Cotter, Kent Lee, and Tony and Linda Mines. My ego is more fragile than one might think and putting one's thoughts and self description out there is daunting. Without my friends' kind words and support I would not have found the courage to publish the Delaney Kids' story.

Thank you too goes to my wife, Lynna Ruth, for her tremendous efforts in compiling the genealogy records. Building on the materials presented by Paula Cope, Lynna Ruth has created a very complete and authoritative body of genealogy research. She also graciously answered my many mundane questions concerning grammar, word choice, spelling, and other details of wordsmithing; she is a patient and generous better-half.

Thank you is extended to James Douthat for his early preproduction assistance and for the suggestion to use "Bought and Paid For" in the title. Thanks go to Brenda Boyar for relating stories about her and Jeff. Finally I extend my sincere appreciation to all those friends and family who have stood by me through times of loss occurring beyond that of my brother and sister. Thank you for being there.

# Foreword
## John Standridge, A Delaney Kid

Family. One almost always hears the word "family" and then pauses for a moment as the memories and emotions flood. For some of us, the memories are a warm wrap that brings immediate comfort. Smells. Textures. Flashes of color. In less than ten seconds, we're back at Grandmother's house for a holiday dinner surrounded by the smells of cinnamon, nutmeg and allspice. We're cocooned in blanket, snuggling with Mom and listening intently as she reads a favorite story. For others, the memories strike a swift blow to the solar plexus, the heart begins to race and it feels as though all the blood has drained to the bottom of the feet. The memories are more confusing and the emotional distress causes physical discomfort.

For my friend, John, the word "family" encompasses the gambit of emotions. It's no surprise to those of us who know him as the master physician that he was the child prodigy who had the unconditional love and support of his parents, the Standridges. John, the artist, enjoyed the idyllic childhood surrounded by hazy morning fogs and brilliant evening sunsets while John, the gifted musician, was serenaded by the sounds of the countryside. Looking back, this almost perfect childhood propelled John toward his own almost perfect family life as an adult – a rewarding partnership and loving marriage to Lynna Ruth and the nurturing of his sons and grandchildren.

And, yet, there's another facet to John's childhood. As an adopted child, he knew there were biological parents out there "somewhere", but he was not consumed by the mystery of his birth. It was not until years later that he learned about his first family, the Delaneys. The story of that discovery forms the basis of his narrative.

John's story is unique and, yet, it is symbolic of the story of hundreds of other stolen children. As a friend, I was excited when his sister, Paula, found him and they began to reassemble the family. As a historian, I was intrigued by the Tennessee of the mid-20th century that allowed a woman like Georgia Tann to operate an "adoption" agency within the view of the courts. Through a combination of skillful deceit and masterful entrepreneurship, Georgia Tann earned a fortune plying on the social ills of those families who had fallen on hard times. Countless babies, toddlers and young children were offered for adoption to childless families whose circumstances were often examined no farther than to ascertain that funds were available for the "adoption". Some of those children like John were delivered into the arms of loving parents. Others were little more than pawns in a game that attempted to construct the perfect picture of a family. If that picture never developed clearly for the new parents, then love and affection were withheld and the emotional manipulation of the child began. The harsh reality was that these children had no control of the situation and many found themselves leaving deprived homes where love was present only to land in lush surroundings devoid of the true meaning of family.

Several years have passed and I have watched from a distance as John and his siblings found each other, loved each other and marveled at their "alikeness" in spite of their early separation. John's generous heart grew as he welcomed the extended members of his new family and that same generous heart grieved when his family was all too soon separated once again.

The story of the Delaney children is a universal story of family, love, acceptance and the unanswered questions that plague many relationships today. The story of Delaney children has the added poignancy of a modern legal drama that one might find touted in the evening news. In this case, the good news is that the Delaney children survived. The sad fact is that Georgia Tann was never held accountable for her crimes.

John Standridge's research unraveled much of the history of Tennessee's "stolen" children and his insightful rendering of his journey from only child to beloved baby brother offers a glimpse into the importance of family at any age. His story combines the best aspects of personal memory and unvarnished truths. It is a story that you will not quickly forget as you find yourself shifting between tears of joy, tears of sadness and tears of empathy. But John's greatest gift to his readers is a reminder that the human spirit is eternal. His positive nature remains unvanquished and the moments shared by the Delaney children enrich his life forever. His personal history is the history of mankind. We can – and the Delaney children did – overcome and persevere.

*Linda Moss Mines*
Chattanooga and Hamilton County, Tennessee Historian

## Chapter 1
# In the Beginning

*Sometimes I feel like a motherless child*
*Sometimes I feel like a motherless child*
*Sometimes I feel like a motherless child*
*Long way from my home*

*Sometimes I wish I could fly*
*Like a bird up in the sky*
*Oh, sometimes I wish I could fly*
*Fly like a bird up in the sky*
*Sometimes I wish I could fly*
*Like a bird up in the sky*
*Closer to my home*

*Motherless children have a hard time*
*Motherless children have-a such a hard time*
*Motherless children have such a really hard time*
*A long way from home*

*Sometimes I feel like freedom is near*
*Sometimes I feel like freedom is here*
*Sometimes I feel like freedom is so near*
*But we're so far from home*

– Southern Spiritual

I am the only one left to tell our story. So I shall tell it true and to the best of my ability.

The process of adoption can be a good thing for all parties or it can have many unintended consequences. Here is the story of three siblings whose fate was literally cast to the wind. The twists and turns of very different lives until their reunion fifty-some years later is a fascinating study of the human condition in the second half of the twentieth century in America. Mostly though, it is a good and dramatic story of lost and found, superficially, and loss and redemption, ultimately. This is the very personal story of the Delaney Kids.

It began for me 60 years ago when in November, 1948, I was born the third of three Delaney children – Marion Richard ("Dickie"), Mary Elizabeth ("Betty"), and me, Jerri Wayne ("baby Jerri") – who were soon to be scattered across the country. My brother and sister were sold to families in the Los Angeles area of southern California, not to know the whereabouts of each other for more than fifty years. I was adopted by John and Juanita Standridge who lived in rural southeast Tennessee.

It must have been a hard decision for our birth mother to give away her babies. My take on it is that our birth mother was emotionally unable to deal with a third child. She was separated from her husband and the two older children and she felt trapped. Her situation defined a "Catch-22" – a self-contradictory circular logic that creates a no-win predicament. She did not have enough money to care for a baby and taking care of the baby prevented her from getting a job and earning some money. Another phrase, less commonly used, is a Morton's Fork, a choice between two equally unpleasant alternatives. She was in otherwords between a rock and a hard place. But make no mistake about it. The adoption was as much about her comfort and security as it was about wanting a better life for her child. The decision to give away the two older children a year later, after she was remarried to then separated from a Mr. Mathis, was a similar dilemma, but still inexplicable to my way of thinking.

The social services worker implied more than once in my adoption record that our birth mother had problems accepting responsibilities. That and the fact that she and our birth father had married, divorced, remarried, and were heading for their final divorce further set the stage. Our birth mother was living with me and her mother in one room of a rooming house, while our birth father and my brother and sister were living with his mother about four miles away, all in what is now downtown Chattanooga. Our parents were 26 years old.

Our birth mother, Imogene Mae Clark Delaney (with the additional surnames Mathis, Boyd, Allen, and Aslinger to be added in the years to come), age 26 at the time of my adoption, was described as 5'1" tall, weight 92 pounds, dark brown hair and eyes. She is attractively pictured in Appendix C – Photograph Album. She was a member of the Baptist Church but was not active in church life. Although Imogene Delaney went only as far as the 7$^{th}$ grade in school, she reportedly gave the impression of having had more education. She had a good vocabulary and used words correctly according to social workers' documents.

Imogene's family history sheds some light on her limited coping skills. Her father, John L. Clark, died in 1922 from complications of a hernia operation. Growing up with no father figure can be an influence that causes a woman to seek support and affection from the men in her life to a greater extent than might otherwise be the case. That might help explain why she eventually became

Imogene Mae Clark Delaney Mathis Boyd Allen Aslinger. Her mother, the 68 year old Mary McJunkin Clark, was on the dole, receiving Old Age Assistance. This can create a certain mind set of entitlement among those who are state supported.

Imogene had six older sisters. Growing up with "seven mothers" might have seemed restrictive as a child who might be unable to get away with anything. Whether this was an influence that led her first husband to describe Imogene as "emotionally and morally immature" is subject for debate. One sister, Elizabeth Davis, age 47, had been in a mental institution in Silverdale, Tennessee, during the first three months of my life, the three months prior to my adoption, the "result of menopause". Perhaps Imogene feared that the stresses of raising me would tip her over the edge and place her in a mental institution with her sister. Her only brother, Bill Clark, age 49 at the time of my adoption, worked in an Alabama steel plant. Twenty-three years older than Imogene, Bill probably served as a surrogate father. Imogene had a brother-in-law who was a salesman at the Goodyear Store and who had given her some financial assistance.

Imogene claimed that her health had been ruined by having her children so close together and she claimed that her doctor said that she "should not have sexual relations" any time soon. She reportedly had a nervous breakdown during her pregnancy with me. She was unable to adjust sexually to a marriage with the father of her children. She said that she had such a fear of pregnancy that she did not believe she could ever "be a wife" again. She was fitted with a diaphragm by her doctor after Betty's birth but it was not successful and five months after Betty's birth she was pregnant with me. She may well have had a postpartum depressive illness. Her rejection of her husband was presumed; her later rejection of her children was obvious, and manifest by their adoption. This was our birth mother and her family.

Our birth father, Marion Henry Delaney, was born September 22, 1922, probably in Chattanooga. He was described as being handsome, 6'1" tall, and weighing 212 pounds. He had light brown curly hair, and brown or hazel eyes. He wore glasses. He completed high school. He gave the appearance of being stable and intelligent. Marion Delaney was described in the adoption records as a very handsome young man of 26 years of age. He was dressed in excellent taste, was polite, well mannered, and quiet. His occupations had been as bus and truck driver. He drove a truck for the Atlanta Constitution and quit that job for a position at the Southern Coach Lines driving a bus, a better paying job. He was a member of the Baptist Church. His father, Ralph Delaney, was an upholsterer. His mother was Elizabeth Jones Delaney. Marion Delaney was their first child. His parents were separated according to 1949 adoption records. The Delaneys and Joneses were early pioneering families who were among the more prominent merchants and land owners in the Chattanooga region. A chapter on the Jones family is featured in the book *Hamilton County Pioneers*, by John Wilson, describing the earliest settlers of the Chattanooga area (see Appendix E). The complete genealogy is provided in Appendix D. This was our birth father and his family.

Imogene Mae Clark and Marion H. Delaney were married November 24th, 1941, in Ringgold, Georgia. They were 19 years old. The waiting period was much shorter for marriage and the process was simpler across the state line from Chattanooga, Tennessee. When Dickie was seven months old, our birth parents divorced for the first time on May 26th, 1943, in Chattanooga. They were remarried on September 29th, 1943, in Rossville, Georgia. One possible explanation for such unstable and erratic behavior centers around Imogene's complaints that her husband drank and did not provide for her and the children like he should have. Imogene also felt that part of her marital difficulty could be blamed on "in-laws". Fear of sexual intercourse and pregnancy undoubtedly factored as well. She expressed antipathy to sexual contact with the father of her children. Given the difference in their sizes and that he may have, as she accused him in divorce proceedings, drunk alcohol to excess, the experience may well have been unpleasant for her.

Marion Richard Delaney (Dickie) was born on October 27, 1942. Little is known of his early development, although his birth mother said he was emotionally disturbed. Photographs of the young child suggest a different picture – one of a happy, smiling, good natured child. Dickie had to repeat the first grade because Imogene had moved their residence so often. The extent to which he was affected by the constant parental discord is not known.

Mary Elizabeth Delaney (Betty) was born September 18th, 1947, in Chattanooga, Tennessee, in Erlanger Hospital. She had a normal birth. A pediatrician gave her two immunization shots for diphtheria and tetanus in 1948 and recorded that she had whooping cough. Our birth mother related a vague history indicating numerous illnesses.

Jerri Wayne Delaney (Baby Jerri) was born November 21st, 1948, in Chattanooga, Tennessee, in Erlanger Hospital. He (I describe myself here in the third person) had a normal birth and was healthy with a good disposition. For the first few months, Mrs. Delaney, her mother and Jerri lived in one room of a rooming house at 815 McCallie Avenue in Chattanooga. The room was upstairs and was furnished with a bed, oil stove, a small table, and an old refrigerator. Imogene Delaney's mother, Mrs. Mary (McJunkin) Clark, at age 68 received an Old Age Assistance grant, and was thought to be too old to care for the child in the event that Imogene found employment. Unemployable as she was, Imogene undoubtedly felt trapped by her situation.

Jerri was described as a fine baby but was not getting certain things that he needed because Imogene did not have the money with which to buy them. Her husband, Marion Henry, provided her with $15 per week. Imogene did not have the money to take Jerri to the doctor, nor to buy cod-liver oil, baby goods, etc. that she thought he should be getting. She thought that it would always be that way. Believing that it would always be impossible to adequately support Jerri and give him the things every child needs was the reason Imogene articulated for deciding to give away her baby. "We could not give up the older children because they already know us but the baby will not know the difference," she said seriously. What she was saying seemed to indicate that she had deliberately arrived at this decision.

Imogene had the promise of employment at a new orange drink stand that was opening on Market Street in Chattanooga. She felt that if she did not have the responsibility of the baby and could get out and meet new people she would be able to regain her health more quickly. Staying at home and looking after Jerri had apparently made her very unhappy. Imogene felt that she was so mentally and physically run down that she could not be a good mother to her children. She considered that if she got to feeling better she might petition the courts in order to regain custody of her two older children after she obtained a divorce. Otherwise she would leave them with her husband and his people.

Jerri Wayne Delaney was given up for adoption on February 28$^{th}$, 1949. It was the birthday of his adoptive mother, Juanita Dees Standridge. Marion Delaney said he had seen Jerri only twice. The first time was on the occasion of his birth. When Jerri was born, Marion came to the hospital to see Imogene but she refused to see him. She later said that she knew it hurt him terribly but that her mental attitude was such that she could not bear the sight of him. Marion Delaney said he had seen Jerri only one more time since he was born and the way in which he said it led the adoption officials to believe that he had no feeling whatsoever for the child. At the time of the adoption, Imogene was already planning to divorce Marion Delaney for the second time. They were officially divorced on April 21$^{st}$, 1949, in Chattanooga.

After the divorce, Imogene moved about so often that Dickie had to repeat the first grade. A year later when Imogene applied to the Hamilton County Branch of the Tennessee Children's Home Society for the purpose of giving up Dickie and Betty, she stated that Dickie was repeating first grade because she had moved their residence. His report card from Sunnyside elementary school in Chattanooga for 1949-50 verifies his satisfactory progress in the first grade. At the time Dickie was released for adoption he was repeating the first grade of school at H. Clay Evans. Prior to their placement in California, Dickie and Betty had lived with both grandmothers; and after their parent's second divorce, in the autumn of 1949, they had

## In the Beginning

been placed for three months in the Vine Street Orphanage. Happy birthday, children!

Imogene Delaney married a Mr. Mathis whom she had left by March 1950. Little is known about Mr. Mathis other then he had one arm. It is unlikely that it was he who placed the children in the Vine Street Orphanage. Recall that it was our birth father that had custody of the two older children when Imogene placed me for adoption. More likely it was a recently remarried Marion Henry Delaney (both he and his second wife were gainfully employed) who placed them. It was likely that it was Mr. Mathis who helped get the children out of the orphanage. After Imogene was married to Mr. Mathis the Court modified the alimony decree December 19th, 1949, so as to give Imogene custody of Dickie and Betty and reduce the alimony to $6.00 per week. Imogene thought Mr. Mathis would make a good home for them, but this marriage failed too, after a few months, and she was again unable to make a home for the children. She, her children, and her mother were then living in a basement apartment on West 5th Street. Imogene was working part time at a dress shop but her earnings together with the alimony were not adequate to provide a decent home for the children. Marion related that Imogene's physical and mental condition made it necessary for him to take the two older children to his mother's. The sequence and dates of their stay with relatives is not recorded, but it remains that no one in this large extended family was willing to take on the upbringing of these children.

The extent to which Dickie and Betty were affected by parental discord is not known. Our birth mother described Dickie as emotionally disturbed and Betty prior to the time of surrender as emotionally upset. Dickie was old enough to remember living with both grandmothers and with various relatives. He remembered poor treatment and horrible food at the Vine Street Orphanage. He also remembered holding hands with Betty at the Vine Street Orphanage. I can imagine that the children knew even then, that all they each had in terms of a loving caring family, was each other.

Marion Delaney had become so involved in debt that it became necessary for him to declare bankruptcy. He gave as the reason medical bills and court costs which his wife had caused. He resided with his mother at 2809 East 47th St. in Chattanooga. He had been employed for the 16 months prior to the adoption of the older children as a bus driver for the Southern Coach Lines. Although he had a good job and made a fairly good salary, he could not keep up two homes.

Marion indicated that he knew the children were not being properly cared for but that it would be impossible for him to assume the responsibility for them at the time. He indicated that he was very happily remarried. His new wife was employed, and he was earning $30.00 per week driving a truck for Merten's Dry Cleaners. If he accepted custody of the children again he felt they would have to place them in the Vine Street Orphanage again. Imogene said she would never consent for Marion to have custody of the children again because she knew he would place them in the orphanage. Marion Delaney said that Imogene had cost him his good job at the Southern Coach Lines, kept him upset all the time, and forced him to pay attorney's fees and court costs numerous times. He expressed the concern that if he took the children and employed someone to look after them during the day, their mother would never cease to interfere. He went on to say that she was emotionally and morally immature, and actually not fit to have the care of the children.

Imogene Mathis indicated that her former husband probably would not consent to releasing the children to be adopted. Marion Delaney explicitly said to the social worker involved in the case that he would never consent to releasing the children for adoption.

Our birth mother, now Mrs. Mathis, apparently brought some action against our birth father, Mr. Delaney, to affect the transfer of Dickie and Betty to the Tennessee Children's Home Society. Since there is no copy of her petition we do not know precisely what pleading was made. There is no copy of a document approving the placing of the children with the Tennessee Children's Home Society for adoption placement. The court order indicated that Mr. Delaney agreed to this placement. The court, however, in making its order made reference only to the removal of custody from the petitioner, Imogene Mathis. It did not indicate in its order that custody of the children was also taken from Mr. Delaney. Legally, the court documents never eliminated Marion Delaney's parental rights by actual court decree. Regardless, only three months after regaining custody of her two remaining children, Imogene rid herself of them permanently. Without an appointment, on March 15$^{th}$, 1950, she walked in unannounced to the office of the same social worker who had been so helpful the year before and asked, "Do you remember me?" How sociable everyone was in 1950. There was the minor problem of a father who was willing to place his children in an orphanage, perhaps as a temporary measure, but was not willing to have them permanently placed for adoption. This was no major obstacle for an agency running low on children at a time when demand was robust and business was good.

The court system was compliant, the machinery was well oiled, and justice was swift. The civil and legal processes of the surrender of Dickie and Betty took a mere eight days to complete; the date was March 23, 1950. As a footnote, Marion Delaney's new wife, Mary Joy Ridge Delaney, to whom he was very happily married, died at the age of 32, on August 24th of that same year.

The irregularity of the father not having been named in the court order removing custody and not having signed documents surrendering the children is exactly the type of abuses typical of the Tennessee Children's Home Society during the scandalous Georgia Tann era. In a similar action in other parts of the country, he would have been named and there would be documents with his signature. As it was, the Delaney children joined the ranks of thousands of other children from disadvantaged homes who were sold to more affluent families. Under the collusive consent and auspices of judges in the Tennessee court system and officials with the Tennessee Children's Home Society, children were sold under quasi-legal pretext, usually to a market of eager families in the Los Angeles region.

The adoption records and other documents are gathered together in Appendix B. They represent an amazingly detailed accounting of the legal and judicial process of extracting children from their birth families, ostensibly with good intentions, and resettling them with adoptive families, gambling on an uncertain fate, an unknowable outcome. The aspect of stealing and selling children was just a sidebar. The documents seem cold and impersonal at times; to the Delaney kids they were cold but quite personal.

## Chapter 2
# Stolen Babies

Throughout the 1940s, Georgia Tann, the charismatic head of a local adoption agency, became a millionaire running a black-market baby ring behind the Tennessee Children's Home Society. Among the earliest exposés of this travesty was an episode of the television show *Unsolved Mysteries* which aired in 1990. An article titled, "The Woman Who Stole 5000 Babies", by Barbara Bisantz Raymond, appeared in *Good Housekeeping* in March, 1991, revealing to the country the heartache and misery wrought by Ms. Tann. A program on 60 Minutes and a docudrama, the made-for-cable *Stolen Babies*, which first aired March 25, 1993, over the Lifetime Cable service, were follow-up fact-based stories of the supposed "angel of mercy". Mary Tyler

Moore was cast as "the purse-lipped, bespectacled, quietly sinister" Georgia Tann in the *Stolen Babies* docudrama. It came as no surprise when Ms. Moore won an Emmy award for her chilling performance.

From the mid-1920's throughout the 1940s, Ms. Tann oversaw the adoption of children from her Tennessee orphanage. Since as the superintendent of the Shelby County Division of the Tennessee Children's Home Society, she was considered a pillar of the community, few questioned Tann's methods. As her power grew under the protection and endorsement of the politically powerful Memphis mayor, "Boss Crump", no one *dared* to challenge Tann's methods after questions of irregularities did surface. Tann organized the Tennessee Children's Home Society in Memphis to remove children from the slums and put them into the hands of the rich, who would educate them. She took children out of hospitals, homes, parks, anywhere she could find a poorly dressed or dirty child.

One story, told in exposé terms by Barbara Bisantz Raymond, involves Alma Stipple. In July 1945, Ms. Stipple was living with her two young children in a one-room apartment in Memphis, Tennessee. Georgia Tann, in her role as director of a respected local adoption agency, had called on Alma to ask about a case of possible child abuse involving a neighbor. Georgia Tann had now returned unexpectedly to Alma's apartment "just to chat". Georgia had seen the impoverished children and was stalking them like a lioness.

Alma was an unemployed waitress. She had little if any in the way of savings. She was divorced and ill-educated. Georgia, authoritative and clearly knowledgeable when it came to children, directed her attention to Alma's

10-month-old baby, Irma, and said with heartfelt concern, "She's sick – she should see a doctor."

Alma was terrified. She had assumed her active, happy daughter's runny nose was due to her teething. If it were something more serious, Alma and her daughter were in a terrible bind. "I can't afford a doctor," she said hesitantly.

With cunning instincts Georgia pounced, "I can get her treated for free at the hospital. We'll just pretend she's one of my wards." Georgia told Alma she would not be permitted to accompany her daughter to the hospital or visit her there. "If they know you're her mother, they won't treat her," she explained conspiratorially. Then, with a reassuring smile, she scooped up Irma and departed. Alma would never see her baby again.

A few days later, Georgia called Alma to say that Irma had developed pneumonia and died. Alma begged to see her daughter one last time, but was told that the state had "put away" the baby's remains. At Georgia's adoption agency, the Shelby County Division of the Tennessee Children's Home Society, Alma could get no further than the receptionist. "The case is closed," she was told. When Alma reported the incident to the Memphis police, indicating that her child had hardly been sick, she was dismissed as an hysterical mother who just couldn't accept reality.

In their turn, waves of grief and frustration and alcohol abuse congealed into a form of learned helplessness. Alma moved with her older child to be near her mother in Covington, Ky. Eventually, she stopped drinking, remarried, and had more children, but the grief and frustration and hope never died.

In fact, Irma *was* alive and living just a few miles away, across the Ohio River in Cincinnati. Irma's new name was Sandra and she was being raised by loving parents who believed they'd legally adopted their adorable blonde, green-eyed daughter. They had, in reality, been unwitting co-conspirators with Georgia Tann in stealing this child.

I have shared the details of this unrelated family to demonstrate how our story – the Delaney children – is not unique. Dickie grieved in frustration and hope for Betty, while for years they were raised only a few miles from each other in Los Angeles. Georgia Tann, one of America's foremost adoption experts in the 1940s, was in reality a ruthless kidnapper who stole and sold more than 5,000 babies. Our Delaney children story was repeated far too often. Babies were literally being stolen off of front porches.

How could Georgia Tann become such a monster? Again Barbara Bisantz Raymond, herself an adoptive mother and undoubtedly America's foremost expert historian with respect to Georgia Tann, informs us. Her extensively researched volume is titled, *The Baby Thief: The Untold Story of Georgia Tann, the Baby Seller Who Corrupted Adoption*. Barbara Raymond's investigation took her to a very xenophobic part of Georgia Tann's home state of Mississippi. Her attempts to interview locals who could give first hand reports of the Tanns were met with suspicion, intimidation, and threat of bodily harm. Deeper digging was required to discover what motivated Georgia's need to steal babies.

Georgia enjoyed a charmed upbringing. Her mother, Beulah Yates Tann, was from a prominent Philadelphia, Mississippi, family – a frontier lineage with deep roots.

My, what a small world! My adoptive mother, Juanita Dees Standridge, was from a prominent Philadelphia, Mississippi, family – a frontier lineage with deep roots that at one time owned thousands of acres of antebellum farm land. My maternal grandmother, Mae Crawford (Mama) Dees, might have enjoyed tea with Beulah.

George C. Tann, Geogia's father, had a truly distinguished lineage. George's grandfather served at the battle of Tippecanoe with William Henry Harrison. George's father was a Confederate war hero, and George, the most highly educated man in the region, was judge of the Mississippi Second Chancery District Court. An arrogant, argumentative and domineering womanizer, George may have been respected, but he was not liked. He was an emotionally cold father. Stern and insensitive, George may have wanted a son. He almost had one in Georgia, who was never interested in marriage, but was described as having a wide brow and low set ears, like George, and as being big-boned, broad-shouldered, and generally masculine.

George's chancery court was given the responsibility for homeless children. Asylums and workhouses were poor alternatives in an area that lacked orphanages. Frustrated by his lack of options, George even adopted one son, Rob Roy Tann. Rob Roy may have turned into Beulah's favorite child, but Georgia was Daddy's girl.

Every child seeks to curry favor and affection. When parents lack the ability to show affection, children sometimes look for ways to receive praise or attention. George was frustrated by his lack of options concerning the disposition of homeless children, and Georgia liked to arrange adoptions. When she was just a teenager, she found a home for two orphans she encountered in the court of her father, the judge. The adoptive family was wealthy. Because Judge George forbade Georgia to enter the legal profession to which she aspired, her only remaining courses, suitable for the proper young Southern woman, were teaching and social work. Georgia chose the latter, and after applying herself to the study of social work at Columbia University in New York, she arrived in Memphis in 1924 at the age of 33. In Memphis she headed the newly established Shelby County Branch of the Tennessee Children's Home Society, which was headquartered in Nashville.

Initially she operated legitimately, placing children who had been legally surrendered by their parents with adoptive families in Tennessee exactly as was her mandate. She derived much satisfaction from her work and it matched her aristocratic world view. The birth parents of the children she placed were usually poor, the adoptive families comparatively rich. Like many people at the time, she believed that wealthy people were harder working and more worthy than poor people. She honestly felt that the wealthy families deserved the beautiful babies they received. It is likely that, in part because Georgia herself was childless, she felt that the poor families did not deserve to keep their own babies. Tennessee was a relatively poor state: plenty of poor babies, not so many wealthy families. Georgia soon realized that more wealthy people were to be found elsewhere. California was a virtual gold mine in the minds of a nation that had witnessed the dust bowl migration and was seeing glamour in the Hollywood films. It dawned on her that she could become wealthy too. She in fact could do quite well while "doing good" with her own brand of social engineering.

Georgia's only fixed expense was the $7 Tennessee adoption fee which had to be deposited in the Children's

Home Society treasury. A child shipped to California or New York could fetch $750 or more in home investigation, transportation, and adoption fees. These monies, too, would have to go to the Children's Home Society, but economies of scale meant that if she shipped seven babies at a time, and made it appear that only one baby accompanied by an aide was making the trip, she could charge transportation and adoption fees seven times over. This is what she started to do. She put the money from one transportation and adoption fee in the Children's Home Society treasury and kept the rest for personal gain.

Georgia began marketing her young wards in earnest. To increase demand outside of Tennessee, Georgia distributed booklets featuring pictures of her Memphis Home, a former mansion at 1556 Poplar Street. She persuaded a reporter friend to write an article titled *A Baby for Christmas* for a Memphis newspaper. The story, accompanied by pictures of an adorable girl with ringlets in her hair, was picked up by the wire services. Soon newspapers across the country were unwittingly engaged in Georgia Tann's campaign.

Before long, Georgia was sending children throughout the country, but especially to cities like New York and Los Angeles. There were many couples seeking to adopt: there were many prosperous couples who could meet her price. Her adoptions went through so fast because she asked so few questions of prospective parents. Many couples found they could mail her a signed form stating, "I'd like to adopt a baby," and receive a child practically on the next plane.

Georgia encouraged couples to tell her in detail exactly what kind of child they wanted. She provided a match for the desired characteristics when she could and made the adoptive parents either believe they were getting a match or made them happy with who was available when she didn't have a match at the time. She definitely aimed to please her customers. She encouraged them to refer their childless friends and relatives. Routine requests, such as for a girl with blonde hair and blue eyes, were easily met. More difficult orders – such as for a baby with "a musical background" or one who had "college-educated parents" – were dealt with by lying. She would describe the child of a tenant farmer as the daughter of a debutante. Protestant babies, such as Dickie (my brother Jeff), were passed off as Jewish. And Georgia wasn't above selling the same baby more than once. When Georgia advertised the "Baby for Christmas", she met the heightened demand by providing several sets of adoptive parents with adopted look-alikes. The adoptive parents believed that they had gotten the one baby who was advertised, but in reality, all but one couple had the next closest appearing baby in Georgia's dwindling inventory.

Georgia was a highly competent self-promoting artist. Her marketing skills created a demand for her babies that soon outstripped her supply. Just imagine her success if she could have commanded today's technologies and media. She tackled her supply problem by expanding operations. She contacted doctors in Arkansas, Mississippi, Missouri, and Kentucky. By offering to pay the hospital expenses of any unwed mother who would come to Memphis to have her baby, she attracted many ill-advised and desperate young women. They usually accepted the offer when they were told that after the delivery Georgia would keep the baby for 30 days while the mother decided whether she wanted to keep her child. The reality was that while the mothers were still half-anesthetized from a mixture of morphine and scopolamine – a mixture preferred by doctors of that era for routine childbirth because of the amnesia it produced – Georgia would have the mothers sign what she called "routine papers." Later, when the young women tried to claim their infants they would discover to their horror that they had signed papers that relinquished their baby. Their babies had already been placed with adoptive parents: their babies were gone. Desperate and distraught young women who dared to dispute this treatment were threatened with exposure as unwed mothers. The shame that these young and poor women had experienced to this point was enormous. The public humiliation that lay ahead was cumulative and seemed unbearable. The women soon realized Georgia was too strong; they couldn't fight her.

Tactics of threats and intimidation did not stop there. Georgia also blackmailed adoptive parents who dared to question her high fees. They might be told, "Your son's birth mother called last week. Should I tell her where he is?" The pattern was that the adoptive parents generally quickly paid up rather than face the wrath, indignation, and potential legal challenge from a mother fighting for her true child. Doubtlessly some of these adoptive parents had some suspicion that the transaction was shady. After all, the unusually large fee she charged them – $1,500 and up – was not typical of a state agency. If threats failed she often punished a couple who wouldn't pay by not finalizing their adoption process. Then, after a year, she could take back their baby to sell to someone else.

Though she usually bought silence through coercion and threats, some birth and adoptive parents did complain about her to the police, judges, and the welfare department. Nothing was ever done about her because she had some very important friends. One of these was the then-well-known E. H. "Boss" Crump, a power broker who controlled one of the most efficient political machines in the country and could deliver 95 percent of the local vote to the candidate of his choice. The other ally Georgia had was the *zeitgeist* – a German word, literally time spirit, that referred to the mood and morays of a time in history. Post-depression era Tennessee was a time and place all to itself. The next chapter seeks to help us understand why doctors, attorneys, state agencies and judges would seemingly conspire to rip children from their impoverished birth mothers and, with hushed conspiratorial fervor, seek to place them in a setting of security. No one knew at the time if the Great Depression hunger would return with an even greater vengeance.

Most Memphis political figures were fiercely loyal to Boss Crump. They had been appointed by him and they served at his pleasure. They dared not question the behavior of his friends. Birth mothers who went to court to try to recover their children found their cases summarily dismissed for "lack of evidence."

Georgia Tann was clever and careful enough to cover her tracks as long as no one looked too closely. In 1941 she obtained a charter of incorporation for another institution, separate from the Tennessee Children's Home Society. If there was ever any doubt about how much of her behavior was well-intentioned and to what extent she was a criminal con artist, all bets were now off. On paper and in her closely guarded books, she was now the director of two institutions. Georgia Tann was now able to receive children through one institution and dispose of them through the other. Now no one could track exactly how many children she was placing, or with whom. The checks flowed faster than ever into her private Memphis post office box.

Georgia Tann lived a privileged life since birth. During the 1940s, she had accumulated more than $1 million (at least $10s of millions by today's standards) from stealing and selling babies in the guise of adoptions. She bought property in Mississippi; she purchased a West Coast hotel, and a 25-acre Memphis estate, where peacocks strolled around her carefully tended lawns. She made frequent gambling excursions to Cuba. She bought two limousines, therefore she needed a chauffeur. In order to maintain appearances, she had him drop her off each work morning at a bus stop near the Memphis Tennessee Children's Home Society. Then Georgia would walk to work from the bus stop, like a normal social worker – just another dedicated public servant.

She never married and never demonstrated interest in men. At one point she adopted a "sister", a woman one year younger than she. Later she adopted a daughter, June, whom she dominated and treated sternly. June eventually married a man and, of course, Georgia disapproved of the marriage and clearly didn't like the husband. To express her distaste, she tore up all of June's clothing. Later however, to express her forgiveness, when June later suffered a miscarriage, Georgia gifted her with an adoptive child.

Nationally, Georgia Tann's fame as a legitimate adoption expert grew. In speeches across the country she stressed the importance of adopting only through recognized agencies and railed against the very black-market adoption operations that she herself had perfected. Georgia's fame and self promotion were highly successful. More people than ever wanted to adopt her babies. So many wanted to adopt that, even with the babies she stole locally and the contacts from surrounding states, she was running out of "product." She would have run out, in fact, if it were not for her good friend and co-conspirator, Judge Camille Kelley.

Camille Kelley was a Shelby County Juvenile Court judge during the years Georgia's Memphis Home was in operation. Like Georgia, she had a sterling reputation and she also had a dark side: She supplied Georgia Tann with approximately 1, 000 of the more than 5, 000 children she placed.

Judge Kelley accomplished this by having an informant in the Welfare Department. Her informant would ask parents who were applying for financial assistance the names and ages of their children, and he'd then relay this information to Judge Kelley. She in turn would order the removal of the youngest of the children because of a "poor home environment." A quick court proceeding would then result in the child being declared a ward of the state. Throughout the proceeding Georgia Tann would often be seated in the back of the courtroom like a predatory lioness with her eyes fixed on her future ward. It may be hard to imagine today, but Georgia Tann and Camille Kelley positively terrified Shelby County families in the '30s and '40s.

The children seized by Camille Kelley were among the most tragic of all those sold by Georgia Tann. At ages usually between two and eight, they were, like Betty and Dickie, old enough to remember and grieve for their parents. Georgia also routinely split up siblings, as she did my brother and sister, and would tell adoptive parents they were getting an only child. If the children told their adoptive parents the truth about their real mother, father, and siblings, Georgia would explain that they must be confused because of the time that they had spent in an orphanage or foster home before being adopted.

It's impossible to conceive of these children's suffering, as well as the very real culture shock they went through. These children were born, typically, to uneducated parents. Their lives were abruptly disrupted. They were dislocated in an orphanage briefly and then they suddenly found themselves with adoptive parents who were professionals, college professors, or movie stars, like Joan Crawford for example. High achieving parents expected what they had paid for and what Georgia Tann had promised – a child with "musical ability" or "a gift for math," or "very bright." At best, many of these children grew up with a terrible feeling of never being able to measure up. At worst, they were utterly rejected. This was totally the case with Dickie – my brother Jeff.

Some of the children were returned several times to Georgia Tann to undergo these disruptions over and over again. Some were given up by their adoptive parents and handed over to the custody of Juvenile Courts hundreds of miles from the state of their birth. Some children were placed with alcoholics; some in abusive homes. Some, like my brother Jeff, were placed in verbally and physically abusive homes only to be abandoned to the cruel indifference of the streets.

In addition, there are children, now adults, who remember being abused in Georgia Tann's care. One former resident of her home remembers that children who did not finish their oatmeal for breakfast got it served again, cold, at dinner. Another recalls having to stand barefoot, for hours, on tiptoe, with her nose pressed against a circle drawn on a blackboard – if she faltered, she was warned, she would be beaten.

Though local pediatricians were assigned to Georgia Tann's Home, none fully investigated her operations. Therefore they could not have understood what she was doing, but all were appalled by what they did know. At least four pediatricians resigned their position as her "baby doctor," citing numerous problems: the frequent drunkenness of a Home worker; Georgia's insistence upon taking babies from the hospital when they were only an hour old; her giving some infants medication against doctors' orders; and her refusal to give others medicine doctors had prescribed, among other grievances. Despite a physician's warning, she shipped desperately sick babies across the country – one infant died two days after reaching its adoptive home in New Jersey.

A Dr. Clyde Croswell warned Georgia not to continue to bring children into the Home during a 1945 epidemic of diarrhea. She coldly ignored the pediatrician's warnings and more than 40 babies died. "There were lots of deaths no one knew about. Even the Board of Health didn't know," Dr. Croswell wrote in 1945. He himself didn't know the exact numbers and, at that time, he was the doctor who should have been signing the death certificates. Georgia, however, didn't always bother with death certificates, or even funerals. She dealt with a local crematorium. The babies just disappeared.

Cruelest of all was the plight of the parents who *knew* that their babies had been stolen by Georgia Tann. Despite their knowledge of how they were wronged, they still did not recover their children. Some tried, but it took years for a case to come to trial. By the time it did, the courts often regarded "the [birth] mother as a stranger," as one presiding judge put it. He left them in their present "good American homes," despite the tearful pleas of their mother.

More than 5, 000 children were separated from 10, 000 birth parents and countless siblings by Georgia Tann. Her methods may have been well-intentioned initially, but as huge profits mounted, she turned the system into outright baby trafficking with little regard to what kind of person the purchaser was. Tann was accused of fraudulently persuading pregnant mothers to relinquish their children. She in fact became a notorious dealer in black-market babies, literally stealing infants – mostly from poor single mothers – and selling them to wealthy patrons. A number of Hollywood celebrities adopted children through the home, namely Joan Crawford (remember the "Mommie Dearest" baby?), June Allyson, and Dick Powell.

Georgia Tann took babies from desperate families looking for temporary assistance and had them sign away their rights without them even knowing that they were doing so. Ms. Tann lied to large numbers of the birth parents and told them their babies died. Couples who had large quantities of money ($5, 000 or more was a lot in the 1940s) were given the babies. Exchanges were made in empty fields and other places that would allow no witnesses. Many of these babies placed for adoption were taken from their birth mothers without the mother even knowing that her baby was still alive. New mothers would be told by Ms. Tann and the doctor that the baby was stillborn or had died of pneumonia. Ms. Tann would then ask the mother to sign papers that would allow for her to make arrangements for a proper burial for the infant. In reality, however, the mother would be signing forms giving custody of the child to the Tennessee Children's Home Society. Growing old and physically (as well as emotionally) very ill, Ms. Tann destroyed most of her records before she died.

Only when dedicated social worker Anne Beals began stripping away Georgia Tann's veneer of respectability did a terrible truth come to light. During the investigation, local attorneys and justices were found to be part of the scandalous network of black market adoption. Details of the culture and politics, the corruption, investigation, and exposure are presented in the next chapter. In 1950, the newly elected Governor of Tennessee, Gordon Browning, called for an investigation of the Tennessee Children's Home Society's illegal baby adoption operations. Georgia Tann left behind a legacy of hate, broken families, stress, disease and death that would have put her in prison if she hadn't died before the Tennessee Attorney General could divulge the outcome of his investigation. Ms. Tann's death in 1950 from cancer prevented not only her exposure as a criminal during her lifetime, but also any in-depth probing of her deeper motives. Could it be that this childless woman held an envious loathing, not only for the mothers she victimized, but also for the children who represented the one thing her fortune could not grant her?

The story is dramatic and shows southern politics at its worst – congenial, respected public figures running shady deals in the back room. Thousands of children were uprooted, often literally stolen, and placed in adopted homes during the agency's operation. Each case is a fascinating story: sometimes involving the search and reunion of adopted children with their natural families, and sometimes involving a life made hollow by tragic loss and never set straight.

In the case of the Delaney children, despite adoption documents that indicate that our birth father *said* that he would agree to the adoption and that it would be in Dickie and Betty's best interest, there is no proof that he ever signed any documents relinquishing the children. In fact there was significant difficulty finalizing both adoptions in California because of improper documentation. As one example, the court proceedings in Tennessee named our birth mother as the only party to the adoption and failed to contain language that stated that our birth father agreed to the adoption. That was highly irregular.

The Delaney children – Dickie, Betty, and baby Jerri – represent but one such story. Our birth mother was poor and divorced. Our birth father, though poor, was gainfully employed, remarried, and said repeatedly that he would never relinquish Dickie and Betty for adoption, in contrast to what the adoption paperwork says. He re-iterated this stance years later to my sister Paula (Betty) prior to his death. Nevertheless, they were taken and sold to Los Angeles area couples who were better off financially.

In Chattanooga where I now live, there are billboards along the highways displaying beautiful, smiling, perfect, white, chubby, three month old babies with a caption that asks, "WANT ONE?" Another billboard, advertising yet another fertility clinic, carries a similar message: "There's hope". Effective fertility treatments were not an option in Los Angeles in 1950. Adoption, however, *was* an option. If Georgia Tann could be marketing her babies today, one can only wonder at the prices she could charge and the devises she could bring to bear to promote her wares. The emotional tug on a childless couple's heartstrings is powerful enough; but combine this emotion with social rewards and approval for having and raising children, pressure from parents wanting to be grandparents, the knowledge that friends and neighbors are adopting children, and the ease and convenience of having the baby packaged neatly and legally enough and brought to your home, and it is little wonder that demand exceeded supply. The whole arrangement became irresistible, even without the mass media marketing that is so prevalent today. One can further project that many couples in Los Angeles at that point in time were searching for the Promised Land there in the Golden state. The promise of prosperity might seem empty without the other accoutrements of the American Dream. Georgia Tann certainly filled a need if not a void at a point and time in American history when all things seemed possible and, because living standards were rising rapidly, the *potential* life style ideals were yet to be established.

CHAPTER 3
# Tennessee in the 1940s

What was Tennessee society and government like in the 1940s that could account for not only Georgia Tann's brazen behavior but also the assistance she received from doctors, attorneys, and justices? The courts and the state bureaucracy clearly facilitated Tann's efforts to redistribute children. The local power structure granted her a certain level of immunity that was undoubtedly a spillover from the underlying corruption that was imbedded in political machinery. Tennessee history reveals the perfect setting for Tann's ambition and opportunism.

One must consider first that Tennessee, like most of the Deep South, had never fully recovered from the reconstruction era that followed the Civil War. The poverty of a defeated people not only lasted for generations, but encompassed beyond the material poverty and into the realms of spirit and pride. A resignation of powerlessness allows corrupt political bosses to fill the void. Good people everywhere understood that things were as they were and they had no choice but to accept the system. A conquered people accept that, indeed, might makes right.

Even the state's constitution contributed to the political quagmire. An editorial in the Washington Post recognized in November 7, 1949, the embedded difficulties facing the citizens of Tennessee.

> "The people of Tennessee are living under a rigid constitution adopted 79 years ago and not since amended. The dangers inherent in such ironclad legalism have often been demonstrated through the State's unsuccessful efforts to get rid of the poll tax, which is embedded in its basic law. So difficult is the amending process under this post-Civil War constitution that an effort is at last being made to assemble a limited constitutional convention."

Let us focus now on the West Tennessee region and Memphis. With broad expanses of Mississippi River bottom land for farming and a huge river for transportation, West Tennessee was the planters' region of Tennessee. Cotton, soybeans, corn and other row crops thrived in the powdery topsoil of West Tennessee. Memphis – home of the Memphis Cotton Exchange and the Cotton Carnival – was a major market for buying and selling crops. Memphis was a river city driven by racial mistrust, and all of West Tennessee still bore the scars and legacies of slavery. More than any other part of the state, West Tennessee belonged to the cotton south of Mississippi, Alabama, Georgia and South Carolina.

> *You want to be my man,*
> *You gotta give me forty dollars down.*
> *If you don't be my man,*
> *Your baby's gonna shake this town.*

W.C. Handy wrote what came to be known as "The Memphis Blues" in 1909. The song was originally titled "Mr. Crump" and penned for Memphis political boss Edward Hull Crump's mayoral campaign. Crump won that 1909 mayor's race and served two terms, but his influence was felt for almost 40 years. He could deliver upwards of 50, 000 votes – including black votes – to his handpicked candidates.

Edward Crump came to Memphis in 1893 at age 18 from Holly Springs, Mississippi, with 25 cents in his pocket. He had dropped out of school at fourteen and after working at a variety of jobs he took a course in bookkeeping and was able to advance from clerical jobs to a managerial position. He joined social clubs and at age 27 he married the daughter of a socially prominent family. His wife's family provided him with the funds to buy out his employer and go into politics. Tennesseans could appreciate Ed Crump's rags to riches story. The people could internalize some hope for themselves that if Crump could go from poverty to power, then why couldn't they or their children. Today a neighbor, or more likely a stranger on the local newscast, is paraded as the latest winner of the lottery, and the people gain hope that next time it might be them. Lottery ticket sales continue to reflect social hope for a better life, rather than a tax on those who cannot do math. So it was with the acceptance of and occasional admiration for Boss Crump. He gave the people individual hope and social progress, rather than a tax on those who could not smell corruption.

> Mr. Crump won't allow no easy-riders here,
> Mr. Crump won't allow no easy-riders here,
> I don't care what Mr. Crump won't allow,
> I'm gonna barrelhouse anyhow.
> Mr. Crump can go and catch hisself some air.
>
> – W.C. HANDY

In 1909 there was a poll tax of $2 that discouraged many people from voting. Many black people could not vote in the South. In Memphis, which was 40 percent black, blacks did vote because it served the interest of the White politicians to have a substantial black vote they could control. The White politicians bought blocks of poll tax receipts which they provided to the black voters with instructions of how to vote. In return for their efforts, black voters received barbeque, Coca Cola, whisky and watermelons.

Boss Crump was a Memphis legend. Like most of the South, Tennessee was a Democrat stronghold after the reconstruction era. In the 1940s, Tennessee politics was dominated by regional political machines, and the king of them all was Ed "Boss" Crump of Memphis. The Crump machine was the equivalent of Tammany Hall in New York City or the Daley machine of Chicago in its ability to deliver patronage and votes. Allied with other political bosses, Boss Crump could control most statewide offices. A key to the power of the Crump machine was an unholy alliance with East Tennessee Republicans led by 1st District Congressman B. Carroll Reece. The essence of the deal was that the Republicans would cede statewide power to Crump and the Memphis boss wouldn't mess in East Tennessee politics and patronage. Seats in the Tennessee Legislature had not been reapportioned to reflect Census trends since the early part of the 20th century. This gave Democrats, who have controlled the Legislature from Reconstruction until today, an advantage in everything partisan.

Time magazine wrote in 1936 that Boss Crump "controls all offices in Tennessee's largest city." In 1945, Time wrote, "Crump has bossed Memphis so long (36 years) that many Memphians hardly know they are being bossed."

With Georgia Tann's dominating personality and eagerness to inform Boss Crump about anyone who threatened his (and with it, her) power, Georgia was soon as powerful and feared locally as Crump himself. Those who promoted legislation that sought to reform adoption practices were of particular interest as targets of the Crump/Tann political machinery. Though Georgia Tann's wiliness and political connections offered her significant protection throughout the 1940s, word of her wrongdoing was leaking out. As early as 1941, the Tennessee Children's Home Society was drummed out of the respected Child Welfare League of America for "major weaknesses". The citations included "failure to perform important duties" of home investigation and "the advertisement of particular children for adoption."

In 1946 Probate Court Judge Samuel O. Bates, one of the most respected jurists in Tennessee, manually typed a single-spaced, six-page letter to the Commissioner of Public Welfare, complaining about Georgia Tann's Home and calling for action. Nothing more than a superficial, in-house investigation was ordered, however, and naturally this quickly cleared Georgia of all charges. Judge Bates was incensed by her blatant misconduct and especially by her apparent immunity from justice. He responded by refusing to approve any more adoptions, but Georgia Tann responded to this by making her operation even more secret.

When some local residents had noticed and confronted one of her baby couriers at the airport with two children, Georgia became anxious to avoid any further such incidents. She began booking 3 a.m. flights for her babies being shipped out for adoption. Additionally, to escape Judge Bates' wrath and scrutiny, she began pressing her adoptions through the courts in small rural counties, where few questions were asked.

By 1946 discovery was becoming inevitable. Georgia had acquired and "placed" over 5, 000 children. She was becoming ill with cancer, yet despite her illness and despite the growing numbers of people wondering about operations of the tree-shrouded Home at 1556 Poplar Street, she continued her operations over the next few years.

Political change and reform were coming. The war was won; people were more optimistic. Many felt empowered to do what was right. The year 1948 brought the election of Estes Kefauver as U.S. Senator and Gordon Browning as governor of Tennessee. These leaders had heard the rumors about Georgia. They were not only staunchly anti-Crump, they were not afraid to take on his friends. In August, 1950, Governor Browning appointed a special prosecutor to investigate Georgia Tann. The job fell to 35-year-old attorney, Robert L. Taylor. Now retired, Judge Taylor says today, "I didn't know what to do with the case."

Taylor says it became the most fascinating case of his career. He began by contacting a former police chief who at that time ran a detective agency. Through him he met Ila

Huff, once assistant to Juvenile Court Judge Camille Kelley, and the appalling truth began pouring forth. Suspicions became facts as details surfaced and names were named. Taylor learned about the frequent 3 a.m. flights that one of Georgia's workers, a Mrs. Walton, conducted regularly to Los Angeles. On one occasion when she was traveling with six tiny babies, he caught the next plane after hers to Los Angeles. Arriving hours later, he hurried to the Hotel Biltmore, where she had already disposed of her infants. Taylor confronted Mrs. Walton in her hotel room. The special prosecutor began by bluffing. Taylor told her he knew "everything" about Georgia Tann. Bursting into tears, Mrs. Walton felt the enormous guilt of years of baby smuggling. She agreed to cooperate in an investigation.

Soon Robert Taylor *did* know almost everything! Not only did he learn details about Georgia's Los Angeles baby runs, but also about another courier's regular New York runs. Taylor talked to dozens of adoptive parents on both coasts, including actress Joan Crawford, who'd gotten some of her children through Georgia Tann. He investigated the terrible means by which Georgia obtained the babies.

Six months after Dickie and Betty were whisked to Los Angeles, on September 12, 1950, Robert Taylor made his findings public. His report created a sensation and generated a great deal of publicity, but the results were not satisfying. Georgia was in the last stages of cancer. She had been in a coma during the public announcement and died two days later. She was never even aware that she'd been exposed. The state of Tennessee eventually sued her estate to recover some of her blood money (no one knows for sure how many babies died while in her custody), but Georgia Tann must have died thinking that she had literally gotten away with murder. Georgia's chief accomplice, Camille

Kelley, was allowed to resign her judgeship, which she'd held for 30 years. In return Kelley was granted immunity from prosecution. Robert Taylor's requests to be allowed to expand his investigation beyond Georgia Tann, herself, and into the larger operations of the Tennessee Children's Home Society were thwarted. Boss Crump had lost much of his power with the 1948 election of Governor Browning, but he still had enough to kill further exploration of this explosive scandal.

Crump's statewide influence began to wane in 1948 when his onetime protégé and now political opponent, Gordon Browning, was re-elected as governor, and Estes Kefauver was elected to the United States Senate. Estes Kefauver's election broke the back of the Crump machine, taking advantage of post-war political forces plus confusion and division in the Crump ranks to win the three-way Democratic primary for U.S. Senate by a plurality. The Crump machine declined until the boss's death in 1954.

Congressman Albert Gore Sr. – father of the former vice president – ran for the Senate in 1952 against Kenneth McKellar, dean of the Senate and a formidable political lion. Gore's victory was the beginning of the end for the old political order. Kefauver and Gore Sr. were an enlightened pair of senators. In 1956, they were the only Southern senators who refused to sign the racist Southern Manifesto.

That was Tennessee politics. The Tennessee economy was another matter entirely. Both African Americans and whites from the rural South lived in poverty during the 1920s, long before the Great Depression struck the rest of the country. Farm markets were suffering after the free fall of prices following World War I, and many families were forced to leave their farms. The 1930's Depression hit Tennesseans and their state finances particularly hard. Even by Depression standards, Tennessee was in sad shape in 1933. Thirty percent of the population was affected by malaria, and the income was only $639 per year. Much of the land had been farmed too hard for too long, eroding and depleting the soil. Crop yields had fallen along with farm incomes. The best timber had been cut, with another 10% of forests being burned each year.

Lacking the necessary financial resources, few Tennessee farmers adopted the technology that had become available in the 1920s and was revolutionizing agriculture elsewhere in the country. Plowing with mules instead of tractors, and unable to afford trucks, hybrid seeds, and commercial fertilizers, Tennesseans continued instead to use the less efficient animal-drawn machinery, hand tools, and cultivation techniques from the nineteenth century. The man in overalls behind the single blade mule-drawn plow is a valid image.

The Great Depression of the 1930s exacerbated conditions with the precipitous drop in already depressed prices. The federal government fashioned schemes to reduce commodity surpluses through limitations on acreage and quotas on marketing. When Tennessee farmers participated by cutting back even further on cotton and tobacco cultivation in return for government subsidies, a welfare class and mentality began to emerge. Furthermore, federal programs had the unintended effect of reducing tenancy, aggravating the swelling ranks of the nation's homeless and dispossessed citizens. Many landlords chose to idle land they had previously rented out, often forcing their tenants to leave agriculture altogether. The depression persuaded farmers to place renewed emphasis on subsistence production, resulting in a modest return to household self-sufficiency. The hint of prosperity felt from 1900 to 1940 in Tennessee agriculture proved to be short-lived and illusory and was followed by stagnation and economic hardship.

My adoptive father, John Standridge, was a supervisor in the Civilian Conservation Corps (CCC) during the 1930s. I was told by those who knew him then that he had a reputation for fairness and for helping others in their time of need. He went the extra mile to use the emerging system to raise people up out of their poverty. Was Georgia Tann so very different in her initial well-intended social work? The CCC employed men in various types of work, including forestry, erosion control, dam construction, parks construction and development, and more. More than two million out-of-work men were given jobs under this program. Those between the ages of 18 and 25 whose families were on relief were eligible for work. They were paid $30, $25 of which went directly to their families. Workers were also provided with free room and board, although facilities were quite simple.

Layered on the setting on wrenching poverty came the greatest crisis of our time, World War II. Rationing and self-sufficiency became the order of the day. Ration cards were distributed during World War II so Americans would consume certain foods, such as meat, sparingly. The Rationing Pledge read: "I pay no more than top legal prices, I accept no rationed goods without giving up ration stamps." Tennesseans were also among the approximately 20 million Americans who tended their Victory Gardens during World War II. Americans were encouraged to grow and preserve their own food in order to help in the war effort. A week after the bombing of Pearl Harbor on December 7, 1941, gardeners stopped talking about their Defense gardens, and began calling them Victory gardens. As food became scarce and prices increased, more Americans planted vegetables in their Victory gardens. The Hero generation was mobilizing.

In addition to the events of the day, there is a larger social and historical context of the 1940s era. In their remarkable 1997 book, titled *The Fourth Turning*, Strauss and Howe describe a series of recurring 80 – to 100-year cycles – known to the ancient Etruscan culture as the Seculum. The "Seculum" is commonly defined as a generation, an age, world, times, or a century. Each cycle of the Seculum has four "turnings" – a High, an Awakening, an Unraveling, and a Crisis. This is analogous to the annual cycle of Spring, Summer, Autumn, and Winter.

Georgia Tann lived and brought forth her mission during the Crisis that arises once each Seculum in response to sudden threats that are now perceived as dire. Great worldly perils provide a hero generational archetype with a focus around the imperative that society must prevail. A solid public consensus develops aggressive institutions and an ethos of personal sacrifice. The great depression and America's Civil War are prior examples of this level of crisis. Public order tightens, families strengthen, and child-rearing reaches a smothering degree of protection and structure. Children realize that events of great magnitude take precedence and they are relegated to the background while their parents do what must be done – even give away their children. Some people even steal.

In the next generation (the artist archetype) a renaissance to life (the High) occurs and a new civic order evolves. The High is followed by an Awakening (a social epiphany; the prophet archetype) that arrives with a dramatic challenge against the High's assumptions about benevolent reason and congenial institutions. An Unraveling begins as a society of nomad archetypes, saturated by the liberating cultural forces set loose by the Awakening, tires of spiritual rebirth, moral protest, and lifestyle experimentation. Individuals assert an ethos of pragmatism, self-reliance, laissez faire, and chauvinism. The Unraveling has been reflected in Generation-X recently, and by the flappers of the roaring 20s, the "lost generation", before that. Child-rearing regains the attentive nature that was lacking in the previous era, again as result of parents wanting things to be better for their children than it had been for themselves. The Nomads thus spawn the next Hero generation, whose destiny it will be to take on the next Crisis era. These young adults will do whatever is necessary to preserve society. Tom Brokaw in his 1998 book, *The Greatest Generation*, eloquently depicts the Americans who came of age during the Great Depression and fought World War II – the Hero generation that went on to build modern-day America. Who will write the story of our *next* greatest generation, probably the greatest since Lincoln's time. Who will chronicle our newly evolving Crisis? More to the point, who will take advantage of the next Crisis atmosphere to corrupt the good intentions of a determined people? Who will be the next Georgia Tann?

In real life history Alvin C. York of Pall Mall, Tennessee, heroically led the seven remaining men in his platoon to kill 25 and capture 132 German soldiers in the trenches of World War I. The movie version starring Gary Cooper as *Sergeant York* was released in 1941 and helped to instill in a downtrodden people the idea that one person's action can turn wrenching adversity into a new tomorrow. The popular culture of the times accurately reflects the mood of society. The popular notion of Georgia Tann, "the angel", as savior of impoverished hopeless children was undoubtedly compelling in the same vein. Tann's idealized storyline reflected this idea that one person's action can turn wrenching adversity into a new tomorrow. The woman converted waifs into well-fed, well scrubbed, fresh faced darlings with a bright future. Who wouldn't be compelled to assist in this grand mission? And if the laws and social mores had not yet caught up with the noble intentions of the fine lady, well it was easy enough to look the other way long enough for the new social justice to prevail. With Boss Crump's blessings, there was the additional justification that "might makes right".

World War II ushered in a new period of transformation and advancement. War-induced demand ended the depression, reinvigorated commercial activities, and brought a return of agricultural prosperity. It stimulated production of the state's traditional market commodities as well as soybeans, a crop that farmers had grown earlier primarily as forage and green manure. The decline in acreage devoted to cotton and tobacco, a trend begun in the 1920s and temporarily interrupted by the war, resumed in the late 1940s. Driving the postwar trend were worldwide oversupplies in both commodities. Low prices in cotton and tobacco kept rural Tennesseans "dirt poor."

Politics, the Seculum, and the economy aside, there was society. Mr. Crump had the support of the church groups in Memphis, the Parent-Teacher Association (PTA), the local American Federation of Labor, the American Legion and the Chamber of Commerce. He was a legitimized force that projected legitimacy, support, and protection to Georgia Tann and her mission of removing children from impoverished homes, even by theft, and placing them among the more affluent. If Georgia Tann became a millionaire in the process, well that sort of thing happens as one ascends the power curve of the socially elite and politically connected. Doing good and doing well were not mutually exclusive in the zeitgeist of Boss Crump's 1940's Tennessee.

It was this terrible mixture of generational poverty and emerging optimism that played into a social acceptance of dislocating children, even by cruel and illegal devices. For the promise and the hope of providing the children with a better life – more security, a better standard of living, healthcare, education – the things each of us would want for our babies, society gave its seal of approval. Georgia Tann was an "angel", as some called her in the 1940s, and she clearly was a "monster" as history now reveals her to be. She was a bit of both depending on who writes the history books. I choose to be slightly generous, despite the undeniable fact that she separated me from my brother and sister for 50 years. She was a fallen angel in a tragic society. She steadily became more evil while society recovered much of the goodness inherent in people. She and society, and society's justice system, finally split with all of the dynamics of a stretched rubber band breaking. Ms. Tann was perhaps fortunate that she succumbed to cancer in the early 1950s, before the state's attorney general could bring her to trial.

CHAPTER 4
# Tennessee's Right to Know

Paula Cope's search for her brothers began after the television program *Unsolved Mysteries* ran the story about Georgia Tann and the stolen babies. As Paula watched that episode in 1990, forty years after her adoption, she started piecing together the possibilities. Could she and her brother "Dickie" have been among the stolen babies sold to the more privileged class of Americans? How could she go about finding out the truth?

Paula recalled seeing documents at a courthouse in Los Angeles that she later indicated she was not supposed to have seen. These documents told her the name she was given at birth, Mary Elizabeth Delaney, and the name of a place of origin, Chattanooga, Tennessee.

Paula and her husband, Larry Cope, traveled from their home in Cincinnati to Chattanooga, making their first stop at the Hamilton County, Tennessee, courthouse and the second stop at the Chattanooga public library. Paula reasoned that with her researching skills, the vast array of documents contained in the legal documents at the court house and the vast historical and genealogical tomes to be found in the library would start her in the right direction. Fortunately she was able to find exactly what she needed – both address and phone number of one Marion Delaney, our birth father.

When Paula called our birth father, he cried for joy. "Yes", he said. "You should come over right now." During this first visit with her birth father, Paula learned about his life and story. He had been in the Navy for 28 years. He had been married six times to five different women. After a life of heavy drinking and smoking cigarettes, Marion Delaney was not in good health. He suffered from emphysema.

Marion Delaney was clear that he never agreed to the adoption of the two older children, Dickie and Betty. It was during this first meeting with our birth father that Paula also learned about me. I was born just 14 months after Paula was born. Our birth mother was so small and frail that the two pregnancies so close together were very difficult for her, both physically and emotionally. Marion Delaney came to the hospital after I was born and our birth mother refused to see him. This rejection must have hurt him deeply. He later indicated that he was not my birth father, although our birth mother scoffed at this when Paula visited her, and stated that at five months after Betty's birth there was no one other than Marion Delaney who came near her. She had indicated in the adoption records that they had practiced birth control but that nothing worked satisfactorily and that it looked like each intercourse meant a baby. The denial of paternity was the excuse that Marion gave for signing adoption papers for baby Jerri – that plus it was not the same as it was with the older children who knew their parents and had formed strong bonds. It was strange though that Marion Delaney told Paula about me, her younger brother, and not about the other children of Imogene – at least not in the context of "you have another brother that you do not know about". Certainly all records and documents show Marion Delaney as my birth father, and photographs comparing his features with my features leave little room for doubt. As I indicated earlier, the rejection at the hospital after my birth must have hurt him deeply. The assurance of rejection in the bedroom was another thing entirely. It may have been easier on Marion Delaney's ego to explain Imogene's rejection of his sexual advances by imagining that there must be another man. However with an infant girl demanding all of her time, a new relationship – a love affair – would be so unlikely that it was beyond ludicrous; it was impossible. Jerri Wayne Delaney was conceived in February, 1948, somewhere between bottle feeding and changing diapers on my 5-month old sister. Marion and Imogene Delaney divorced for the second time five months following my birth and two months after my adoption.

Paula also discovered where our birth mother was living and went to see her. That resulted in a rather unsatisfying visit. Although our birth mother did tell her about baby Jerri and did talk about herself some, Paula indicated to me that it was her impression that she couldn't have cared less about meeting Paula. It was Paula's perception that our birth mother was not welcoming to her but instead rather self centered and socially "limited". Paula never bothered to visit her again and indicated to me that I might not want to meet her either.

Paula (Betty) was only one year old when I was born, and two and one-half years old when she herself was adopted. There was no way that she could have remembered "baby Jerri" the way that Dickie did. So when Marion Delaney told her that she had a younger brother, it came as a complete surprise. It was not until this revelation that Paula began her search for me.

At this point we must acknowledge Georgia Tann's role in helping our family to find each other. If Georgia Tann had not been so egregiously wicked in stealing over 5,000 babies, the Tennessee legislature might never have been compelled to pass a bill creating a law known as "Tennessee's Right to Know". This legislation allows adopted children to unseal adoption records in order to discover whether they were among Georgia Tann's victims. The adoption records search is actually broader in scope than I have described, but the original impetus is as I did describe. The intent of the law is to facilitate the reunion of families illegitimately torn apart. In the case of the Delaney kids, the law did just that for Paula and me.

Most families affected by the Tennessee baby theft and marketing campaign of Georgia Tann continued to suffer long after the dislocations themselves. Most family members, anxious to find the loved ones they lost 40, 50, even 60 years ago (and aware that if they didn't act soon, few of their relatives would be alive), ran into a stone wall. The customary practice of the states was to permanently seal adoption records. In 1980, however, a woman named

Denny Glad became the director of Tennessee's Right to Know, an organization devoted to helping adoptees find their roots. Because of her location in Memphis, Denny frequently dealt with victims of Georgia Tann. Aware of the suffering affecting so many, she and her organization lobbied for four amendments to the state laws, which now make it easier for separated families to find each other. Over the past 10 years, Denny has helped more than 500 people hurt by Georgia. Three of those benefactors are my brother, my sister, and myself.

The information about baby Jerri from our birth father, combined with the legislated access to adoption records, gave Paula all she needed to determine that I had been adopted by John and Juanita Standridge who lived at that time (late 1940's, early 1950's) in Benton, Tennessee. She also discovered that Dickie had been adopted by the Boyars of Los Angeles. *Her brother had grown up only 3.1 miles from where she had been raised, and she never knew it until just then!* Armed with this knowledge, Paula then obtained a CD ROM containing names, addresses, and phone numbers of everyone living in the Eastern United States. Looking in the phone directory had proved useful before when Paula was searching for our birth father. It made sense that the same method should work again in her search for me and Jeff.

With the information from the adoption records obtained and unsealed through the authority provided by the "Tennessee's Right to Know" legislation, Paula was able to discover that I had been adopted by John and Juanita Standridge of Benton, Tennessee. Using the census and address information provided on the CD listing people living in the Eastern United States, Paula was able to create a data base of everyone named Standridge who was living in East Tennessee. She then wrote a letter of introduction, which I have enclosed in Appendix A. She narrowed her search parameters and mailed five letters to five Standridge households with East Tennessee addresses. One of the five letters went to my previous address in Kingsport, Tennessee. The postal service would eventually forward it to me. A second letter was sent to my son, Adam, who lived in Benton, Tennessee.

Adam read the letter from Paula with interest. He did not know what to think. Could this be a scam? It sounded legitimate. Adam gave the matter some thought, and then he decided that the best way to check it out was to call Paula himself. He did call Paula and, after becoming convinced that her story sounded sincere, he told Paula that he would share her story and letter with me and that I would call her if I wanted to follow up on her initiative. He chose not to give Paula my address or phone number.

Adam called me as soon as he hung up from talking with Paula. "I don't know what you want to do with this," he began, "but there is someone claiming to be your sister. She sent out some letters and one of them came to me." He proceeded to read from the letter. He said, "I told her that you would call her if you were interested."

Well, I didn't know what I wanted to do with this new life development either. I had not asked for this. One of my dominant thoughts, after the shock of having a sister started to sink in, was that I didn't need this. I had a wonderful upbringing by loving parents whom I will always cherish. I had an extended family that I was totally pleased with. I was not looking for another family with a whole new set of entanglements. I was agitated by the news that my son had presented to me.

Furthermore, it did not fit my fantasy view of my adoption circumstances. I had not thought of this for decades, but as a child I had made up a story to explain why I had been adopted. To my way of thinking, it was inconceivable that someone could have "given me up" for adoption. Parents simply do not give away their children. They fight tooth and nail to keep them, to be there for them. My imagination was that both of my parents had died at the same time, maybe in an automobile accident. That was my version of what must have happened. I was an only child in both my fantasy version of life before adoption and during my real life after adoption. I had assimilated this imagined scenario without questioning it, and it required no further testing. It was done once as a child and forgotten as easily as a once read comic book. My adoption circumstance was a tidy story that neatly packaged my world view for a facet of my life that need concern no one else. If I had a sister, and it would seem that I did, then she came with a whole set of realities that not only popped this fantasy bubble, but also would challenge many other assumptions that I quietly held – nameless secrets that even I had forgotten over time.

The next evening I tentatively called Paula's home. We talked for over an hour. At first she shared and I gathered information, then I shared and she gathered. She told me all about the Delaney family and our adoption. Five years of research had made her quite the historian. She told me about Jeff (Dickie) and her futile attempts to locate our brother. We exchanged stories about our families. We exchanged stories about our personal lives, our *selves*, who we were and what we were like *really*. Eventually all this information gathering and sharing evolved into really getting to know each other. I began to get a feeling of who my sister is and

I sensed a lot of myself in her. There was never any doubt about our relationship once the conversation started. The personality, the humor, the quick wit, the logical thought progression, sentence structure, articulation, thoughtful pauses, even the quality of the laugh – she was so much like me that it was amazing. We ended our first hour's conversation by arranging a time and place to meet. It was to be Cumberland Falls State Park in Kentucky, roughly equidistant between Chattanooga and Cincinnati. When I hung up the phone, I had been turned 180 degrees around. I had gone from "I don't need this" to realizing what a gift I had been given. My sister had found me. I did not realize what I had been missing all of these years, but now I felt truly blessed.

We connected through phone calls and emails almost daily. We were still getting to know each other and were counting the days until we could meet one another. I have attached some of those emails. They are posted in Appendix A. The Cumberland Falls weekend would be here soon. We could hardly wait.

The search for Dickie was not as fruitful, even with both of us searching with all the cleverness that internet resources would allow. That search was to continue until *he* found *us*. He had been searching for us his entire life, so it was only fitting that he prevailed.

CHAPTER 5
# The First Delaney Kids Reunion

There were two reunions: one as a result of Paula finding me; the second as a result of Jeff finding the two of us. The first reunion, the one between Paula and me, took place in the winter of 1996. We had talked repeatedly on the telephone, mailed each other letters, and had shared emails nearly daily, but nothing could take the place of actually meeting in person. Paula was living in Cincinnati and I was in Chattanooga. Cumberland Falls State Park, in southeastern Kentucky was a reasonable halfway point and would have cabins that could serve nicely for accommodations.

We were excited. Our emails expressed eagerness, a kind of child-like Christmas eve level of anticipation. But our eagerness was tempered by concerns, too. What if I don't like this person? Or worse, what if this person doesn't like me? The letters and emails suggested total acceptance. We would be fine.

And then we met. We were two peas in a pod. We shared the same laugh, the same twinkle in the eye, the same wicked playful humor, the same facial features, the same gentleness, and more. We were similar not only in facial features, but also in body habitus. We took pictures, and laughed, and ate, and talked and talked and talked. We clearly had a lot of catching up to do. What was most special about our meeting was the feeling that was generated. I not only felt, I *knew* that Paula was my sister. There was no doubt – none – no DNA test needed, thank you. I am a scientist. This level of knowing was new to me, and not at all unwelcome.

We also noticed a string of co-incidences. Admittedly some of these are a stretch. Paula lived in Cincinnati and I was in Chattanooga. Both cities start with a "C" and have four syllables. Both are on a river that bears the name of the state: the Ohio and Tennessee rivers. Cincinnati and Chattanooga are both on the same "road", I-75. Cincinnati and Chattanooga are both in a Hamilton county. Cincinnati has a baseball team, the Cincinnati Reds, and Chattanooga has the Lookouts, a division AA minor league team of the Cincinnati Reds. When Jeff found us, we had to add one more co-incidence. Jeff was living in Centre, Alabama, which is the southern point for "the world's largest yard sale" that takes place every August along U.S. Highway 127. Highway 127 and the yard sale went past my front door on Signal Mountain, Tennessee, where I lived at the time we met, and proceeded northward to end at Cincinnati. Jeff lived at the southern end of the highway/yard sale, Paula lived at the northern extent, and I lived directly on the road in the middle. What are the odds?

Our weekend together at Cumberland Falls State Park was a time of amazing discoveries. Paula had brought photographs of herself and her family from the previous forty-some years and I had brought similar pictures of me and mine. Paula also had photographs of our birth mother and birth father, of her and Jeff as young children, and of other relatives. She brought documents that pertained to our adoption and related issues. She presented me with a whole new genealogy. Most of all she presented me with herself – an all grown up, smiling, warm, flesh and blood, honest to God *sister*.

I found myself adjusting very well indeed to the idea and feelings that were sweeping over me. It was taking some adjusting, to be sure, but I was more than handling it; I was loving it. There were two overwhelming gifts for me that weekend, neither of which I can adequately express. The first and clearest was Paula herself. I immediately liked her and Larry. They were good people, fun to be with, great to get to know. With Paula, however, there was so much more than I could have anticipated. *I loved her instantly.* How can I possibly explain feeling a love for someone that I had never met before and a type of love different from any other experience I had ever known? This was not like the love I had for my parents, nor like that which I have for my children or grandchildren, and nothing like the deep and abiding love that I have for Lynna Ruth, and have had for nearly four decades. My love for my sister Paula was unconditional, protective, nurturing, and knowing that it was totally reciprocated. This mutuality was so damn comforting that we could have just sat and grinned at each other with our secret understanding. Instead we talked and talked. There was so much catching up to do, so much getting to know each other that we hardly knew where to begin. But begin we did. We learned a lot about each other that weekend and we began the process of really, truly, deeply learning more about each other and about our selves than we could have imagined. Larry and Lynna Ruth completed us, as our mates and as a perfect balance to the foursome. We learned a new co-incidence: we had each married spouses whose parents were from the same small out of the way place on the earth – Scott County, Tennessee. What are the odds?

I mentioned two overwhelming gifts. The first was, of course, Paula herself and the inexplicable feelings of reciprocated love, and the feeling of truly, deeply knowing her. The second gift was a sense of family, but more than that, the knowledge that I am not alone, that I have someone that I can turn to, no matter what. Paula will forever and always be my sister and we will forever and always have those special bonds. The closest similar relationship I had was with my mother, especially after my father died. I knew I could always go to her with any problem, any dilemma, and she would listen, sympathize, and above all be supportive. After my mother's death, I had no parent and never *had* had a brother or a sister. I was *it* – the head of the household. Paula's second gift to me was as a blood relative. I was not *all there was* any more. I had an older sister. I don't mean to take away from Lynna Ruth or diminish how much she means to me or the sum total of all things that she represents. She is and always will be my sun and my moon. Lynna Ruth and I chose each other to be our life mates for our lifetime. Paula and I are full fledged

## The First Delaney Kids Reunion

family with no choosing and no going back. It is different from anything I had ever known and it felt very right.

Overflowing with these new and wonderful feelings, we had an intense visit. We took pictures, and ate our meals together, and enjoyed the scenery of Cumberland Falls. We also planned our next get together. We knew we could not discover all that was important to know about each other in such a short time – and that weekend did seem to be much too short – but we also knew that we had time and that we would get to know each other very well indeed. We just thought that we would have more time than we did. Still the time we had was more than just *good*. It was a very special *gift*.

In June Paula came to visit me in Chattanooga. Next it was my turn to visit her in Cincinnati. On these occasions we met each other's children and grandchildren – more gifts! I have a lovely, sensible, thoughtful niece, Beth, who is married to the amazing Paul. Beth and Paul have three beautiful, sweet, warm, funny and loving children – Jacob, Benjamin, and Mary. These three sweeties have absolutely got their "Uncle John and Aunt Ruthie" wrapped around their proverbial little fingers. Our children and grandchildren had the same effect on Paula, garnering affection and absolute acceptance from the first moment they met. Now! *This* was a family!

There was, however, a piece missing. After the initial excitement of finding each other and discovering all of this magic, Paula and I sent out with a vengeance to find our brother Jeff. Internet searches turned up some morsels of information to tease us. For example an amateur radio license had been issued to a Jeff Boyar, but there was no contact information and no way to determine if this was *our* Jeff. Later I learned that it was indeed. We searched for Marion Richard Delaney as well as for Jeffery Dean Boyar. Paula kept telling me that she had heard from our relatives in Chattanooga that Jeff had been through rough times, and there was no telling what kind of person he had turned out to be. There was no way of knowing even if he was still alive, and *if* he lived was he someone that we would regret finding. Still, we had to know if we had a brother Jeff, if he was alive, what life had brought his way, and who he had become. We had to know!

Meanwhile the mention of our relatives in Chattanooga – aunts, uncles, cousins, our birth mother who was still living (and may be alive still for all I know) – allows me opportunity for a segue that explains why these relatives were not a part of our reunion. In fact I have not tried to contact or meet any of them. It is as simple as the older family members collectively could have kept us and kept our family together. There was a failure of the will or a failure of the imagination. I admit that I am curious about any half brother or half sister I might have, but the older family had their chance. This is especially true when it came to Jeff. Jeff found his way back home as an emancipated minor. He was looking for support – someone to take him in. He needed love and acceptance, but he expressed that need poorly by acting out like only an adolescent could and by challenging those family members who did try to reach him. Instead of finding sanctuary, he ended up in prison. As a result of these things, I eschew the penumbra of the local Delaney family. If I were to reconnect with them now, I might be a curious family footnote, peripheral to the family circle. I think it is best for everyone that I just don't go there.

To be fair, there were family members who did care and deeply regretted what happened to the children, but they felt powerless to do anything. The abrupt decision by Imogene in 1950 and suddenness of our birth mother's action, and the swiftness of the Tennessee Children's Home Society and the courts, left few options for a stunned extended family. I am told that our grandmother, Elizabeth (Mrs. Ralph) Delaney, kept a doll in a child's chair for Paula for when she came back, which was hoped for if not expected. Many in the Delaney family were victimized by the Georgia Tann organization just as we children were. Life has its conflicting demands, I know, but would it have been too much to ask for the family to have found a way to keep the children together? Instead the subject became something that they just didn't discuss.

For me, Jeff and Paula were a different matter all together. We three were different from the rest of the family in so much as we were all in the same boat. We were each adopted out during a time when we were totally dependant on the family to care for us. I speak now for the three of us when I ask you guys how could this have happened? Where were you when we needed you?

Allow me to interject one more thing while I am at it. I know the presumption is that we were adopted out because our birth parents could not provide for us emotionally and financially and wanted what was best for us. I have had a decade to sift through that argument and I am fairly certain at this point that the argument that the adoption was something that was done with our best interests at heart is fallacious. No one was thinking of us and our needs or best interests during the time of our adoption. The three of us are proof that the adoption process is a crapshoot – a roll of the dice. I had a good outcome, Jeff had a rough time of it, and Paula had a mix of those outcomes. Nobody knew ahead of time if we would be better off or worse off. All anyone knew for sure was that we would be torn apart with essentially no chance of ever seeing each other again or, in my case, of even knowing that we had a brother and/or a sister.

Children of impoverished backgrounds frequently strive, thrive, and amaze. We were *very* bright kids. We had each other. We would have made it. What I would have failed to achieve because of a lack of nurturing support would have been more than compensated for by Jeff's accomplishments and enhanced stability. What I have done with my life is fine. I am grateful and have no regrets. But my outcome in life does not compensate for ripping a bright, sensitive, seven year old boy from his sister and extended family and selling him to some asshole in Los Angeles. This is the point where my friend Karl would have said, "But tell us what you really think. Badumpbump." But I digress.

Paula presented me with the adoption papers that she had obtained through the powers of Tennessee's Right to Know legislation. Not only did I have to adjust to the idea of having a sister, but I got to meet – in a manner of speaking – my birth parents when they were at their most dysfunctional and incapable parts of their lives. The adoption papers may not have been pretty, but they were telling. The following is a narrative account of some of the documents Paula gave me when we first met. Appendix B has the actual wording of the documents themselves.

In sharing some of the more important documents, I may repeat some essential facts describe earlier, especially from Chapter one. There is great richness of detail in the documents, however, and at the risk of being redundant on occasion, the documents do advance and enhance our story.

The first document I encountered was one titled, "CHILD'S OWN FAMILY" In it my siblings are named and recorded as Marion Richard Delaney, birth date October 27, 1943 (not the true birth year of 1942), and Mary Elizabeth Delaney, birth date September 18, 1947. The birthplace for both was given as Chattanooga, Tennessee. The birth mother, Imogene Mathis, age 29 of West 5th St., Chattanooga Tennessee, and the birth father, Marion Delaney, age 27 of the Overman Apts., West 6th St., surrendered their children on March 21st, 1950, according to social worker Margaret Hall, the TCHS Field Secretary. The problem with this dry information was that it was not true in important details. Not only was Jeff's (Dickie's) birthday manipulated to make him appear one year younger, but most importantly, our birth father was excluded from the adoption process in all aspects other than the faulty paperwork.

The story goes that on 3-15-50, Mrs. Imogene Mathis did appear in the TCHS office without an appointment. Unannounced and while she was still walking forward, she asked, "Do you remember me?" The TCHS worker, Mrs. Hall, did remember Imogene from the encounter one year previous. In February of 1949, she and her husband had released Jerri Wayne Delaney, age 3 months for adoption. She then stated that she had 2 more children she would like to release for adoption. She explained that Mr. Delaney had been given temporary custody of Marion Richard, age 7 and Mary Elizabeth, age 2. Shortly after obtaining custody, he had placed them in Vine Street Orphanage for a period of three months. After Imogene was remarried to Mr. Mathis the Court modified the decree. On December 19th 1949,

Imogene regained her custody along with $6.00 per week alimony. She said she thought her husband would make a good home for them, but this marriage had failed too and she is now unable to make a home for the children. Her children, and her mother an OOA recipient, were living in a basement apartment on West 5th Street. Mrs. Mathis said she was working part time at a dress shop but that her earnings together with the alimony was not adequate to provide a decent home for the children. She had moved about so often that Dickie had to repeat the first grade.

Mrs. Mathis indicated that her ex-husband, Mr. Delaney, probably would not consent to releasing the children in spite of the fact that he showed very little interest in them outside of paying the alimony. Mrs. Hall agreed to contact him and to review the court record to see what could be worked out. Imogene said she would like placement to happen as soon as possible because the children were both unhappy and emotionally disturbed.

Mrs. Hall later reviewed the Circuit Court divorce record and verified the facts as presented by the mother. She also contacted the father, who at first said he would never consent to releasing the children for adoption. He said he knew they were not being properly cared for and that it was impossible for him to assume the responsibility of them at this time. He said that he was very happily remarried, his wife works, and he is earning $30.00 per week driving a truck for Merten's Dry Cleaners. If he accepted custody of the children again he felt they would have to place them in Vine Street Orphanage again. Imogene told Mrs. Hall that she would never consent for him to have custody of the children again because she knew he would place them in the Orphanage. Mr. Delaney said his former wife had cost him his good job at the Southern Coach Lines, kept him upset all the time, and forced him to pay attorney's fees and court costs numerous times. He seemed to think that if he took the children and employed someone to look after them during the day their mother would never cease interfering. He went on to say that she was emotionally and morally immature, and actually not fit to have the care of the children. He said the baby they released in 1949 was not his child; therefore he had no hesitancy in releasing it. He said he would think the matter over and get in touch with Mrs. Hall later. The paper work filed by Mrs. Hall indicates that following day he called and said he had reached the conclusion that if the children were to have a chance in life they would be better off in an adoptive home. He consented to a hearing in the Circuit Court. The veracity of this next day change of heart cannot be confirmed. The agency workers had many years of experience in making the paperwork *look* "right".

Soon afterwards, on March 23rd, 1950, Mrs. Mathis and Mr. Delaney were present at a Hearing. The court was presided over by the honorable Judge L. D. Miller. As decreed by the judge, Order (#83617) awarded custody of the two children to the Tennessee Children's Home Society to place said children for adoption into proper homes. It is recorded that both our adoptive mother and father also signed a surrender, which became part of the court record. This part is in strong dispute by our birth father when he was visited by Paula (Betty) in the early 1990s. There are documents with excellent credentials suggesting his lack of presence in the courtroom and there is no signature on the court documents, but this court record, signed by a court clerk (but not a judge) does exist. Because it does, it provides us with two potential truths, two conflicting and mutually exclusive pieces of evidence. An official document suggests Jeff is a year younger and the birth father signed the adoption papers. Other testimony and documents disagrees with both of these assertions. Marion Delaney told Paula the official court document was a lie. He never agreed to relinquish Jeff and her for adoption.

Pending relinquishment of the children, the Tennessee Children's Home Society paid our birth mother board for the children's care. On the day the court released them, the children were transferred to the Memphis Receiving Home for placement. The birth parents were told that they would not be placed in this community. Perhaps that explains why family would not take in Jeff when he came back to Tennessee when he was a teenager. He had broken somebody's rules and violated someone else's understanding when he came back. The court had assured the family that he would not be *placed* locally; no one ever said he would not try to come back home.

The records have a lot of detail concerning the social history of me as well. Here I am presented as Jerri Wayne Delaney. I accurately reflect the social workers documents in Appendix B. Skip to this section and scan some of the Appendix B section on records if that interests you. The narrative resumes in the next chapter and evolves to include our three life stories before and after our reunions; reflections on gaining and losing siblings; reflections on gaining a culture and turning Irish; and reflections on life – reflections brought on by becoming one of the Delaney Kids.

## Chapter 6
# Mary Elizabeth Delaney

*September 18, 1947 – October 25, 2006*

I am most fortunate to have for this portion of the narrative an essay that Paula wrote for a freshman English course at Clermont College at the University of Cincinnati. Paula took college courses perhaps with an eye toward a college degree someday, perhaps to qualify for promotion in her long time profession as computer programmer at Blue Cross Blue Shield of Ohio, and perhaps just for fun. I was never clear on the issue. Nevertheless her essays (I have two) stand today to reveal thoughts and feelings that may have otherwise never have been made clear. Here is "Mail Order Baby" by Paula Cope.

# Mail Order Baby
### by Paula Cope

My parents had always told me I was adopted, explaining that I was special because I had been chosen. I was born in Chattanooga, Tennessee in 1947, and was placed through the Tennessee Children's Home Society with a family in Los Angeles in 1950. I would joke that I was a "mail order baby" because the first time my parents laid eyes on me was when I was flown in from Tennessee and placed in their home. I was a very grown up two year old and quickly adapted to my new surroundings and lost all memory of my previous life.

As I grew, the feeling of being special faded and was replaced with resentment at not knowing anything about my background. I grew angry every time I was asked to complete one of those family medical history forms at a doctor's office. My parents were very uncomfortable about discussing my past and denied knowing anything more than the fact that I had a Scotch-English-Irish heritage.

While pregnant with my first child, I decided to find out what information was available to me at the courthouse. I believe I ended up seeing more that day than I was supposed to. I saw some microfilm which revealed three important facts: my birth parents had been married and divorced, I had a brother, and my birth name had been Mary Elizabeth Delaney. I knew then that I probably had enough information to enable me to find my parents, if I really wanted to. My biggest obstacle was the little voice in my head that kept telling me, "They didn't want you, so why should you find them? Why set yourself up for rejection again? They don't deserve you!"

This inner battle went on for most of my adult life. I resented the fact that I had not been given up as an infant before my bond had time to form. Someone had raised me for 2½ years, had gotten to know me, and then gave me away. There were pieces of my life that were missing, and one of those missing pieces was a brother. Did he look like me? Did he even know I existed?

In April of 1990, I saw an exposé of the Tennessee Children's Home Society while watching the television show "Unsolved Mysteries". The home's director was running a black market baby ring during the time of my adoption. Some children placed for adoption had been obtained through deception, falsification of records, and even kidnapping. I felt I no longer had a choice; I had to find out the circumstances surrounding my adoption.

My husband and I began making plans to go to Chattanooga. Our first stop was the courthouse where I learned, through my parent's divorce papers, that some information had been falsified on the adoption records I had seen. We left the courthouse and headed for the Public Library to wade through city directories. Two hours after my search began, I had all the information I needed, including my father's address, phone number, marital status, and occupation. I knew there was no turning back now, but how was I ever going to find the courage to call him? What would I saw to him? My husband just kept saying, "Speak from your heart; the words will come". It took all the nerve I could gather together, but when we returned to our motel room I called him. When he answered the phone I announced, "My name is Paula Cope, but I was born Mary Elizabeth Delaney". I asked him if that name meant anything to him, but there was no answer, only silence. I took a deep breath and repeated my question. Finally, after what seemed like an eternity, a shaky voice on the other end of the line said, "My God! If that's true, you do not know how long I have been looking for you! Where are you?" An hour later, we hugged for the first time in forty years. He took us back to his house so that we could talk. He was a big man, but very frail. He suffered from emphysema and a heart condition. After talking for about an hour, he announced that he had something for me. His wife disappeared into the next room and returned carrying a large baby doll. He explained that the doll had been mine when I was a little girl, and he had saved it all those years in the hope that he could return it to me some day.

My father passed away a year and a half later, but I am very grateful that we had the chance to get to know each other before he died. Finding him has led to several other reunions with relatives. As recently as three months ago, I found a younger brother who was placed for adoption almost a full year before I was. He knew that he had been adopted, but having a sister came as a complete surprise. I now have one remaining brother left to find.

It's very hard to describe what it feels like to see baby pictures of yourself for the first time when you are forty years old. I did not grow up with people who looked like me. I now have relatives whose features I inherited, and somehow that gives me a sense of belonging.

The stories my parents told are filled with half-truths and remembrances. Time has reshaped and clouded the circumstances in each of their minds, and the truth lies somewhere in the middle of a divorce struggle. I will probably never know the exact circumstances that led to my adoption, but I have at last made peace with it.

---

Here Paula is presented as Mary Elizabeth Delaney: With this passage I quote the social workers document.

---

# Mary Elizabeth Delaney

SUMMARY

Taken from the Records of the Hamilton County Branch and Shelby County Branch of the Tennessee Children's Home Society August 6, 1951.

THE CHILD: Mary Elizabeth Delaney, born 9-18-47 (verified) in Erlanger Hospital, Chattanooga, Tennessee.

Placed in the Shelby County Branch, Tennessee Children's Home Society Receiving Home 3-23-50.

Guardianship removed from the parents, Marion H. Delaney and Imogene Mathis, and placed with Tennessee Children's Home Society by court order #83617, Circuit Court, Hamilton County, Chattanooga, Tenn. On 3-23-50.

Placed: 3-28-50 for adoption by Shelby County Branch of Tennessee Children's Home Society in home of Paul R. Crippen, age 41 in August 1949, of English descent, occupation sales engineer, no church affiliation, and Janet Allan Crippen, age 39 in August 1949 of Scotch descent, housewife, member of Quaker sect.

3941 Ridgelay Drive, Los Angeles Calif.

PREVIOUS APPLICATIONS: State Social Welfare placed boy 4 ½ years of age (in August 1949) Children's Home Finding (no address given)

New Name: Paula Allan Crippen

CHILD'S HISTORY

Mary Elizabeth Delaney was born 9-18-47 (verified) in Chattanooga, Tenn. According to the Hamilton County Branch record, she was diagnosed as normal at birth in Erlanger Hospital. Nothing is known of her early development and little of her physical condition, except that a pediatrician gave her two immunization shots for diphtheria and tetanus in 1948 and recorded that she had whooping cough. Her mother gave the Hamilton County worker a vague history indicating numerous illnesses.

The extent to which Mary Elizabeth was affected by parental discord is not known. Her mother described her prior to the time of surrender as emotionally upset. Apparently, when not with her parents, she lived with both grandmothers and was placed for three months in 1949 in Vine Street Orphanage. She lived with her mother and stepfather briefly after that. There were no dates given indicating when and how long she lived with various relatives. Her custody was removed from the parents by court order at the parents' request, March 23, 1950, and transferred to the Tennessee Children's Home Society.

---

Five days after the court action placing Paula with the Tennessee Children's Home Society, less that two weeks after Imogene Mathis walked into the adoption agency unannounced and unexpected, Paula was in Los Angeles, California, and was officially placed in the adoptive home of Paul A. and Janet E. Crippen. The Crippens were, compared with Imogene and Marion Delaney, a relatively older couple when they adopted Paula. Janet Crippen was a forty year old housewife; Paul Crippen was forty-two. He was a sales manager with General Metal Corporation. Janet and Paul Crippen were of the Quaker faith and Paula was raised as a Quaker just as Jeff had been brought up in the Hebrew faith. I suppose their Baptist birth parents were o.k. with that.

The Tennessee Children's Home Society commissioner, J. O. McMahan, expressed concern with the rapid placement, especially in view of the birth mother's attestation that the child was "emotionally upset". Documents from the Crippens, however, attest that Paula had a very happy disposition and adjusted to the new home well and quickly. Paula was precocious from the minute she stepped off the plane and was so independent that she wanted to do everything herself. The Crippens were undoubtedly quite pleased with their good fortune at acquiring such a smart and pretty daughter. A letter from Mrs. Crippen dated April, 12th, 1950, stated, "She seems to feel very much at home and is very happy." Visits to the doctor gave Paula reports of excellent health and I.Q. testing, which seemed to be a common practice in adoption situations. The IQ testing revealed Paula to be very bright indeed.

An attempt to enroll Paula in school was complicated by the inability to provide the school system with a birth certificate as required by California law. Janet Crippen wrote several letters specifically requesting resolution of the process and transfer of necessary documents. One letter dated June, 1951, indicated that the matter should have been resolved the previous March. As with Jeff, there were numerous irregularities with the adoption paperwork that delayed finalizing the adoption process for years. Among these irregularities was that the court order that transferred guardianship to the Tennessee Children's Home Society had been signed by the clerk but not the judge. That does not sound like routine procedure. There was no signature by either parent that was either witnessed or notarized. Further complications resulted from the permanent closing of the Tennessee Children's Home Society as a result of the black market baby scandal. Many records were lost or destroyed. After a delay of several years, a "Petition to Modify Decree" and an abundance of communication between Nashville and Los Angeles agencies allowed adoption agency officials to finalize adoption procedures so that the matter of Docket No. 83617 could be closed.

The cottage on Catalina had been in the Crippen family since before the turn of the century. Apparently, a great-grandfather staked out a plot of land back when squatters could still lay claim to parcels. A grandfather, who was a doctor, continued the tradition. Janet Crippen, Paula's adoptive mother, came to their beach house regularly while growing up, and had wonderful pictures from the 1920s of bathing beauties at the beach. Janet's sister, Aunt Dot, said they used to get cited for Public Indecency if they were seen anywhere other than the beach in their bathing suits. The original house, I believe built in the early 1900's, remains today with only a few modifications. Paula recalled that they still had an "outhouse" up until her teens. She mentioned that this was the only vacation spot that they went to, and she became bored with it. It was popular with celebrities, though, so she did get to see many on the island. Paula recalled a beautiful ballroom in a casino that had dances in the summer.

Paula apparently had a good childhood but she had a rough first marriage. She married a marine from Ohio. She indicated to me that he was "not the same after Vietnam". My understanding was that he was abusive verbally and physically. Largely because they had two children, Paula stayed married to him for fourteen years.

Paula undoubtedly had her struggles raising two teenage children as a single mother. Her son was nineteen and living with her ex-husband when he was killed in an automobile accident. Her daughter, Beth, and she had many opportunities to hone their coping and survival skills.

A second marriage, to Larry Cope, fared much better. Larry brought stability, security, and love to a relationship that flourished for more than twenty years. After Paula found our birth father and before she found me, Beth married her high school sweetheart, Paul. It meant so much to Paula that our birth father, Marion Delaney, and his wife, Billie DeFriese Delaney, were able to attend Beth's marriage before his death.

Paula's career for more than three decades was as a computer programmer for Blue Cross and Blue Shield of Ohio. She was highly competent but could not advance in her position or pay grade because she did not have a college education. Her coworkers remember her for her ability to stay calm and collected when there were crises. The old adage goes, "If you can keep your head when all around you are losing theirs, you obviously don't understand the situation." Such was not the case with Paula, however. She was simply that veteran who had been there, done that, and could reassure the others that this latest computer crash would be all right.

Other than her family, on whom she doted, Paula's other great love was her times spent with her friends in the Red Hat Society. Paula looked great in her red hats and purple outfits, but more than that, she loved her red hat ladies. These friends were an important part of Paula's social circle. I appreciated them, not only for the joy that they brought Paula, but also because it made my life so much easier at gift giving times – a red hat here, a serving platter with an image of red hat lady there. Life was good.

CHAPTER 7
# The Second Delaney Kids Reunion

Six years had passed since Paula wrote the first letter that brought us together and still there was no sign of Jeff. Then one day it happened. Jeff had tried for so long and so many times to reconnect with family that he had just about given up. He had never given up looking for Betty and Jerri Delaney, but those people did not legally exist and there were no clues on the internet or anywhere else to suggest to Jeff what names we had been given after our adoptions. He had been down many a dead end road in his pursuit of his sister and brother, whom he did remember. Jeff decided that he would try one last time to connect with family in Chattanooga. He knew them. He had their telephone numbers. He just never felt wanted. But he would try one more time. Jeff called our cousin, Sharon Osborn Blevins, who is the daughter of our birth father's sister, Emma Gene Osborn. Sharon, her mother Emma Gene, and another of our birth father's sisters, Anna Lee Dietch, were the closest contacts Jeff had and were the only ones of the Delaney family that I know who seemed to care about him. Sharon had become close with Paula (who was much better than I about integrating with the family in Chattanooga). After she had discovered our birth father and his extended family, Paula came to Chattanooga every June to spend a week visiting and shopping with Sharon. So when Jeff called this time, Sharon was able to tell him about Paula. It is not clear to me if Sharon knew Jeff's number and somehow failed to tell Paula where she could find him. Surely she did not. On this occasion, however, Sharon did not feel comfortable, or perhaps empowered, to give Paula's telephone number to Jeff. Instead she took down Jeff's number and told him that she would give his number to Paula. If Paula wanted to call Jeff, then she would. That was the best she could comfortably do, and they hung up. Days went by and Jeff received no word and no telephone call from Paula. He thought to himself, "Well, damn! Nobody else in the family has ever wanted anything to do with me. Why should I expect anything different now from my sister?" Those were the exact words Jeff told to me when we first met and were telling our stories. That was what he thought and he was more dejected and felt more rejected than ever before.

Sharon had gotten the number wrong when she relayed it to Paula. When Paula finally did connect with someone at the number she was given, she realized her mistake. Finding Jeff's true telephone number was easy for our sister the expert sleuth. She called Jeff, who answered, and they talked and cried and shouted and went on this way for an hour. What joy after all these years of knowing and not knowing, of searching and not finding! What joy! Of course Paula immediately called me with the same arrangement. Because of my reluctance to meet my family locally, Paula chose not to presume my preferences when it came to Jeff, although we had both been searching for years. Paula knew quite well how I felt when it came to the three of us siblings. Still she thought she was doing the right thing by telling Jeff that she would give me his phone number, and that if I wanted to call him that I would (she told him she was sure that I would). Of course I immediately called my long lost brother. I had a brother! Holy Mother of God!

All I can say now is "Wow"! There is no way to express how we felt. Jeff sounded exactly like me on the telephone, except he laughed more. We had the same inflections, the same stupid humor, and so much more. I could tell, I could feel, this was my brother – some other very real part of me. We talked and cried and shouted and went on this way for an hour. We started telling each other our stories – our life stories, the things that made us who and what we had become. I could tell early on that Jeff's life was way more interesting than mine, but so much of it you had to drag out of him. Paula and I both had trouble believing everything he told us. Some of it was truly incredible – or at best marginally credible. How much of it was an embellishment? Medical school? Really? Still, I could tell that he had been around the block. He had an honorary Ph.D. from the school of hard knocks. How could he still be so upbeat, optimistic, and irrepressible? How could he be so frilling funny? I do not know, but he was. Jeff was great and I could not wait to meet him.

I could not wait to be united with my brother and my sister. The three of us would be together for the first time ever and it could not happen soon enough. We decided that Chattanooga was middle ground. I was eager to play the host. Jeff and Brenda could stay in our guest bedroom. Larry would never stay at our house. Paula simply explained to me that he was not comfortable staying at other people's houses and never had been. I guess he felt like it would be an imposition. At any rate Paula and Larry would stay at the Howard Johnson Plaza in East Ridge as they always did. Larry's comfort level being high was a good thing. We set a date and prepared to paint the town red, as they say.

The next thousand words are on the cover of this book. Our group hug says it all.

The six of us got together for the first time (ever) at the Howard Johnson Plaza in East Ridge, Tennessee. It was everything you could imagine. Allow me a little copy and paste action: We talked and cried and shouted and went on this way for an hour. We started telling each other our stories – our life stories, the things that made us who and what we had become. Only this time it was live and in person. We kissed and hugged and cried for joy and literally beamed. It was as joyous as this life gets. We were reunited and no one, no way, no how could tear us apart again. Take that, World!

I wonder now if the victorious solidarity that we felt then, the overcoming of adversity and doing it against impossible odds, was magnified by our Irish heritage. I wonder if some Jungian Irish zeitgeist was at work. We Delaneys thrive on oppression but you cannot keep us down. We will persevere and we will emerge victorious.

Us against the world, man, bring it on, is that all you've got? I'm just saying.

We visited until the late evening. The next day we toured Chattanooga, but it did not matter where we were geographically, we were together, and that was all that mattered. We started off the day with breakfast at the Cracker Barrel restaurant. Paula and I had that as one of our little traditions. No one seemed to mind. We went to the Chattanooga Choo Choo. There really is such a place, for those of you not from around here. Rose gardens fill the station tracks, an old time, brightly painted train still makes runs around the grounds, and a large domed restaurant occupies the former station house. My younger son, Aaron, was able to join us there for lunch. It was such a joy to have him meet my family. We toured a large model train lay out. We went to Coolidge Park with its merry-go-round and its fountains. We went several other places then capped off the day with a surprise at the city's newest hotel, the Chattanoogan. I had arranged a reserved area of their bar, the Foundry. There was a pool table. The area was already set up with a fruit and cheese tray and heavy *hor d'oeuvres*. We also had coffee and soft drinks (neither Larry nor Jeff drank alcohol), pink fru-fru drinks, and wine. We had the space all to ourselves, and Jeff, Brenda, and Larry could smoke. I am fairly certain that Jeff beat me at pool. It was a great setting for the first of our many reunions.

The next day we spent mostly at our home on Signal Mountain. We visited with each other as well as other family and friends. Aaron was there as well. Later we went to my older son Adam's house where Jeff could meet the rest of the family. The important thing was that we were starting to get to know each other and we loved each other unconditionally. It was a truly magical reunion and the feelings ran deep. The book's cover and Appendix C reveal some nice photographs of our reunions.

CHAPTER 8
# Marion Richard Delaney

*October 27, 1942 – September 5, 2006*

Here is Jeff as Marion Richard Delaney: With this passage I again quote the social worker's document. This chapter begins with a few important documents. These and additional documents are transcribed in Appendix B.

---

SUMMARY taken from the records of the Hamilton County Branch

And Shelby County Branch Tennessee Children's Home Society

THE CHILD: Marion Richard Delaney, born Oct. 27, 1942, in Chattanooga, Tenn. (verified).

Placed by Circuit Court, Hamilton County, Tennessee, Court Order No. 83617 under guardianship of Tennessee Children's Home Society for adoption placement, March 23, 1950.

Placed: 4-5-50 placed for adoption in home of Herbert M. Boyar, age 38 in 1950, Jewish, store owner, and Fannyetta Niederberger, age 37 in 1950, Jewish housewife, (old address 856 So. Montebello Blvd., Montebello, Calif.) now residing at 1758 Preuss Road, Los Angeles 35, Calif.

PREVIOUS APPLICATIONS: Los Angeles County Bureau of Adoption

NEW NAME OF CHILD: Jeffrey Dean Boyar

CHILD'S HISTORY

Marion Richard Delaney was born on October 27, 1942 (verified). Nothing is known of his early development. At the time his mother applied for help from the Hamilton County Branch of the Tennessee Children's Home Society she stated he was repeating first grade because she had moved their residence. His report card from Sunnyside School in Chattanooga for 1949-50 verifies his satisfactory progress in the first grade. His mother said he was emotionally disturbed. The extent to which he was affected by the constant parental discord is not known. Prior to his placement in California he had lived with both grandmothers and after his parent's second divorce in April 1949 he had been placed for three months in Vine Street Orphanage. He then

# Marion Richard Delaney

lived with his mother and a stepfather briefly. The sequence and dates of his stay with relatives is not recorded.

On 3-15-50 his mother, Mrs. Mathis, who had custody of Marion Richard, sought help from the Hamilton County Branch of Tennessee Children's Home Society in releasing him and his sister for adoption. The father agreed to relinquish the children, and on March 23, 1950, Mrs. Mathis and Mr. Delaney went for a hearing before the Hamilton County Circuit Court. An order (#83617) awarded the custody of the two children to the Tennessee Children's Home Society to be placed for adoption.

His sister, Mary Elizabeth Delaney, born 9-18-47, was considered normal at birth. She was also placed for adoption by Tennessee Children's Home Society through court order at the parent's request.

CHILD'S DEVELOPMENT AND ADJUSTMENT IN FOSTER HOME

Although the Boyars had requested to adopt a girl, the letters from Mrs. Boyar indicate an acceptance of this boy. Mrs. Boyar in several letters implied a close relationship between their natural daughter and this boy and expressed surprise in how well and quickly he adjusted to his new mode of living. She expressed pride in his good physical condition, in his interest in Sunday religious school, and his completion in June 1951 of the second grade with good comments from his teacher.

In February 1951 and subsequently they requested information regarding the completion of his adoption.

In the last letter mention was made of having taken him to an optometrist who prescribed glasses.

Mr. and Mrs. Boyar were delighted with their son; they could hardly believe their own eyes when they saw that Dickey had dimples just like they did! Their little daughter was so pleased with her new brother and told him she had an Easter surprise for him down in the car! All left looking very happy.

Alma Walton

| | | |
|---|---|---|
| AREA OFFICES | **Earl Warren** | STATE HEADQUARTERS |
| LOS ANGELES OFFICE | **Governor** | SACRAMENTO |
| MICHIGAN 8411 | | GILBERT 2-4711 |
| MIRROR BUILDING | | 616 K STREET |
| 143 SOUTH SPRING STREET 12 | STATE OF CALIFORNIA | 14 |
| SACRAMENTO OFFICE | **Department of Social Welfare** | |
| GILBERT 2-4711 | | |
| 924 NINTH STREET | CHARLES I. SCHOTTLAND | |
| 14 | DIRECTOR | December 15, 1952 |
| SAN FRANCISCO OFFICE | Los Angeles | |
| EX BROOK 2-8751 | December 11, 1952 | |
| GRAYSTONE BUILDING | | |
| 948 MARKET STREET 2 | | |

Mr. J.O. McMahan, Commissioner
Department of Public Welfare
State Office Building
Nashville 3, Tennessee

ADDRESS REPLY TO:
145 South Spring Street
Los Angeles 12

OSC "D"

Adoption of Marion Richard Delaney
By Herbert M. And Fanny N. Boyar

Dear Mr. McMahan:

We have recently completed our investigation in the above-mentioned adoption case and are glad to be able to forward to you this report.

The child, whom Dr. and Mrs. Boyar call Jeffrey, has made a nice adjustment in this home. They report that when he first came they had some behavior problems, but appear to have given expert consideration and understanding of the factors of the child's background that might lead to this rather poor adjustment at first, and have been most successful in their handling of the problem.

When Jeffrey was placed in their home they were given a paper with a scant amount of information regarding his background, and on this it gave his birth date as October 27, 1943. They have been proceeding on this supposition, and were considerably surprised when agent informed them that the birth certificate gave his birth date as 1942. They had been told he was in the first grade when last in school in Tennessee, so had given no thought to it, and had no reason to question his age, as he progressed normally in the second and third grades in school, and is now in the fourth grade. Mr. and Mrs. Boyar's natural daughter, Stephanie, was born in 1942, and they state that in every way Jeff seems to be about a year younger. They realize, however that it is difficult to judge at this particular age. They have just had a psychometric test of Jeffrey, which has indicated that he has an intelligence of a very superior nature: that if at the age level of nine, he would have a full scale I.Q. of 146, and if at the age level of ten, he would have a full scale I.Q of 133, so there seems to be no question but that Jeffrey is a brilliant child.

In considering the question of the age, Mr. and Mrs. Boyar feel at this time that they will make no point of the age difference, and will not change his age in any records. They realize that his birth certificate will be the correct one. They think it very probable that between now and college age he may skip some classes, as he seems to do well in school, and in that way he will possibly make up for the year he lost earlier. It is interesting to note that the doctor making the psychometric test stated that Jeffrey is definitely college material and should experience little difficulty academically.

```
Mr. and Mrs. Boyar and Jeffrey have all
had recent medical examinations, and in every
instance were reported to be in good general
health and physical condition. Mr. and Mrs. Boyar
both had serological tests and chest x-rays, all
having negative results.
```

Marion Richard Delaney (a.k.a. "Dickie") remembered the orphanage and did not have any good thoughts or feelings about the place other than holding hands with his sister Mary Elizabeth (a.k.a. "Betty"). They were at the place about three months and they were with various relatives. Then came the airplane flight to California. Dickie was adopted by a Beverly Hills carpet merchant and real estate developer named Boyar. His most memorable line to his new son was, "Shut up. You are bought and paid for." The going rate in 1950 was probably less than the $10,000 that Jeff had repeatedly been told that his adoptive parents had paid for him.

There you have it. The title for this book is based on Jeff's adoptive father's phrase that indicated to Jeff that he was "bought and paid for." I have no way of knowing how many times daddy Boyar spoke these words to Jeff, but I do know that the words stayed with Jeff for his entire life. The words were so much more than smug, superior, authoritative, and cold intimidation. They also served to destroy any vestige of self worth remaining in the abandoned and displaced child. They were dehumanizing in the most direct and concrete way. The words did not merely *imply*, they stated in the clearest terms that Jeff was an object rather than a person, a commodity to be purchased, a plaything for Boyar's daughter. Furthermore, in naming to Jeff the $10, 000 purchase price, Boyar set the bar at an impossibly high level for Jeff to measure against his perceived self worth. That was an enormous amount of money to a child in the 1950s. Did Mr. Boyar not get the goods that he was promised? Did Mr. Boyar mean to imply that Jeff would need to pay the money back to him? Was there buyer's remorse when Jeff failed to live up to expectations? To an unenlightened person whose own ego could be inflated by tearing down someone else, Jeff must have seemed to be an easy and available target. This child must have been emotionally devastated on a regular basis.

Marion Richard Delaney was chosen because of his age and appearance. Like many prospective adoptive parents, the Boyars were promised certain characteristics that could not be delivered. In the case of Richard Delaney, the Boyars requested and were promised a female Jewish child about the age of their natural daughter. They were buying a playmate for their daughter. If the Tennessee Children's Home Society did not have a child with the precise characteristics that were being requested, they at least had a protocol for dealing with the situation – they lied to the prospective adoptive parents. These unfulfilled expectation typically set up a disappointment that could be difficult to overcome. Because Jeff was neither female nor Jewish, he was clearly unable to meet the Boyar's expectations of him and therefore would forever be a disappointment on some level. It is impossible to know whether Mr. Boyar felt that he had been overcharged.

Mr. Boyar had a daughter who was Dickie's age and Dickie's features were that of a good looking child with a good-natured personality. Mr. Boyar was apparently pleased by Richard's dimples that reminded everyone of his own. So Dickie got the job; he became Jeffery Dean Boyar.

Jeff told me he never felt accepted fully by the Boyar family. I am guessing that he also never felt that he was loved. I am guessing that the only true love and acceptance that he ever felt came from his sister Betty (a.k.a. Paula). Neither his birth parents nor his adoptive parents gave Jeff support, financially or emotionally. Jeff's life story reflects the mix of nature and nurture when the nature is a high I.Q. and happy personality but the nurture is rejection, abandonment, and neglect.

The climactic event occurred when Jeff was fourteen. He had gotten up before the others in the family one morning, fixed himself breakfast, washed and put away the dishes, and returned to his bedroom. Mr. Boyar came in, not knowing he had done these things, and accused him of being lazy and worthless for still being in his bedroom that morning. An argument ensued when Jeff tried to explain his actions. Push led to shove and Jeff struck Mr. Boyar, knocking him backwards. When Mr. Boyar fell backwards, he landed in such a way that he hurt his back. Mrs. Boyar, before she drove her husband to an emergency room for medical attention, backhanded Jeff, cutting his face deeply with the large diamond ring she wore. While the two were gone, Jeff left home never to return.

Initially Jeff lived in a closet underneath some stairs at the house of a friend, a teenage female. She would sneak food to him and he lived in this manner long enough for any half-hearted search effort to die down. When Jeff presented himself to the local police, they appeared not to know what to do with him. It is not known whether they contacted Mr. Boyar. Presumably they did. Could it be that Mr. Boyar could simply decline to take Jeff back? Mores were different in the 1950's. A businessman could make certain requests of officials. Favors were granted. People looked the other way. At any rate Jeff found himself being "allowed" to start life on his own as an emancipated minor at the age of fourteen. The police and perhaps a social worker helped him find an apartment and a job.

Jeff had outlived his usefulness to the Boyars. He was purchased as a playmate for their daughter, but now that he was a teenager, the family no longer desired him for that purpose. Jeffrey Dean Boyar, the "Bought and Paid For" commodity, was now to be *discarded*. This to me was the most egregious of the cruelties inflicted upon Jeff; and the most outrageous.

Jeff later indicated that up until the separation from the Boyar family, he had been set up with a substantial banking account in his name. This largess was summarily rescinded by the Boyars, otherwise Jeff would have had a decent grubstake. As it was, Jeff never saw a penny of his "family fortune".

Jeff traveled a lot. He eventually visited most of the 48 states, he later indicated. One of his first trips was to return to Chattanooga, to the family he still remembered, when he was 16 years old. It was not a welcoming homecoming. He visited with aunts and cousins and even saw his birth mother, who couldn't have cared less. No one was willing to take him in. Rejection number three; but at this point, who is counting?

Jeff may have told me, but Brenda reminded me recently of one more incident. Jeff the teenage male opened his wallet and showed a female relative a condom. It may have been his step-sister. She in turn complained to Jeff's father who told Jeff to go back to his family in California. Showing the condom was a little strange, and I am uncertain of the timeframe, but it strikes me as a [snicker, snicker] rite of passage, like showing off the cigarette that you are not supposed to have but are going to defiantly smoke anyway. I believe it was kid stuff; not lewd innuendo. It points out Jeff's lack of guidance growing up. Without loving parents to nurture and mentor him, he was left to find his own way. There must be a lot of trial and error tutelage in the school of hard knocks. It also helps explain some of the difficulty the famiy had in taking Jeff back. He would have been a project, and the family had neither the capability for understanding this awkward young man nor the tools and social skills to make him right. Jeff's healing would take considerable time.

A bit later, Jeff signed up to join the Navy and the enlistment process required not only proof of age but also his parents' permission since he was only "seventeen". Jeff contacted his parents to obtain their permission and a copy of his birth certificate, which over the years and through several moves had been misplaced. *Permission* was forthcoming – no problem. Jeff's mother, Fannie, contacted the Tennessee Children's Home Society to acquire a new birth certificate. It was only then that Jeff discovered that not even his birth date was sacred. The Boyars had changed his date of birth from 1942 to 1943 so as to not conflict with the birth date of their natural daughter who was also born in 1942. Appearances were important in Beverly Hills. Jeff, it turned out, was eighteen years-old after all: he did not need his parents' permission to enlist. Jeff's military career was short. After a diagnosis of enuresis (bed wetting) was established during boot camp, Jeff was rejected for a fourth time. First his birth parents, then his adoptive parents, then his extended family in Tennessee, and now even the military was telling him to go away. Things could not look bleaker for a teenager trying to make it on his own and build a little self esteem along the way.

Documents show that Jeff appealed more than once to the state adoption agencies in order to find out what had happened to his sister Mary, known to Jeff as "Betty", but now in California as "Paula". He gave the agencies "one more chance" to help him locate Paula when he was back in Chattanooga at the age of nineteen. These appeals were taken seriously in the spring of 1962 and a heartfelt effort by Chattanooga adoption officials was met with the inevitable negative results by Nashville agency directors. Jeff was neither the parent nor Mary herself. The law did not permit adoption records to be unsealed for a sibling. Even if Tennessee legal barriers could be surmounted, those pertaining to California jurisdiction would be formidable. Sorry, Jeff, now go away. The genuine sympathy expressed by the social worker in the post Georgia Tann era was evident in the letters. Do look at the Records and Documents section (Appendix B). This social worker's letter is very much worth reading. She appealed to the state citing Jeff as an example of all that could go wrong with the adoption process.

Jeff's stated urgency in discovering the location, name, and status of his sister was that he did not want to accidentally court and marry her, which somehow seemed to him to be a real possibility. Jeff later told me that he would ask every girl that he dated if she was adopted. The need to find Paula was deeper than this one issue, but this aspect was especially relevant during this visit to Tennessee because Jeff was in love at the time and wanted to get married as soon as he could support a wife. He was working at a Kroger grocery store bagging groceries. Before Jeff's teenage plans saw fruition, however, his girlfriend became pregnant by another suitor, and she married that young man instead of Jeff. Rejection number… I really have lost count now.

At this point Jeff must have been a troubled teenager. Alone and abandoned, he was the true life version of a rebel without a cause. Jeff was no Marlon Brando though. Skinny and bespeckled with horn-rimmed glasses, he more closely resembled Buddy Holly.

Jeff stole a car. When he told me the story, he used the term "joyride". It was no stranger's car either; it belonged to the one aunt that he thought cared about him. Jeff had not intended to "borrow" the car for all that long. He and a friend went on a "joyride". When the police captured them, Jeff was not treated as gently by Chattanooga authorities as the police had treated him in California.

Jeff wasn't treated gently in prison either. Jeff took the fall for his friend whose idea it was to take the car in the first place. Maybe Jeff went along with the idea to please his friend. After all, to have a friend was to have someone on your side in life, someone in your corner. Maybe Jeff took full responsibility because Jeff had nothing and no one – no future and nobody who cared – and his friend did care. Maybe Jeff felt responsible because the car had belonged to Anna Lee, his father's sister, the aunt who had taken him into her home. Maybe Jeff took responsibility because he meant no harm and his naïveté prevented him from imagining that the consequences could be very harsh. At any rate Jeff took the entire blame for the "joyride" and received no leniency from the court. He was a juvenile delinquent and an example was set for others.

As I insinuated, prison life was not kind to Jeff. The skinny kid with the horn-rimmed glasses was ill-equipped, physically or emotionally, to deal with a prison population. He told me that he did what he had to do to survive. He hinted at sexual abuse, but he never wanted to talk about it and I never pressed the issue. I have never read where the stages of development move through neglect, abandonment, rejection, and abuse. Nevertheless, that seems to be the tortuous path taken by my brother.

After maybe a year in prison, Jeff was released and found employment doing factory work. Work that is repetitive and mind-numbing to most people could not oppress Jeff's bright and inquisitive mind. Score one for the high I.Q. Jeff saw a way to triple production at the factory and designed a part for the machinery to accomplish this. Rather than applying for a patent that could have made him rich, he sold the design to the company for a lump sum when they made him the offer. With this sum of cash he went to Mexico in violation of his parole conditions.

In Mexico he met a senorita who introduced him to (among other things) the Mexican version of karaoke. He would laugh as he told me how she would teach him the Spanish words to sing to the songs. Out of impishness, however she would teach him the wrong words. For example, instead of "Cast Your Fate to the Wind", Jeff would stand in front of the crowds singing "Cast Your *Farts* to the Wind" in Spanish and would wonder why the audience would laugh. Still, or perhaps because of this, he would usually win these contests.

Jeff used his money that he was awarded for his invention to put himself through medical school in Mexico. With no high school diploma (Jeff "reached" the 12$^{th}$ grade) and no college, he essentially bought his way into the Universidad Autónoma de Guadalajara, the oldest and largest private university in México. It could not have been easy learning medicine in another language and without that little preliminary nicety, college. But he did it. Score two for the high I.Q.

After medical school, Jeff worked with an obstetrician whose name translated to "Dr. Kill" – perhaps a Doctor Matar. In this setting he delivered what must have been hundreds of babies. When Jeff came back to the United States, the degree was not transferable, so he could no longer practice medicine. It is uncertain whether Jeff accomplished all of this as he described it to Paula and me. He may have completed enough medical school to apprentice with or assist the Mexican obstetrician. He also mentions some respiratory therapist training and employment. Jeff was vague about medical school records, and in discussions of medicine, he would display limited knowledge, merely indicating how much had changed since he went to medical school. While that is true, what else was clear to me was that Jeff was very bright. Given a better opportunity in life, I have no doubt that he could have achieved anything that he wanted to achieve.

After Mexico, Jeff went through a period of wanderlust. For a while, he was part of a motorcycle gang. At another time he did carnival work. Mostly, however, he took out on his own. He would drive an old car which would eventually break down, and then he would hitchhike. He would stay in one place long enough to find work and would work long enough to get another car. Then he would take out on the road again. During this gypsy travel, he met and married Connie, who adapted to his lifestyle and even hitchhiked with him. Connie was periodically unfaithful, however, and Jeff was in the process of getting a divorce from Connie when he met Brenda.

Brenda and Jeff met accidentally. Brenda was working for her father doing janitorial work. Jeff happened to engage Brenda's father on the citizens band (CB) radio. They struck up a friendly conversation and Brenda's father invited Jeff to come visit that very evening and also to meet Brenda. Brenda recalled that she was "filthy" from the cleaning that she was doing and her hair was in rollers. Nevertheless, they met. The next night they went bowling and for a car ride. Brenda at that time was a single mother with three children of her own. The first of her previous two husbands was very childish and the second was an alcoholic. One evening while Jeff was visiting, a social services worker called and was quizzing Brenda about her situation of being a single mother with three children. Jeff took the phone from Brenda and indicated that the social services worker would not have to persist in bothering Brenda about this, because he was going to marry her.

A few days later, Jeff formally proposed to Brenda who initially resisted the idea of another marriage. On the advice of her mother and other family, she accepted the proposal of marriage. She always explained her reasoning as "Elvis was dead, and since she had no chance of getting him, she could accept Jeff's proposal". Jeff and Brenda were married September 17, 1977, in a little shack on a farm in Keeler, Michigan, where Jeff worked fixing farm equipment. Jeff and Brenda together had a janitor business and later ran a CB radio shop.

His karaoke talents expanded and he began doing Elvis impersonations. Brenda says that in the beginning, Jeff could not sing. Brenda would close the door to their bedroom and turn up the stereo. Then one day she thought he was playing an Elvis CD, but it was Jeff singing. She made him stop and start again to prove that he was not lip sinking to a recording. He became most popular for his rendition of My Way, for which he received many a karaoke contest trophy.

For a period of time, Jeff worked at Cook Nuclear Plant, maintaining the lighting among other systems. He would be on scaffolding changing light bulbs in a setting where a misstep could be fatal. Jeff was an attentive apprentice and eventually persuaded his supervisors to let him take the electrician certification test. They were reluctant at first and told Jeff that even master electricians had difficulty passing this test. Jeff was allowed to take it, however, and passed it to the surprise of all. Score three for the high I.Q.

Jeff and Brenda lived in an old school bus for several years, which they sold and then acquired a travel trailer. Jeff had a pickup at the time, but was afraid to haul the travel trailer because it swayed precariously. Their next dwelling was a fifth-wheel trailer, which they parked in Rogers Lake, Michigan. Their first winter there was challenging. Even water was hard to come by. They relocated to Florida and stayed in parks, but regulations limited them to two weeks at any given location. After awhile, they went back to the Rogers Lake park setting, where Jeff took on employment in order to be able to stay there. With winter approaching, they started back to Florida, but got only as far as Centre, Alabama. Jeff was doing karaoke in a bar. Everyone was friendly and wanted them to stay, so they did. As in Michigan, they found a park – Alabama Queen – where Jeff could work and they could stay.

Jeff found plenty to do in Centre. For one friend, he provided a sound system for wrestling events. Other friends would provide locations for them to park their fifth wheel trailer, in return for Jeff's handiwork, which included everything from mechanic work to digging graves. This lifestyle proved too difficult, and heart problems experienced in Michigan, provided Jeff with disability income. For awhile, Jeff, Brenda, and Brenda's mother Margaret lived in a small, rented trailer, later moving to a larger 3-bedroom mobile home.

Brenda and Jeff went through a period of separation and lost the mobile home. Brenda at the time was taking care of a gentleman in his 90's, Carl Rayburn, who invited Brenda and her mother to move in with him. After a time, Jeff joined them. When the Colonel (as Jeff and Brenda called Mr. Rayburn) died, he willed his home to Brenda and Jeff. Carl's son "Junior" contested the transfer of the Colonel's property to Jeff and Brenda, so Jeff compiled 1100 pages of evidence that the son had misappropriated tens of thousands of dollars worth of property from the Colonel. Litigation and difficulty with attorneys ensued, but the courts eventually found in favor of Jeff and Brenda, thanks in no small part to Jeff's investigations into the son's wrongdoings. Jeff's efforts led him to a new career interest – private investigator – one of the few things he had not done yet.

In the summer of 2006, Jeff visited me and described abdominal pain, 40 pounds of weight loss, and other GI symptoms. Medical workups by his doctors in Alabama were conducted, but reached a variety of contradictory results. One doctor suggested irritable bowel syndrome. A CT scan of the liver was read as normal, while another physician suggested cirrhosis, although Jeff had not drunk alcohol in decades. A subsequent investigation done in Chattanooga included a biopsy of the liver, which was largely replaced by carcinoid tumor, a slow-growing cancer that typically originates in the bowel.

The biopsy was on a Friday and Jeff stayed at my house for me to watch for complications and for him to recuperate. We had a great visit. We told stories about parts of our lives that the other of us had missed out on. It was probably the best time we had ever had together. Jeff was opiate-naïve (meaning he was not used to the effects of narcotics). His doctor had prescribed oxycodone for pain and Jeff was occasionally giddy. He felt better than he had felt in months. His appetite improved dramatically and he was sleeping well for the first time in weeks. As we talked and told stories, I learned more about his rich and varied life than I had previously known, but more importantly we had a good opportunity to just hang out and enjoy being with each other. It was an opportunity that we had never had before, and would never have again.

I learned fresh details about Jeff. I played the piano and sang Jeff some new songs I was writing. He was amazed. He said that it was exactly his style and not only could he have written it, but that he actually had written a song similar to the one that I just played and sang for him. In his trusting Jeff manner, however, he had sent the song to a publisher and never thought anymore about it until one day when he heard it played on the radio. He nearly wrecked the car simultaneously turning up the radio and screaming to the others, "That's my song. I wrote that." Someone in the music industry had stolen Jeff's song and turned it into a hit. It was not the first time a large sum of money had eluded my brother. This was typical of the stories we shared that weekend. By Sunday Jeff was feeling better. I was on call and making hospital rounds, so Lynna Ruth drove Jeff to Centre. It was Brenda's mother Margaret's birthday, and Jeff did not want to miss wishing her a happy one. Also it was only ten days until Paula and Larry would be down from Cincinnati, and the six of us could be together. Anyway that is how we left it.

## Chapter 9
# Jerri Wayne Delaney

Few people have the details of the first three months of their life so well documented. From the adoption records:

> For the past few months Mrs. Delaney, her mother and Jerri have been living in one room at 815 McCallie Avenue. a rooming house. Her husband gives her $15 per week. She has not had the money to take Jerri to the doctor, nor to buy cod-liver oil, baby good, etc. that he should be having now. She says it will always be that way. She knows that it will be impossible for

them to adequately support Jerri and give him the things every child needs. "We could not give up the older children because they already know us but the baby will not know the difference," she said seriously. What she was saying seemed to be painful to her and yet we recognized that she had deliberately arrived at this decision.

I interpreted the meaning of adoption and she said she fully understood that it meant final separation and that while she regretted this action it was the only solution to the problem. I went into temporary foster care with her and asked if the Family Agency could provide this care until she and her husband worked through some of their problems, she would accept their help. She said no, that temporary care would not solve their problems; that her husband would probably never make any more money than he does now and that it is not sufficient to support his dependents. I asked what her husband thought about the adoptive plan and she said they had talked it over numerous times before, she never got in touch with me and that he had sent her to talk with me about it. She said he would come too when I needed him.

I asked Mrs. Delaney what she planned to do if we took Jerri. She said she had a job to go to on the 24$^{th}$ - a new orange drink stand is opening on Market St. and she has promise of employment there. She feels that if she does not have the responsibility of the baby and can get out and meet new people she will regain her health more quickly. Staying at home and looking after Jerri has apparently made her very unhappy and her mother is too old to care for the child while she works.

Mrs. Delaney said she was so mentally and physically run down she could not be a good mother to her children. In time, if she gets to feeling better she may ask for custody of her two older children when she gets a divorce, otherwise she will leave them with her husband and his people. She also mentioned that part of her marital difficulty could be blamed on "in-laws".

We suggested that she have her husband to come and talk with us before a definite decision was made. She asked if I didn't wish to come and see Jerri before she and her husband signed the surrender. I told her I might drop by there later on during the day.

I did stop by and went on upstairs to the room where I found Jerri lying on the bed. The room with a bed, oil stove, small table and an old refrigerator, was spotless. I met Mrs. Delaney's mother, Mrs. Mary (McJunkin) Clark, age 68. She was very clean and had little to say except that Jerri was a fine baby but was not getting certain things that he needed because they did not have the money with which to buy them. Jerri was kicking his feet in the air and looked like a perfect specimen. Mrs. Delaney remarked that anybody would love him because he was such a sweet baby. He smiled and cooed and all of his reactions appeared normal.

---

The American Red Cross headquarters are sited in a large brick building at 815 McCallie Avenue today. My original home place now has the mission of rescuing many others for whom fortune and fate have been fickle. How ironic is that?

I am clearly fortunate in that my adoptive parents were loving and nurturing. They sacrificed in order to provide opportunities for me to realize my potential. And I have worked hard in life to live up to the standards they set and to meet their expectations of me. I have known security and have always felt that they were there for me. If only Jeff could have had such good fortune!

As Jerri Wayne Delaney I survived three months with a "nervous type" mother who did not want me. I was adopted by new parents – John Brendle Standridge and Annie Juanita Dees Standridge – who very much wanted me, and who were willing and able to care for me and about me in the way every child deserves. For this I am forever grateful.

John and Juanita Standridge met and married in Benton, Tennessee, where John was Clerk and Master for Polk County and Juanita taught senior English at Polk County High School. John was the first in his family to attend college. He graduated with a degree in history from Tusculum College. Juanita graduated in English and drama from Mississippi State College for Women and considered becoming an actress. One of her former students remembered her to me for her dramatic reading of Walt Whitman's "O Captain! My Captain!" to the assembled high school student body upon the death of Franklin Delano Roosevelt. They were both active in Democratic politics and together they edited and published the local Polk County News. It was into this honest, earnest, intellectual, political, and loving environment that I was adopted. Juanita was working as a social worker also at that time, and it was in this capacity that she heard of my potential placement as an infant. She had an inside track, but other than this "insider trading" twist, my adoption appeared to be completely legitimate. It occurs to me only now in fact that by acting quickly when I became available for adoption, my adoptive mother saved me from being sold in the black market baby ring. She got me before they could sell me.

Life in rural Tennessee was actually quite enriching for me. I had a stimulating attentive early life, and as an only child, I was probably overindulged. Examples of this nurturing extremism include my parents driving back and forth through the McCallie tunnel because I would take my bottle better when we were in the tunnel. I cannot make this stuff up. Another example is the year my parents stocked up on beets because I developed a taste for beets. Go figure. Another time was when I went through an entire carton of eggs while sitting in the middle of the kitchen floor, throwing one egg at a time and shouting, "Play ball!" My antics were met with smiles at my cute behavior rather than the spanking that I deserved. That is enough of this embarrassing part of my life. It was not my fault.

When I was five years old, my father was given what I believe was a political appointment. He was the new Director of Finance and Taxation for the southeast Tennessee region (read: chief revenuer). I suspect that our move to Chattanooga was prompted in large measure by my parents' perception of a better school system there. My mother became a stay-at-home mom both in Benton and in Chattanooga for a number of years before returning to teaching. I remember a good childhood with neighborhood friends, bicycles, dogs, toys, TVs, vacations, piano lessons, and books.

I have always done well in school. My first grade teacher took special interest in me after my I.Q. test came back very high. Allow me the dignity of not being explicit. My teacher, Mrs. Ludeman, sold my parents a set of World Book encyclopedias and started sending me home from Sunnyside elementary school with a new book to read every afternoon. My mother would read these with me and seemed to take pride in my accelerated education. At the time, of course, I could not have known that I had a brother who had attended this same Sunnyside elementary school only six years earlier. Perhaps he sat in the same room and had the same teacher that I did.

Throughout elementary school, junior high, and high school I was chosen for "talented youth programs", honors society, Beta Club, and the like. I enjoyed playing trumpet in band, excelled scholastically, and was awarded Tyner High School's math award when I graduated. Whenever I came home with an "A" on my report card, my mother would tease me with, "Why wasn't it an "A+"? Seriously, folks, she was teasing. She had a weird sense of humor that has rubbed off on me.

The sputnik-inspired space race prompted many of my generation to major in engineering and I did major in electrical engineering at Tennessee Technological University for awhile. I also worked as a co-op student at the NASA space fight center in Huntsville, Alabama, assisting with the digital flight simulation of the Saturn V booster rocket. While there I took a night course in psychology at the University of Alabama, Huntsville branch. On the basis of that and other teenage experiences, I transferred to the University of Tennessee at Knoxville and changed my major to psychology, later expanding into pre-med. It was in an honors psychology seminar program that I met the love of my life – one Miss Lynna Ruth Webb. We were married in 1970 and went on to raise two magnificent sons.

Meanwhile, I went on to medical school, family medicine residency, private practice, and eventually into academics. This journey took us from Knoxville to Memphis, to Etowah, to Roanoke, to Ocoee, to Cleveland, to Kingsport, to Signal Mountain, and to Harrison, Tennessee, over the decades. There were many rich experiences in each of these places and we have friends now scattered all over the country. As a family, we played together and worked together. We hiked and camped when the boys were young and went to their soccer games and band performances when they were older.

I am not good at or all that comfortable with providing details about myself like I have done for Jeff and Paula. Again, however, I am fortunate to have an essay written by Paula in 1996 during her freshman English class. This one is titled "Dr. John".

## Dr. John
### By Paula Cope

*His license plate reads "DocJohn", but that is just a small part of who he really is. John and I were having lunch together recently, when his pager interrupted our meal. After returning the call to his patient, he looked annoyed. He explained that the patient had called him "Doc", and he resented being called that because the slang term, by itself, belittled him as a person. He went on to say that doctoring is his profession, but not the sum total of who he is. He is right; John is so much more than just a doctor.*

*I first met John in January of this year, as the culmination of a search that began nearly three years earlier, when I first learned of his existence. John is my younger brother, but we were separated by adoption over 40 years ago. Before meeting for the first time, I was worried that he might be disappointed in me because I don't have the education and professional background that he has. He sensed my nervousness, and he put my mind at east by writing to me, "Don't be worried that I'll be disappointed somehow. This is not a contest. You are my sister and the only one on earth who is. That makes you special in a way no one else could be. It's heart and soul, and humor and kindness, and caring about it all that counts, and I've already picked up on those qualities in you. The way you and your husband look in that picture you sent says a lot, and speaks volumes about what good people you are. You better start worrying about what kind of weird duck your brother is."*

*What I discovered about this "weird duck" is that for all of his accomplishments and such, he is a kind and gentle soul that has, in his own words, "worked hard not to be like other doctors" (arrogant and so forth). "I think character is very important, and I try real hard to be kind, sensitive and compassionate. I think that the profession suffers from a shortage of these characteristics." John is someone I would like even if we weren't related.*

*As a doctor, his accomplishments are impressive. "He served as chief of medicine at both Cleveland area hospitals, as president of the Bradley County Medical Society and as medical director of the substance abuse treatment unit. Dr Standridge has been affiliated with East Tennessee State University Department of Family Medicine and served as program director of the Kingsport Family Practice Residency. In 1991, he received the 'Primary Care Provider of the Year' Award presented by the Virginia Primary Care Associates Inc. Dr. Standridge is a diplomat of the American Board of Family Practice and holds the certificate* of added qualifications in geriatric medicine. He is a fellow with the American Academy of Family Physicians and is a member of several professional societies and organizations" (Chattanooga Free Press).

His day does not end when the last patient leaves the offices in the evening, however. That is when he does evening rounds at the nursing home and occasionally volunteers at the free clinic. His wife, Lynna Ruth, told me that the old ladies at the nursing homes he visits just love him. They refer to him as "the Robert Redford of the geriatric set."

John said in an article he wrote in 1993, "What forms the ideals of the family physician is an ability to keep art in perspective." He also quotes Sir William Osler as saying, "The practice of medicine is an art, not a trade; a calling, not a business; a calling in which your heart will be exercised equally with your head" (Standridge 11-12).

John shares a special relationship with his patients, as evidenced in an article he had published a few years back. He relates a touching account of his oldest patient, Mary, and her death at age 105 ½. "Forget your biased image of a centenarian. Mary was plump and rosy of skin tone and personality. She was gutsy, sharp mentally, and possessed a keen wit. She laughed frequently and easily, and, of course, we performed and joked with her all the more for that" (Going With…). John treated her with dignity and respect, and her last words to him were, "Will you die with me?" Of course he couldn't, but a part of her lives on in the memories John shared with us of that delightful lady.

In his personal life, he lives by the same principles that have made him such a respected physician. He treats people with dignity and respect. While some may mistake his slow style of speaking as just another Southern mannerism, he has perfected the art of thinking before speaking and weighs his words carefully.

On more than one occasion, I have observed him holding back when his wife said something he obviously didn't agree with, and then he would turn to me with a wink and say, "You learn to pick your fights".

John has a full head of straight brown hair, streaked with a few strands of gray that stubbornly falls down across his forehead in a haphazard fashion. A full beard and glasses hide much of the rest of his face, except for what he describes as a rather prominent nose. He has a marvelous sense of humor and likes to play with words. He describes his wife's name, Lynna Ruth, as being a mellifluous and euphonic southern double name. Being overweight myself, I was pleasantly surprised to see that he doesn't always "eat right" and can find as many excuses as I can for not exercising regularly. He likes jazz music, cats, and the beach. He plays the piano, writes a little music now and then, and has oil paintings hanging in his den that he painted himself.

He and his wife share a love and respect of nature, and once built their own log cabin on 40 acres of land that backs up to a national forest in eastern Tennessee. Their son, Adam, and his family now live in it. The house he currently lives in is filled with antiques, but most of them are family heirlooms that he feels are to be used and enjoyed, not hidden away or merely observed like a museum piece. His hardwood floors are covered with beautiful wool rugs that his mother hooked by hand. When I remarked that I would be afraid to walk on them, he said that his mother had always insisted that they were meant to be walked on, and out of a love and respect for her, they continue to do so. The love of his life, other than his wife and two sons, is his two year old grandson, Addison, who calls him Paco.

When asked what I should bring to our very first meeting, a weekend in a cabin at Cumberland Falls State Park, he replied: "Bring a lifetime of experience, a warm and glad heart, a bucket of tolerance for your strange and definitely different brother, ears to listen, arms to hug, and mouths to feed." That pretty much sums up how John approaches life in general.

Works Cited

"Dr. Standridge Opens Family Med Practice." Chattanooga Free Press 13 Nov. 1994. Medical and Regional News.

Standridge, MD, John B. "A Hero's Journey." The New Physician Dec. 1993: 11-12.

—. "Going With Guts." Archives of Family Medicine vol. 2. Feb. 1993. Copyright 1993, American Medical Association: 123.

Starting medical practice in Benton, Tennessee, was based on my perception of what I thought my father would have wanted me to do. Treating the underserved has always appealed to my better self. My father died in 1973, when I was in medical school, and it always struck me that he did not live to see me graduate. My mother lived two more decades. She moved back to the small town of Benton, but continued to teach in the Chattanooga area schools. She rose very early to drive the 60 miles each way, each day. Rather than teaching senior English, she was focused on teaching remedial reading to seventh graders. She initiated Hamilton County's remedial reading program and used my collection of vintage DC comic books to stimulate interest in reading. I miss those comic books. My mother survived one form of lung cancer and its surgery, but became unable to continue working. She retired to Benton where she lived with her mother and my father's sister, Gena. My grandmother died first, at age 93, then my aunt. My mother succumbed to another more virulent lung cancer in 1993. Even now, after their death, I am basically trying to please and respect my parents and live up to their expectations. Not out of fear or obligation, but out of the expectation that they instilled in me when they taught me to believe in myself.

When my mother died, "I was all there was left". I am trying to convey the feeling one has when all of the older loved ones in your family have passed on. The sense of loss compounded with being alone in the decision department and having no one with that special wisdom born of life experience to turn to – this is a special emptiness that no one warns you about. When my sister found me, that void was instantly filled.

Today I am a professor of family medicine with the University of Tennessee College of Medicine in Chattanooga. I am the program director of the UTCOMC's geriatric medicine residency. I am board certified in family medicine, geriatric medicine, and addiction medicine; and a specialist in clinical hypertension. I am the medical director at the Council for Alcohol and Drug Abuse Services (CADAS), a local alcohol and drug treatment facility, and medical director of the Alexian Health Care Center. I am in demand as a lecturer locally, nationally, and internationally. Point being, it is actually a fairly impressive resumé, and to me it just happened that way. I am the first to acknowledge that none of this matters in the larger scheme of things. Here's the point: I have been fortunate. I am fortunate to have all of the work and recognition that one person can handle and still be able to dabble in hobbies such as music, painting, and cooking. I am even more fortunate to have with me in my life an amazing family and wonderful friends and colleagues.

Our sons, Adam and Aaron, and our grandchildren, Addison and Arianna, add a rich tapestry to our lives; and our friends are the greatest people you would ever want to know. Adam and his wife, Betty, are enrolled agents (E.A.) with the I.R.S. Together they own and operate a half dozen franchised income tax offices. They also take care of twenty-four horses at their ranch, Earthaven Equine Rescue and Activities Center, Inc. – a nonprofit establishment for rescuing neglected or abused horses and providing equine therapy for individuals with physical or emotional disabilities. One example is when Adam worked with the people from Hospice of Chattanooga to provide horse rides and fun times to the children who had lost a parent to one of the terminal conditions that call for hospice care. There is no person that Adam will not go out of his way to do anything he can to help. Adam is simply the most amazing person.

---

In January, 2009, Adam described himself rather accurately on his facebook profile in an exercise titled, "The whole 25 things about me".

1) I live in a log cabin on a 50 acre ranch with 24 horses, 30+ chickens, 3 goats, 2 pigs, 29 cats, 5 dogs, 6 rabbits, 2 parakeets, 2 kids, and a red tail in an oak tree.

2) I actually enjoy reading USC Title 26.

3) After close to 30 years owning a computer, I still can't type.

4) Betty and I were married one day less than a month before Addison was born. 15 years ago last fall.

5) We're still best friends.

6) I can sweat copper pipes, frame in windows and doors, hang and finish drywall, rewire the whole

house, build trusses, lay shingles or metal decking, tile the tub, and change a light bulb.

7) I can't spell (despite well meaning attempts by several great English teachers, including my grandma).

8) I enjoy riding horses, camping, canoeing, cooking breakfast in cast iron, and splitting fire wood.

9) Not so much into TV or video games.

10) Matthew is currently my favorite book of the Bible.

11) I let Betty cut 15 inches off my hair in 1996 so H&R Block could hire me as an office manager and still had longer hair than most.

12) I am proficient in Access, Excel, Word, Fortran (once upon a time), Visual Basic and HTML.

12.5) I don't dance.

13) I would rather listen than talk.

14) I have been to five colleges and still just have a high school diploma (and I think they gave me that so I wouldn't come back).

15) One of my degree seeking attempts was auto mechanics. Now hate turning wrenches. Fortunately my son seems to enjoy it for the moment and we have rebuilt two tractors, a 2000 mustang, a '79 Scout, and worked on 100's of others.

16) I have a working 1941 model Frick sawmill powered by a 1957 Farmall H tractor. I have no pine trees left.

17) I have been to all 6 of my daughter Arianna's ballet recitals and seen her perform in the Nutcracker all 4 times. I usually get funny looks in from the other parents in the theater.

## Jerri Wayne Delaney

18) I am the only member of my family that can't play some type of instrument. I am also the only member of my family that doesn't wear corrective lenses.

19) I can skin a buck, run a trot line, cook a whole pig in the ground, and we usually have at least a half acre garden.

20) I drive a white 1995 24' Ford F-350 crew cab with a pickup bed, cattle racks, and a 7.3L Diesel. It has a busted fender and dented bumpers I'm not inclined to replace, close to 190K miles, will pull a mountain sideways, hold in excess of 5K pounds, and does 65 max downhill with a good tail wind. Many times have I enjoyed helping people move things that wouldn't fit in their damn little rice burner after they chided me for the fuel cost or pollution output of my tank.

21) I like frog legs, scrambled eggs with Tabasco, hash taters with onions for breakfast on my birthday. But I'll eat almost anything.

22) I hate crowds and being in the spotlight. So the couple of times I have received awards at conventions with in excess of 2K people present, I tried to escape before they called me up. It has never worked, they keep tracking me down.

23) I am blessed with many great friends and family. Probably one of the few that can say I love my wife's family as my own and am proud they put up with me so well.

24) I enjoy being able to help church family and neighbors with everything from home repairs and hauling things to animal care and fire wood.

24.5) I am 6'1" and 175lbs. I wear the same size jeans I did in high school. I still have some of the clothes I had in high school.

25) I can do algebra, calculate depreciation on an asset with a 7 year class life, long division, fractions, and percentages in my head. And now I'm proud to say I finally (after starting this thing over 3 hours ago) counted to 25 (or so)...

---

The lovely Denise tagged me on Facebook recently with the same exercise. I could bring myself to do it only by limiting the reply to her. If this paragraph and 25 things are in the book, it is only due to surviving editing by Lynna Ruth. Oh, well, if Adam can do it, I can too.

1. I am very impatient.
2. I should have started with something positive.
3. I used to be really good at Name That Tune.
4. I am incredibly nostalgic.
5. Maybe it is because I have had a really terrific life so far.
6. I cry when people I know die.
7. I enjoy playing "washers" (Washers, for the benefit of non Missouri residents is a game similar to horseshoes where you throw a large metal washer (goes on a bolt) into a box from several feet away.)
8. I love to share my opinion on things, no matter their importance. I don't need to convert anyone, and I like to hear counter opinion. I think sometimes this comes off as more forceful than I intend.

## Jerri Wayne Delaney

9. I have a very acute sense of right and wrong. This backfires from time to time because most issues make my eyes water. The neat thing is the way smell translates to memory.
10. I love to cook! I love having a group of good friends over to share some food and a bottle of wine.
11. I started playing music around age 5 – piano at home; trumpet at school. I still dabble in music
12. I am somewhat intellectual.
13. I love to make people laugh. If I can make someone laugh out loud or "snort", I feel like I "won" something.
14. Smart and funny are big turn ons.
15. I use big words a bit more than I should and I love word play.
16. I am in the early process of recording a CD with Aaron. It was his Christmas present to me: a CD of traditional Irish music by the two of us. We'll have a lot of fun, and it is a safe, friendly and encouraging environment to learn and grow. I have self-produced 3 previous CDs.
17. I am still/back in academia. I have the good fortune of a position that doesn't take all my nights and weekends – only most of them.
18. I like to see the big picture, but I like details, too.
19. I have a Beagle named Molly McGuire Delaney. She's a good dog, too.
20. I am not good at keeping in touch.
21. I am still completely nuts over Lynna Ruth!
22. I can wiggle my ears… could ever since I was a kid.

23. My favorite Beatle is Paul. Still getting it done – some great recent CDs.

24. I want to let my little light shine.

---

Aaron and the lovely Denise live, work, and play in St. Louis, Missouri, where Aaron follows his bliss as a computer programmer designing computer games for Simutronics. He was recently promoted to audio engineer and now composes and records music and sound effects for the games, like *Hero's Journey* and *Elanthia*, that he helped to create. Scratch that; as of this last edit, he is now Simutronic's Lead Designer, writing the story line. I cannot keep up with that boy.

Aaron on guitar and every other thing, and Denise on bass and drums, play and record the most amazing music. With their friend, Princess Sara, they comprise the group *Whiskey Tango Foxtrot*. Aaron's solo efforts are sometimes given the band name *Liquid Burning Fish* or *Light Grey Sabbath*. His college band, *Revolution Block*, was outstanding, winning much local recognition, awards, and contests. Their CD is titled *Role Model* – which is also the name of a song on the album written and sung by Aaron. Adam may have 24 horses, but Aaron has a menagerie of musical instruments to rival his brother's surfeit of livestock. Aaron and Denise are exceedingly fun to hang with. According to Aaron's Facebook page as I write this, Aaron is "generally concerned with the state of things," but recently "made a perfectly adequate balsamic vinaigrette dressing."

I am exceedingly proud of both of my sons. I once remarked of my sons that I had a country mouse and a city mouse, in reference to a children's book that we used to read to them. Both of these young men value people over things; both possess a fierce understanding of right and wrong. Lynna Ruth and I are blessed with their love and are fortunate for how each has grown to be self-actualized.

Please do not think of me as too fortunate or conversely a sad case. Things are what they are and I am neither ashamed for being an "overachiever" nor apologetic for my lack of downtime. Whatever I have achieved has come about not only from a lifetime of study, extremely demanding work, and putting in over 100 hours of work some weeks, but also from the support and energy given to me initially by my parents but more importantly for the last 40 years by my wife, who is by all measures amazing. It is hard to be objective about oneself, but I have always considered myself as highly egalitarian. I believe in the inherent worth of every individual. My point in sharing my story of good fortune and achievements in life is to contrast them with my brother Jeff, *who and where but for fortune go I.*

We were so alike in mannerisms, humor, intelligence, and aptitude. Jeff went to medical school in Mexico and delivered more babies than I have, yet he could not transfer that skill set to this country. I went to medical school at the University of Tennessee along a traditional pathway. Jeff passed a master electrician's exam and was referred to as an "electrical engineer" at a nuclear power plant, while I majored in electrical engineering at Tennessee Technological University out of aptitude and interest. Jeff and I both love(d) music. He performed live while I composed and recorded, but the love was the same. We shared a remarkably similar world view, philosophy of life, political leanings, and ethics. And we both loved our sister Paula. What more proof do you need of the power of genetics?

I am not wealthy, but my life of hard work has paid off with typical middle class home, enough money to pay the bills, and strong, smart, and healthy children and grandchildren. Jeff's life also consisted of hard work, but lacking the support system that I had, it granted him none of these satisfactions. Jeff preferred country music and Elvis; I prefer jazz, rock, and classical music. What more proof do you need of the power of the environment?

But enough introspection. I am what I am, but if Jeff had gone to my adoptive parents and I had been sold to the Boyars, I have no doubt that our lives would have been substantially different and quite possibly largely interchanged – Jeff in my shoes and I in his. We had the same shoe size, by the way: 9. Let's get back to the three of us. My life seems boring by comparison.

## Chapter 10
# Our Time Together

We were bonded together as the Delaney children – Marion Richard ("Dickie"), Mary Elizabeth ("Betty"), and Jerri Wayne ("baby Jerri") – but we did not think of ourselves or each other by those names. We were Jeff, Paula, and John. Paula and I had ten years to get to know each other and our families; the three of us had but five years.

I would occasionally notice a continuing medical education (CME) conference that was being held in Cincinnati. I could then use the conference as an excuse to visit Larry and Paula Cope, Beth and Paul Bollman, and my wonderful great nephews and niece, Jacob, Benjamin, and Mary Josephine. In fact I am fairly certain that I became a

Certified Medical Review Officer (CMRO), authorized to make life changing decisions regarding people based on their urine drug screens, simply because there was a one week CME conference on that topic at a time when I wanted to visit my sister and her family. Medical conferences were easier to justify than vacations, and tax deductible as a business expense. I had plenty of available vacation time; I'm just a sick workaholic that needed an excuse to visit. OK? I never have functioned as a CMRO, but you never know when the need to do something like that will arise. Meanwhile I can add it to the ridiculous string of letters after my name.

Paula's excuses to visit me in Chattanooga were similarly contrived. The two more common contrivances were related to the continuation of her annual visits with our cousin Sharon and shopping trips to Pigeon Forge. Glenda Sharon Osborne is our first cousin, the daughter of our father Marion's sister, Emma Gene Delaney Osborne. Sharon was Paula's favorite relative from the Delaney clan. The two of them enjoyed shopping and liked to eat out, but mostly they loved each other's company. Sharon lived on Lookout Mountain, near Chattanooga, and they would visit at her home as well as have their "girls' night out" on the town. Paula scheduled vacation time and came to Chattanooga every year, usually in June, to visit with Sharon. After our 1996 reunion, I could depend on seeing Paula for a goodly part of that week in June.

Larry was not comfortable staying at another person's house. Paula and Larry were more than welcome to stay with us in our guest bedroom. Our home on Signal Mountain was built in 1928. It was cozy but comfortable and accommodating. They did visit us frequently at our home and we would while away many hours in the living room or on the side deck talking, and sharing, and caring. Larry and Paula would always stay at the Howard Johnson's in East Ridge. It was at an I-75 interstate exit and it provided Larry with a dependable and comfortable familiarity. Plus, it was near a Cracker Barrel restaurant.

Our pattern was this. We would visit Larry and Paula at the Howard Johnson motel when they arrived in Chattanooga. We would sit poolside after dinner at the motel, talking into the late evening. We would drive home to sleep then get up to drive to the East Ridge Cracker Barrel the next morning for breakfast. Usually Adam and his family would join us for breakfast, driving in from Polk County about one hour away. We formed a large, happy table of relatives. Then the day laid before us like uncharted waters. We might shop; we might go to the aquarium or any of Chattanooga's many tourist attractions; we might go to Coolidge Park; we definitely would eat again. It never seemed to matter exactly what we did as long as we were together in a place that let us visit and talk and explore and share and, most of all, care. It never ceases to astonish me how much Paula and I loved one another. With genetics I could reasonable expect similarities of body habitus, intellect, even humor, but the immediate and total acceptance, support, and nurturing love was unexpected, and yet the greatest gift of all.

I did take vacation time when Paula and Larry came to visit. I had an old cabin cruser on Chickamauga lake at the time, so one thing we did was to take a boat trip up the river to Hiwassee Island where I could show Paula the estuary of great blue heron. Another time we might go to a play at Chattanooga Theater. Times were swell.

I mentioned too Paula's shopping trips to Pidgen Forge. Many like to visit this resort town with its discount malls to do their Christmas shopping and "get it over with". Paula was no exception except perhaps she enjoyed it more than most. She took Larry along to carry the packages. Larry and Paula were a wonderful couple. They were totally devoted and comfortable with each other. They appreciated in each other the qualities of kindness, genuine affection, and attention to each others needs and comfort. They were helpmates with the sure satisfaction of knowing someone intimately for a long time. Love is long.

Whenever these Pigeon Forge trips came about, usually in the fall, Lynna Ruth and I could depend on Larry and Paula making a side trip to visit with us in Chattanooga. So once or twice a year, we would visit, get to know each other more deeply, and just hang out enjoying the company. At other times we emailed and talked by telephone. Appendix A chronicles these missives.

My visits to Cincinnati were less frequent but no less enjoyable. Larry and Paula lived in an older, solidly built, and comfortable house in a quiet neighborhood. Several miles down the commercial district lived Paul and Beth in a two story house, roomier and of newer construction. We would often eat at Beth and Paul's. They were marvelous cooks and always fixed entirely too much food. Mary Josephine would sit in my lap and Benjamin would entertain me constantly. Jacob played the responsible older brother, looking out for the others but not letting them misbehave either. His definition of misbehaving and mine were not in synch as I was totally loving the children's attention and the older Bollmans thought I might be bothered by the young ones. No such thing; even the dog was great. As we were leaving one evening a grinning, beautiful

Mary Josephine, dressed in a Halloween princess costume, stole our hearts when she spontaneously called Lynna Ruth "Aunt Ruthie". This precious love is my great niece. Benjamin is the happiest, most affectionate creature on the planet; and Jacob is a strong, handsome, responsible, and genuinely fine young man. These are my great nephews. I would not have this amazing family if my sister Paula had not searched until she found me. These children would not be so impressive if Paul and Beth were not such nurturing, responsible, capable, and loving parents. I am blessed many times over.

After Jeff found us and we had our first tearful and joyous reunion, the three of us got together whenever we could. Always in June when Paula came down on her yearly vacation, we would meet according to the pattern already established by Larry and Paula. Jeff and Brenda would get a room at the venerable Howard Johnson, and the six of us would sit around the pool that first evening, with Cracker Barrel plans for the next morning. Then whatever anyone wanted to do, that's what we would do. Want to go see the model train exhibit at the Chattanooga Choo Choo? Sure, let's go. And off we went. Pookie's great adventures, one after another. We were like kids in a candy store. Shopping at antique shops (Junkin') or walking in the park or eating at a good restaurant, we were living the good life together for that week. After being separated for 50 years, who could blame us?

We occasionally arranged other visits, too, but at least once a year we could count on reuniting for our time together. It never got old. Chattanooga was more central. We never made it to Cincinnati or Centre with the three couples.

Lynna Ruth and I visted Jeff and Brenda fairly often in their mobile home in Centre, Alabama. They had lived there since the mid-nineties. Jeff had built a screened-in porch on the back and it was quite comfortable. It was quiet with no close neighbors in the cotton farming community, but Jeff was well liked and popular in Cherokee County, so there were frequent visitors. Jeff and Brenda loved their dogs, too, and were constantly entertained by them. They had a small pack.

Jeff and Brenda would come visit us on Signal Mountain as well. Centre was only a few hours down the road. One very special trip that Jeff made to Chattanooga was when he was booked to play live music in a local music hall. It was then that I met Robin Wooten, Jeff's long-time friend and musical collaborator. Robin has a wonderful singing voice, but I must admit partiality towards my brother Jeff. He loves to sing and his voice is clear and strong. Given an opportunity, he could have made it professionally. He gifted Paula and me with CDs that he had recorded with karaoke music backing him. I have recorded a few CDs myself. Did I mention that Jeff and I had a few things in common?

Then there was the time Jeff came by himself because of some personal issues that he wanted to talk over with me. How special is that? Jeff tells me his troubles and I listen like any brother, eager to help in any way I could. It was not advice, so much, that I had to offer. It was that one thing that is so rare that you cannot dependably find it even in close families – unconditional acceptance. Support and acceptance were what I could offer my brother. He did not need my advice. He was the expert on his life. But I could be there for him. How special was that?

# The Events of September and October, 2006

When the great book of life is written, no one will give a rat's ass about letters – MD, CMD, CMRO, FAAFP, FASAM – or any other achievement. What clearly matters in this world is Our Time Together. I am not talking about just Jeff and Paula and John now, but you and your family too. All of us nurture relationships as only humans can. To be human, to express one's native humanity, is to interact with others with kind and uplifting words and behaviors. Fostering and nurturing relationships is the most fundamental of human gifts, and those who do it well are sought out and recognized for their life-affirming spirit. Ambassadors and presidents require this spark of humanity as well, for wars are waged in the aftermath of their failings.

Our Time Together was precious, but now it's gone. Jeff and I were good at loving and nurturing, grinning and hugging, and being there for each other, but Paula was the best. Women seem better at relationships in all of their aspects than do men. They seem to be better hard wired in that realm and more focused. Maybe that is why the species has been successfully propagated. If it had been up to the men, we probably would have gone extinct during the ice age. Things get a little challenging, and pffft. Who needs this? But women, women have known it all along. I wrote a song about that once, titled cleanly enough, *Relationships*. And there was a song from the sixties called "What's it all about, Alfie?" If Alfie had been smart he would have known the answer. Relationships, and their vehicle... Our Time Together.

I am so thankful for our time together.

CHAPTER 11
# The Events of September and October, 2006

*"Man makes plans, and God laughs."*-Unknown

Paula and Larry arrived at our home near Chattanooga on a Tuesday evening after their long drive down from Cincinnati. It was September 4, 2006, the week of our reunion that we had all been planning for many months. It had been five years since our first reunion, when all of us got together for the first time. No one was more excited about the six of us getting together than our brother Jeff. He had been sick and undergoing tests the last few weeks, but he repeated to me and others that he would be here (in Chattanooga with us) no matter what. Actually, the biggest concern he had was the price of gasoline which had climbed to more than three dollars a gallon that summer. He knew that I would cover his gas expenses and one of us would cover his motel bill – each of us had done so in the past – but accepting financial help from his brother and sister was not something that Jeff enjoyed. Still if it meant the three of us being together, he would take it in stride.

The bigger problem on this date is that Jeff had taken a turn for the worse and was now in the Cherokee county hospital in Centre, Alabama. Two weeks prior, in order to get a handle on Jeff's abdominal symptoms, jaundice, and mixed messages from his Alabama doctors, I had arranged for Jeff to be seen by a doctor friend whom I respect here in Chattanooga, and he had arranged for Jeff to get a liver biopsy. Ten days prior to Paula's visit the liver biopsy was obtained. After the biopsy, Jeff stayed at the house with Lynna Ruth and me, but just for the weekend.

On the following Monday the official pathology report came back announcing that Jeff had carcinoid tumor in every one of his liver biopsies. Widespread metastasis was now the clinical picture. Later that week, Jeff was not feeling well, not eating and drinking enough, and Brenda took him to their local hospital where he was admitted with dehydration complicating his liver failure. I visited Jeff that weekend and talked with the covering physician who had her hands full with what seemed like nearly every patient in the hospital. It was a football weekend in Alabama and she was the lucky doctor whose duty it was to round on the other doctor's patients while those doctors went to the University of Alabama football game. She did not know Jeff's medical history but I was able to fill in some blanks for her. We arranged for Jeff to see an oncologist to begin chemotherapy later in the week. I met some of Jeff's friends whom I had not previously met, and Jeff and I had another good visit despite his weakened condition.

It was in this setting that Paula arrived at my house the following Tuesday. This stop was simply an overnight pause on the way to our reunion with Jeff the next day. Jeff was to be transferred to another hospital where there was an oncologist, and Paula, Larry, Lynna Ruth and I would visit him Wednesday wherever he was. Paula, Larry, Lynna Ruth and I were just starting to get caught up on family and other events going on in our hectic lives when we received a phone call from Brenda. Jeff had taken a turn for the worse. Brenda sounded uncharacteristically calm.

Paula got to see a side of me that she hadn't seen before that night, and one that Lynna Ruth has seen all too often. I became demanding and commanding. I drilled the hospital nurses about Jeff, demanded that they move him to an intensive care unit if the hospital had one, and I called his attending physician on his cell phone. Jeff's doctor basically told me Jeff was dying, but that he would go to the hospital soon and check on him. That's when it started to sink in. Jeff *was* dying.

Jeff was dying and there was nothing I could do to change that. This is not a position that I am comfortable with or one that I can accept. I am used to being able to make things right. Jeff's doctor did come to visit Jeff shortly thereafter; and soon after that Jeff did die in Brenda's arms. We were all in shock. Paula and I had arranged vacation time for one of our reunions, not our brother's death! It had been five years since he found us, but now it seemed much shorter than that. Jeffrey we hardly knew ye.

Jeff had had an unusually rapid and progressive downhill course and died in his local Alabama hospital on

## The Events of September and October, 2006

September 5, 2006, eleven days after the biopsy. His wife Brenda was at his side.

Carcinoid tumor is typically slow-growing and treatable. At the time of diagnosis, most patients already have metastases to the liver. Even so, from the time of diagnosis most patients live at least five years. Jeff's death so soon after his diagnosis was highly unusual. It gave his family and friends no time to adjust to the idea of life without Jeff.

Still, we said good-bye the best we could.

We drove to Centre the next morning, mostly to comfort Brenda and help with arrangements. It surprised me, given his limited means, that Jeff had taken out a small insurance policy a few years back. It would take care of Jeff's cremation expenses and still leave some for Brenda. At the funeral home we were given the opportunity to view the body. The room in the mortuary was as clinical and sterile looking as a surgical suite. There were no rich woods or coffin, no flowers, makeup, or suit. Jeff was lying on a stainless steel slab and he was very yellow. He had been jaundiced in life, of course; his bilirubin had risen to 25 toward the end (normal is less than 1.0). But I was not expecting the bright yellow that is left when the life blood has departed and there are no competing hues. Paula had not seen Jeff since he became ill. She had even less time to adjust to our new reality than I did. It was a hard viewing. No way was this corpse our vibrant brother, who was always so funny and animated and full of himself. His eyes should be twinkling; there should be a gleam. We cried hard.

Paula and I carried on with our planned reunion, but it was mostly a little support group. We arranged another get together next month. I had meetings scheduled in late October in Gatlinburg which just happens to be near Pigeon Forge – Paula's favorite place to shop. Six weeks would give us a little time to heal. Life goes on...

――-Original Message――-
From: John/Lynna Ruth Standridge
Sent: Saturday, September 09, 2006 7:32 PM
To: Paula Cope
Subject: Re: us

Paula,

I did call Brenda. She sounded OK but subdued. I told her you had made it back and I confirmed the memorial time (2 pm central) 9/17.

She said "Jeff" was ready to pickup, but she wasn't in a hurry to get the urn – wants to prepare a place for it with pictures and flowers. I also ordered a spray of flowers from us – "Love You Bro" on the ribbon.

I really enjoyed our visit. All the more due to circumstances.

Yeah, the resemblance in Marion's picture is for real.

Love you, Sis.

John

*I really enjoyed our visit, as well. Let me know what I owe for my half of the flowers, and please let me know how the memorial goes. I am sorry I can't be there, but my thoughts will be.*

*Love you, too.*
*Paula*

## The Events of September and October, 2006

Paula was not able to come back down for Jeff's memorial service which was held a few weeks after his death. I was able to attend that Sunday as were many friends and family. I was asked to say a few words and I mostly reminisced about the Jeff I knew and about our story of lost and found. I also read a poem by John Donne, who wrote this about 400 years ago.

> DEATH be not proud, though some have called thee
> Mighty and dreadfull, for, thou art not so,
> For, those, whom thou think'st, thou dost overthrow,
> Die not, poore death, nor yet canst thou kill me.
> From rest and sleepe, which but thy pictures bee,
> Much pleasure, then from thee, much more must flow,
> And soonest our best men with thee doe goe,
> Rest of their bones, and soules deliverie
> Thou art slave to Fate, Chance, kings, and desperate men,
> And dost with poyson, warre, and sicknesse dwell,
> And poppie, or charmes can make us sleepe as well,
> And better then thy stroake; why swell'st thou then;
> One short sleepe past, wee wake eternally,
> And death shall be no more; death, thou shalt die.

Lynna Ruth told me she thought that the poem might be over the head of some who attended the service, but I am fairly sure that I chose that poem more for myself than for anyone else there. It gave me comfort to articulate so assertively that with our brother's passing it was death itself that ceased to exist for our brother. Death for Jeff, who could not die again, was no more, and therefore of no more concern. So there, death; take that!

Life goes on…

## Jeffrey Dean Boyar Eulogy
### By Robin R. Wooten

*We are here today to celebrate Jeff's life and I would like to take a moment to tell you about my friend.*

*Jeffrey Dean Boyar passed away on Tuesday September 5th at 8:40pm in the Cherokee Baptist Medical Center. He is survived by his wife Brenda of Centre, AL, three step children Roger Rutz of Coldwater Michigan, Ruth Ann Klimawitz of Berrien Springs Michigan and Howard Duke and Traci of Centre AL, eight grandchildren Michael, Jimmy, Dustin, Jacob, Kylee, Sandy, Stephanie and Lucas, one great grandchild Jacob and mother-in-law Mrs. Margaret French of Benton Harbor, Michigan who now resides in Centre AL, his sister Paula Cope of Cincinnati, Ohio, his brother Dr. John Standridge and wife Lynna Ruth of Chattanooga, Tennessee and many friends.*

*Jeff was 63 years of age and was born in Chattanooga, TN on October 27th, 1942 as Richard Delaney. He lived there for eight years before moving to California with his new adopted parents who were from Illinois. Jeff lived in California until his teenage years. He then became a free spirit, as he called himself, and began to travel around the US. Those of us who knew him well were always intrigued by the numerous stories he could tell of his travels. He eventually wound up in Mexico where he went to college to obtain a Medical Degree.*

## The Events of September and October, 2006   135

One afternoon we were talking while we were setting up equipment for a rehearsal and his medical experience came up. I just stopped what I was doing and I said "you are kidding me right"! I knew that he had done a lot of things and I was aware that he was an electrical engineer but I never dreamed that he had studied medicine as well. He looked at me with this serious expression and said "Kid you shouldn't let these old worn out jeans and t-shirt fool you, or..." in this long pause, which seemed like an eternity, I thought, oh Lord, I have offended him. You know I was just thinking how could anyone have accomplish so much in one lifetime and maybe he is just teasing me, but he was not smiling! Then that "or" and again he paused then continued, "or these striking good looks of mine" to which he gave one of those sheepish grins of his. I had been holding my breath because at that time I had only been working with him a few months and I hadn't gotten quite accustomed to his crazy antics. Since that time I have fallen for several more of his pranks.

Jeff had a great sense of humor and a quick wit about him that made those around him feel good. He loved people and had a good heart. He always went out of his way for everyone and seemed to have a strong desire to love everyone and to be loved.

Jeff and I were in the music business together and due to that fact my husband Dave and I got to spend a lot of time with him and his family. In May of this year we finally came up with an idea of how we thought we could pull off a good prank on him. We had a show to do in Lafayette, GA and had to go up early to work on putting the stage together. After several hours we were tired and hungry and so we decided to go over to the local Mexican Restaurant. Our waiter was really new to this country and didn't speak English very well. Jeff tried speaking Spanish with him because he was fluent in the language but apparently the waiter didn't speak that language well either. Anyway, we had to leave early I told Jeff and apologized for leaving him eating. I went to the front and told them that it was his birthday. We paid for the birthday cake and went to hide and watch. The guy took this 50 gallon sombrero with fringe on it to the table along with the cake. He shoved it on Jeff's head and began to sing, in whatever his language was. The look on Jeff's face was priceless. For once the man was speechless. Then he began to try and explain to the guy that it wasn't his birthday. The waiter kept saying yes, because it was one of the few words that he apparently knew and he just sang louder! The more Jeff shook his head in denial the more the fringe bobbed and the lower the hat slid down on his head. We were standing behind him by this time and everyone in the room was now watching. They could see us and the fact that we were hysterical and they began to join in on the fun. Finally someone pointed to us and Jeff looked around. With tears rolling down my face I could hardly catch my breath long enough to say anything more than "Gotcha"!

Jeff was a good sport as well as being smart and talented. He loved to laugh and he loved to make people laugh. I heard him say that he hoped that people would not grieve at his passing but would rejoice with him and remember his life with a smile. There is a poem that I think was sent our way with a special message to Jeff's family and friends and I would like to read it.

## I'M ALWAYS WITH YOU

When I am gone, release me, and let me go.
I have many things to see and do.

You must not tie yourself to me with too many tears,
but be thankful we had so many good years.
I gave you my love, and you can only guess
how much you gave me in happiness.
I thank you for the love you have shown,
but now it is time I travel on alone.

So grieve for me a while, if grieve you must,
then let your grief be comforted by trust.
That it is only for a while that we must part,
so treasure the memories within your heart.
I won't be far away for life goes on,
and if you need me, call and I will be near.
And if you listen with your heart,
you'll hear all my love around you soft and clear.
And then, when you come this way alone;
I'll greet you with a smile and say "Welcome Home".

*Jeff performed over the years doing musical shows and was also a Karaoke DJ. He loved Elvis and even did a tribute show which included his Elvis costumes.*

*Jeff and I worked together on building a program for our new group. We had been traveling some and performing. I know only enough about a computer to mess the thing up and so he spent a lot of time performing miracles for me as he always like to say. I would ask him for something and I would say "is that impossible" to which he would reply "impossible, no but a miracle like this one may take me a little longer"! I never knew how he accomplished all that he did but he would make it happen. He would kick off all of our songs as we performed and the opening line that I would always say to him was "maestro if you please"!*

*Jeffrey Boyar, a man we are all proud to have called brother, husband, dad, grandpa and friend! He was my partner and I was glad to be called his friend! So, today as we say goodbye and pay tribute to his memory I consider it an honor to once again be able to say, "Maestro if you please".*

With that, Robin then played a recording of Jeff singing, "Where Could I Go but to the Lord". It was eerie to hear my brother's strong clear voice singing at his own memorial service.

Robin also sent Paula a copy of the eulogy since Paula was unable to attend the memorial service. Paula replied by email:

*Yes, I did receive it, and thank you so much for sending it! It really brought a smile to my face and I could just picture Jeff at that Mexican restaurant. Jeff was a special person, and in the short period of time I knew him, he became a big part of my life. He was my big brother, and I was the little sister that was taken away from him all those years ago... He called me nearly every Saturday, and not a weekend goes by now that I don't expect the phone to ring and hear his voice... I miss him terribly.*

---

——-Original Message——-
From: John/Lynna Ruth Standridge [mailto:jbslrs@bellsouth.net]
Sent: Monday, September 11, 2006 8:15 PM
To: Paula Cope
Subject: Out of sorts

Ditto for me and I think John has been kinda off balance, too. And, man oh man, was it quiet here today!

The more I've thought about it, the more I think a weekend in Pigeon Forge (or some place closer to you, if you can think of a spot) is a great idea. We sort of have to plan about 2-3 months ahead, because of John's schedule (and Jan – Feb and April are out for me). So, give that some thought...

The genealogy stuff is pretty similar, except I filled in some kids and grandkids, mostly from census.

LR

*Okay, I have decided to push my October vacation back a week, from the week of the 16th to the week of the 23rd. Paul's surprise party is Saturday the 21st, but Larry and I can drive down to Pigeon Forge on Sunday the 22nd and stay a couple of days. We would have Sunday evening and all day Monday together (except for John who has to be in meetings). When were you planning on leaving to head home – Tuesday?*

*Love,*

*P*

———-Original Message———-
From: John/Lynna Ruth Standridge
Sent: Wednesday, September 13, 2006 8:49 PM
To: Paula Cope
Subject: Re: Out of sorts

*John says he doesn't have meetings on Monday – just Tuesday at 1:00 and then we have to drive back for him to be on call. So, that sounds great! I had gone ahead and made us reservations in Gatlinburg at Glenstone Lodge, which is the Days Inn just above the Convention Center. I think the Arts & Crafts festival will be going at the Convention Center until Sunday (at least Saturday). It will be great to see y'all!!*

*LR & JB*

*I know neither one of you are home this evening because I just talked to John while he was waiting to board his plane. Larry made our reservations for next month, but he made them at the Grand Resort in Pigeon Forge.... that's where we always stay, that's where he feels comfortable, so that's where he made the reservations. What can I say, he is a creature of habit and doesn't like change. As John always says, 'you gotta pick your battles', and I figured this one wasn't worth fighting over. We'll still get to spend most of our time together, we'll just have a slightly longer ride to get there.*

*Love you both and looking forward to next month!*
*P*

---

The morning of October 22, 2006, was spent keeping ourselves busy while we were waiting for Paula and Larry to arrive from Cincinnati. Lynna Ruth and I had just finished driving a "motor trail" through a section of the Great Smoky Mountains. I thought the autumn foliage had never been more resplendent. The cell phone rang and it was Paula. She and Larry had arrived at the Grand Resort in Pigeon Forge but it was too early for them to check in to their room. I said we would be there in 15 to 20 minutes.

Eating, shopping, and simply hanging out together were on the agenda. It was a marvelous three days! Paula and Larry took us to one of their favorite restaurants, the Bullfish Grill. I had the Parmesan Crusted Grouper. Our first shopping destination was in search of a "princess wallet" at the Disney store. They were no longer carried at the regular Disney stores but were supposed to be at the discounted "warehouse" mall stores for which Pigeon Forge is famous. A certain little girl in Cincinnati needed a princess wallet and Paula's first priority dealt with finding one for her daughter Beth to then present to this certain little girl. I don't even think it was intended for Beth's gorgeous little three year old daughter Mary (I am a great uncle, you know). Rather it was for one of Beth's friend's certain little girl. But it was Paula's number one priority, so after sustenance, we set out for the mall with its crowded parking and lots of walking only to find that the Disney Princess Wallet was not in stock. Was it no longer a hot item or was it too hot to keep in stock? I may never know.

Next we are off to a beading shop. I think it was Lynna Ruth who got Paula interested in making beaded necklaces, earrings, and bracelets. Lynna Ruth's handmade beaded necklaces and earrings are some mighty handsome pieces of jewelry, I must admit. Paula was more interested in making earrings and bracelets. I was all about finding the beading shop, so when it was found to be out of business (strike two, Paula), I surreptitiously found out from a sales clerk about the Purple Cat. I cannot just tell someone where we are going. What's the fun in that? I would rather hear confusion about why we are in Sevierville. And "Are you lost?" Perfect timing, that question was, as I parked near the Purple Cat. "Where are we?" they asked. "Only at the finest bead store around," I smart off. I totally lost them and a good chunk of our bank account over the next hour or so. That's OK. I had not yet shopped for the world's most comfortable boots. That was high on my agenda. As it was, I hung out some across the street from The Purple Cat at a shop called Second Thoughts. I found a card to send to Brenda. The four of us struggled to find encouraging words to write. Paula wrote hers before she read mine and noticed that she had written the same message that I had – wishes for Peace and Happiness.

It was like this for days. I did find my perfect boots – a pair of ostrich skin Lucchese. I also had the opportunity to retaliate for Larry and Paula's marvelous restaurant selection with one of my own – the Greenbrier Restaurant. The Greenbrier is set in an historic log cabin up in the hills (away from the crowded town) and overlooks the colorful fall leaves that show the Smokies at its best. The best food we found was for a luncheon at the Old Mill Pottery House Café in Pigeon Forge. We feasted on garden fresh salads and hearty homemade soups. Their delicious sandwiches featured freshly baked breads made with whole grains stone ground at the historic Old Mill across the road. Even their stoneware plates were of pottery made on the premises. Did I mention that it was our agenda to eat and shop and take in the scenery and simple hang out together? That is exactly what we did and it was perfect. Oh, I *did* say that.

Tuesday morning I found out that my meeting was not until three in the afternoon. With more time than I had anticipated, we drove towards Cades Cove but were distracted by an empty gasoline tank and the promise of fried apple pies in Townsend, Tennessee. It was a fine out of the way snack, complete with apple cider, at a picnic table on a covered wooden porch. The music playing overhead was a fine collection of 1970's cover tunes performed by talented musicians and performed on traditional acoustic instruments. I purchased the CD for myself and Paula, and we listened to it as we drove through the Smokies that afternoon, along a roaring river with waterfalls and cataracts, and among the ever brilliant fall colors. What a great day!

Later that afternoon we went into one of those old timey photograph places where they dress you in period clothing and take amusing photographs of you, documenting forever and always how silly you can be. I think Paula enjoyed that more than anything else that we did. That evening, after my meetings, we dined at the Applewood restaurant in Gatlinburg. Paula thought the Applewood restaurant in Pigeon Forge had been better. I took a photograph of her

## The Events of September and October, 2006   143

beautiful smile for the last time. After dinner Lynna Ruth and I drove back home to Harrison (near Chattanooga). The following morning I went to a 7 a.m. meeting where the chancellor of the University of Tennessee Health Science Center was describing proposed changes to the policies governing promotion and tenure. I did not think it pertained much to my status since I had already achieved the rank of a full professor and there was really no mechanism for additional promotion, but I was there like a good soldier.

I went back to my office and my cell phone rang. It was the manager of the Grand Resort Hotel trying to tell me that something had happened to my sister. At first she was tentative, giving me time to take it in. The manager told me, "She has had some sort of spell." I am thinking, "She passed out?" She asked softly, "You are a doctor, aren't you?" She was verifying this for a reason before she continued. "Yes." I replied, now more uneasy. "I think your sister had had some sort of cardiac arrest. It doesn't look good. She is on life support. They will move her from the local hospital to the U. T. Medical Center in Knoxville if the helicopter can land. There is a lot of fog this morning." She continued. "I am so sorry." The fog wasn't limited to Pigeon Forge: I had more than my share of another kind of fog in my head about that time. I was in a daze, unable to fathom the change that had occurred from one day to the next. My sister: something has happened to my sister. I had to precept the residents. Stuff at work had really piled up in the two days I had been away. An old friend and former partner in a medical practice dropped in unannounced. He didn't fully understand when I told him that I couldn't think of anyone I would rather see right now. For five, maybe ten minutes, I could pretend none of this was happening. But not really; and we chatted about our families but I also caught him up on Jeff and Paula, and now this morning's events. We parted and I made hasty arrangements with my fellow faculty to cover for me.

Lynna Ruth had joined me in my office by this time and we were about to head out the door to be with Paula when I received the second telephone call from the manager. She was on the phone in another part of the building and I hurried to hear what I was afraid she was about to say. She was so sorry to tell me, but "Your sister has died." She was calling from the U. T. Medical Center in Knoxville where she had driven Larry in his Chevy Blazer, at rather remarkable speeds I later learned. "Are you on your way here?" she needed to know. "Yes. We are leaving now." I assured her. It had all happened so fast, so suddenly, and so unexpectedly. She indicated that she was very worried about Larry. He was so unprepared for this, so pitiful in his grief, and so lost without Paula. He kept saying that he didn't know what to do; and the manager thought that he was disoriented at times. With the reassurance that we were on our way, the manager indicated that she was going back to Pigeon Forge in a car that she had follow her and Larry to the U. T. Medical Center. She would have Larry wait for us at the hospital in Knoxville.

I was so thankful that Lynna Ruth was waiting in my office. She must have known the moment I walked in. My face was twisted in emotional pain and my eyes locked with hers in a plea for understanding. I held to her and I cried – long and hard. "Paula's gone," I sobbed, but she already knew.

Larry was a tragic figure. It was all he could do to keep his face from distorting with grief, especially when he related the events. Paula and Larry had decided to stay an extra day in Pigeon Forge in order to get in some more shopping. They had mapped out an itinerary. Maybe they could find some nice Christmas presents for friends and family. They had showered and Paula was sitting on the bed getting dressed. Larry was looking out the window at the view of the river that ran beside their motel room. He turned around and did not see Paula. He thought she had gone back to the bathroom so he started in that direction. Then he saw Paula lying between the beds. He went to her and she said that she felt like she was going to throw up. Then her eyes rolled back and she was gone. Larry called for help and only a few minutes elapsed before emergency medical personnel arrived. Chest compression, endotracheal intubation, mechanical ventilation, drugs, an ambulance to the local hospital, and a helicopter ride to the U. T. Medical Center in Knoxville all amount to a picture perfect cardiopulmonary resuscitation attempt. But she died in Pigeon Forge between the beds. Paula's sudden cardiac arrest probably was the result of a coronary thrombosis with ventricular fibrillation, or possibly a ruptured aneurism. No one really cared about those sorts of details. She died in Pigeon Forge between the beds, quickly and without pain, after the most wonderful three day vacation anyone could have wanted.

 The day before coming to Tennessee, Paula helped Beth throw a surprise birthday party for Beth's husband Paul. Her grandchildren were there also. Then we had our time together. All in all, it was not a bad way to go. As Beth said, when she goes she would want it to be after a vacation, not just before one.

 The funeral arrangements were decided at a funeral parlor in the Anderson suburb of Cincinnati. The weather was dreary with rain taking its toll on the autumn foliage. This weather event happens every year as a cold front moves through after a period of crisp blue skies. I thought that it needed its own special name, so I labeled it "Paula's rain". I wrote a little poem as we drove along Beechmont Avenue.

> Late October's coldest rain,
>
> The one that steals her gold from her trees,
>
> Now gift I thee with thou own name.
>
> Gone today are sunshine and smiles;
>
> Replaced by cold tears and dark trials –
>
> God's gift now named: "Paula's Rain".

At the funeral parlor my mood was depressed further by the "business" of itemizing choices from a fee schedule – implements of a traditional funeral service from the selection of the memory card to the choice of a coffin. Larry and Beth made the decisions and everyone held up well, even through the obituary details.

The funeral was early Saturday afternoon and the rains had given way to a cold damp day. It was no less dreary and somehow seemed appropriate for saying "Goodbye" to Paula. The throng of mourners was a comfort to the family. Larry's family of sons, daughters, and grandchildren came down from northern Ohio. Beth and her husband Paul and his many brothers and sisters, mother and cousins, nieces and nephews were all there. Paula's grandchildren were beyond precious. Jacob Daniel, now 13 years old, was quite the young man. He was probably the only one of the three that really understood what was going on. He grieved and sometimes shed that tear that men are not supposed to have. Half-way through the reception period, he stood up and walked over to where Beth and Paul (and Larry and I) had formed a reception line to greet the well-wishers. He took his place with us and went through the motions of shaking hands, smiling sweetly, looking down, looking in eyes, comforting and accepting comfort. I thought at that moment, Jake was a real man indeed. Benjamin Paul and Mary Josephine were fine as well. Dressed in a suit from his recent communion, Ben took in everything very attentively. Both he and Mary were curious about the crowd and the ceremony, and their grandmother's body, and they appreciated being held and hugged.

Paula's coworkers and family produced an overflow crowd. I heard one coworker relate that Paula was the one that everyone could count on to remain calm when things became crazy with computer crashes and system meltdowns. But it was much more than her competence at work that brought so many to her service that day. Paula was loved for who she was, and she was missed in a big way by so many people who realized it already but knew that it was still too soon to fully sink in.

For me one of the more gratifying moments was when the entire troop of Paula's Red Hat Ladies came in together, dressed resplendently in bright purple outfits and scarves, and wearing impressive red hats. This defiant movement of women who are all about living life and building relationships brought to the scene an affirmation of getting on with life that was extremely refreshing and welcome. Paula loved her involvement with the Red Hat Society. Paula's outfit, chosen by Beth and Lynna Ruth, was purple; and next to her in the coffin was a favorite red hat. It was so touching that a final tribute from this group of best friends was a collection of long stem red roses, placed on her body one by one by the Red Hat Ladies as they each said goodbye.

As with Jeff, Paula's death occurred so suddenly and unexpectedly that it gave her family and friends no time to adjust to the idea of life without Paula. As with Jeff's memorial service, the funeral for Paula helped us move through the loss. As the psalm says, we go *through* the valley of the shadow of death. And again, we said good-bye the best we could. And again, life goes on.

Chapter 12
# God and Job
# (Making Sense of Fate)

Do you remember the Old Testament book of Job? Job is a pious and loyal servant of God, and to test him God brings a series of tragic events. Job's cattle and crops, family and fortune are all destroyed, and yet Job remains steadfast in his devotion to the Almighty. Toward the end of the book Job beseeches God to explain why God would do all of this to such a worthy servant as himself. Whereupon God lets Job *know* in no uncertain terms that He is not to be questioned. Job could not have understood that he was God's test and demonstration of Good over Evil.

Clearly there are things that we cannot know. One of those things is whether God will want us here to serve some purpose tomorrow.

There are some things we can know, however. Some of those things are the love we felt from those who have gone before, and the love we feel for and from those who are with us now.

And thank God for that.

I have been asked more than once if Jeff was bitter that his life had not turned out better. It is true, I believe, that Jeff did not realize his full potential. I do not believe that he was bitter, however. He expressed no regrets and he identified with the song, *My Way*, popularized by Frank Sinatra and Elvis Presley. Certain phrases in that song stand out. Jeff certainly "lived a life that's full" and he "traveled each and every hightway". He may have had some regrets, "but then again, too few to mention". Finally, Jeff was truly one who could say that he "took the blows and did it my way!"

Paul Anka rewrote "My Way", re-interpreting the original French lyrics specifically to fit Frank Sinatra's persona. The lyrics tell the story of a man who reflects on his life as he is nearing death. He declares that he has few regrets for how he lived his life, especially considering the challenges he has faced. He is comfortable with and takes responsibility for how he dealt with all the ups and downs of his life while maintaining some respectable degree of integrity. This man is comfortable is his own skin and offers no apologies or excuses. Likewise he does not hold the world or anyone in it to blame. This was profoundly Jeff.

Jeff was describe by people who knew him as warm, generous, kind, caring, funny, mischievous, and many other adjectives; but never bitter. This brings me to my

## God and Job (Making Sense of Fate) 151

second point about the book of Job. In Job, Satan tells God that it is easy for a man to love God when everything is going well and God protects him from misfortune. The true test of a man's devotion to his Maker comes when hardships abound and losses multiply. This challenge led God to test Job, who did live up to God's expectations. Jeff was surely tested in this way and still he loved the Lord without question.

It is difficult, to say the least, to try to make sense of the events that life throws your way. Hardships and bad outcomes in life have four origins, according to my friend, Mack Worthington. The first is a result of poor choices that we make in life. The second is a result of poor choices that others make that impact us. The third is a result of being in the wrong place at the wrong time. The fourth is a result of doing the right thing in service of family, God, or country, and being placed in harm's way as a consequence. I am not trying to write some new version of *Why Bad Things Happen to Good People*. I happily surrender to God the issue of "Why". But still, one strives for closure. One wishes to understand how events unfold in a particular manner. One wishes to establish ones place among humanity, and from that reference point, one hopes to establish a value-driven purpose and meaning to ones existence.

In conscious consideration, I recognize that all of us have misfortunes in life. I am moved to compassion and love for my neighbors, my fellow man and woman as well as my siblings. I grieve for all around me. But unconsciously, a "there-but-for-the-grace-of-God-go-I" thought appears. And with this thought I find myself with an expression of relief couched in the language of God's grace – divine action that starts or stops cancer, creates or prevents floods. Grace is an unexpected gift. Grace is free. It is not earned.

The absence of grace is not a statement of moral depravity or anything moral at all. The experience of grace is not a statement about righteousness. Anything free, loving, and kind is grace. And it is abundant.

Poet Marilyn Chandler McEntyre tells us that Grace takes us by surprise. "It comes in odd packages. It sometimes looks like loss, or mistakes. It acts like rain. Or like a seed. It's both reliable and unpredictable. It's not what you are aiming at. Or, what you thought you deserved. It supplies what you need. Not necessarily what you want. It grows you up. And lets you be a child. It reminds you you're not in control. And not being in control is a form of freedom."

Jeff and Paula were a gift of grace. When Paula found me, my mother had been dead three years and my father had died many years ago when I was in medical school. I was alone with no family other than my wife and descendants. Because I was raised as an only child, the loss of my parents gave me no one to turn to for the reassurance and moral authority and acceptance and unconditional love that sit silently across the table from you when you need it. Lynna Ruth is all wise and all knowing, is calming beyond belief, runs quiet and deep, and is the Queen of my universe. But she represents that mutual, chosen, work things out, adaptive, supportive, nurturing love that works over a period of time; or not. Ours certainly has worked but it is not the blood relation that accepts another as part of your own self, no matter what.

The "you can pick your friends but you can't pick your family" kind of commitment is the level of *acceptance*, and the "I will be there for you no matter what" kind of commitment is the level of *support*, that Paula and Jeff brought to me, and that Paula and I brought to Jeff, and that Jeff and I brought to Paula. That is the level of the gift that finding out that you have a family is all about. Except… Paula died last week [ed. The first draft of this book was written in November, 2006], suddenly with no warning; and Jeff died the month before that, unexpectedly, too soon. I am again head of my family with no "big brother" or "big sister" to turn to. Who do I see about that?

After not even knowing that I had siblings, I am thrilled to have had Paula as my sister for ten years and to have had Jeff and the reuniting of the three of us for five years. To have discovered them – learned of their existence – after their deaths would have been bittersweet indeed. The photographs collected within these pages reveal the joy and pride that we felt for one another.

The special bond that I felt and still feel for my brother and sister is not possible to describe. It is a kind of knowing that transcends words. Before my sister found me and Jeff found the two of us, I did not know what I could not have known – that there was a connection of such a quality that could exist between people. This connection and bond were not the most intense, nor the most emotional, nor even of the greatest love. Those bonds belong to my wife, children, and grandchildren. But the connection with my siblings was perhaps the most real and the bonding was without question, without qualification, just pure acceptance. I have now proven to the world that indeed, words are inadequate to describe our attachment.

For those of you reading this that have had brothers and sisters for your entire life, you may well take your siblings for granted and may judge with skepticism what I am trying to say. You may even be mad at your brother or sister for perceived slights or jealousies or some unresolved competition or other issue. I hope that someday you will be able to rediscover that gift of God, that natural best friend, your brother or your sister. Rediscover while you can the closeness as if you are experiencing it for the first time. That was one more unexpected gift: experiencing the powerful brother/sister natural bond for the first time, not as a toddler, but as a middle aged and sentient adult.

As for me, I shall treasure always the memories of Paula and Jeff. I know that I am better for having known them. I know that I carry a part of them with me. I know that I shall see them again. And although I find reasons to get up and go to work every day, I know that from this time forward I am living each day as if it could be my last. The sudden unexpected death of Paula the morning after our great time together and following just six weeks after Jeff's unexpected death has thrust me into my *endgame*. I am not looking to run off to Maui seeking silly pleasures. Rather I am looking to treat everyone I meet with the affection and respect that all people deserve. If I can be a kinder friend, a better husband, father, and grandfather, and the best physician that I can be for my patients, then perhaps my life, well lived, can be part of Jeff's and Paula's legacy.

To the extent that we maximize our relationship with others, that action can be described as God's love. Along the lines of this thinking, a process school of theology has given the western world a concept of a compassionate kinship with all that *is* – mutuality, a relatedness. Where love abides, God abides also. That is the genius of theology. In so far as you weep and are moved to some action with others – no matter how tiny or insignificant – you are participating in this mutual activity which adds to a greater good. "The world breaks everyone," wrote Hemmingway, "and some are made strong at the broken places." "The heart that's broken," writes Maya Angelou, "can hold the whole room." Welcome the stranger. Practice the art of hospitality in whatever way you can, and by doing these things, we transform the world. This, too, would not be an unfitting legacy for my dear brother and my dear sister.

CHAPTER 13
# I Am Becoming
## *Hibernicis Ipsis Hiberniores*

> *"I do not think this country will afford sufficient allurements to the citizens of other States ... The children of Irish parents born abroad are sometimes more Irish than the Irish themselves, and they would come with added experience and knowledge to our country..."*
> – SEN. PATRICK KENNY, 1924

From Wikipedia, "More Irish than the Irish themselves" (Latin: *Hiberniores Hibernicis ipsis*) was a phrase used in the Middle Ages to describe the phenomenon whereby centuries of foreigners who came to Ireland attached to invasion forces tended to be subsumed into Irish culture and society. They adopted the Irish language, Irish culture,

# I Am Becoming Hibernicis Ipsis Hiberniores

style of dress and a wholesale identification with all things Irish. While this phenomenon was associated with earlier invaders, the phrase is still commonly used, both colloquially and in the media, in reference to immigration and assimilation in Ireland, and in my situation and the case of all Irish diaspora, the maintenance of Irish heritage.

I hold no illusions about the extremes that people go to in order to cope with hardships and losses. If accepting my Irish heritage is a coping mechanism that somehow seems to me to be an appropriate tribute to my brother and sister, then so be it. To me it seems a harmless enough obsession. Certainly the writing of this book has been seen by myself, my family, and my friends as a means to cope with the loss of my siblings, one then the other. Some have said it is a good way "to vent", others told me it will help "get it off your chest", and even I see the process as helping to "make sense of it all". Mostly though, I see the book as a rich story; a tragic joy with deep and rare emotional bonds. What does all of this have to do with turning Irish? I wonder that, too.

I can pinpoint the beginning of this *Hibernian* turn of mine to the early afternoon of October 24, 2006; Paula's last full day. We – Paula, Larry, Lynna Ruth and I – were in Gatlinburg cruising the shops in The Village when we came upon The Celtic Heritage. I was looking at silver rings when Paula came up to me with a Delaney lapel pin – a little family crest that I could wear. "No, I don't think so." I told her and she put it back. Celtic traditional music was playing on the store's stereo, Lynna Ruth was looking at a pretty knitted woolen wrap, and I was distracted. "A couple of CDs would be nice," I was thinking to myself. Then I started thinking more about the lapel pin family crest that Paula had shown me. She was getting one, so I decided that

I would get one too. It would be something different and a symbol of solidarity with my sister. As for the silver rings, I wanted the one that had "Ireland" engraved around the band, but alas, they did not have it in my size.

My confusion about my genealogic status has been entrenched ever since my sister found me in 1996. Prior to that, I was a Standridge and I had researched the Standridge line back to the Revolutionary war soldier *James Standridge*. I received regular *Standridge Kith and Kin* newsletters and had traveled, with my son Adam, to national Standridge family reunions. I was looking forward to the genealogy book that Francis Jones was publishing on the Standridge family tree. I had hosted a very large family reunion myself and I considered genealogy to be one of my hobbies. All of that changed when my sister found me in 1996.

Suddenly I felt like a man without a country, or more precisely, a man without a family heritage. I was no longer *Standridge*. In fact I had previously received independent confirmation of this fact. I had submitted extensive material to the Francis Jones genealogy book that listed eight generations of the Standridge family and the details of our western North Carolina and southeast Tennessee pioneer heritage. Word came to be that I had been relegated to the status of a footnote in the book. My adoption by John Standridge was noteworthy but neither I nor my children had Standridge blood, so my children would not be included in the genealogic records. It finally struck me on a level deeper than the intellectual understanding, the superficial and comfortable level, where I customarily dwell. Genealogy means that it is from the same gene pool. I had known that, of course, just like on some level I had known that I was adopted. It just had not mattered before. It was reality but it was not real, at least not to me. The day

# I Am Becoming Hibernicis Ipsis Hiberniores 159

by day structure and course of my life had allowed me to be *Standridge* with zero contravening nuances. Then my sister found me.

An equally acceptable response by me would have been to adopt both family lines out of intellectual curiosity. On the one hand there is the Standridge line. Isn't it interesting? It is the line of those nice people who took me in when I was three months old and abandonded by those who bore me. On the other hand is the Delaney line. Isn't it interesting? It is the line of those people who gave me away when I was three months old and abandonded me because they could not have cared less and couldn't feed, clothe, and nurture me or my brother and sister.

I understood from Paula that there were many relatives in the Chattanooga area that I could meet and get to know. But, I thought, what's the point? Furthermore, they had their chance fifty-some years ago. Family could have taken us in. Now it was my turn to reject them. That reasoning may seem petty to some but it felt right to me. Jeff and Paula were different. They were in the same boat as me. We had all been set adrift and we had been reunited by our own means. We had each other and that was all I needed. Paula was more generous with herself and her time. She regularly visited aunts and cousins, but I saw that as her thing.

We had the three of us. We were the Delaney kids. Then Jeff died. And in Gatlinburg that day, we still had the two of us. If Paula wanted me to wear a Delaney family crest as a lapel pin, then not only "yes" but "hell, yes". We were the Delaney kids! Solidarity, man! Then Paula died the following morning.

If as I stated earlier, I eschew the penumbra of the local Delaney family, it is equally true, and not at all contradictory, that I embrace the Delaney Irish ancestry. That ancient and noble blood of scholars and poets, of saints and sinners, courses through my veins and indeed my heart. I may be *Hiberniores Hibernicis ipsis*, but moreover it is with the greatest respect for my Delaney brother and sister that I now recognize that I, and they – we – are of Ireland. *Is D'Eirinn Mé.*

*Delaney* – About 1150 A.D. the northern section of Ossory (Co. Laois) held the sept of Ua Dubhslaine (O'Delany or O'Dulany) of Coill Uachtarach who were noted as chiefs of Tuath-an-Toraidh. Delany is a surname never seen today with the prefix O which probably belongs to it. It is O Dubhshlainte in Irish, Delaney being a phonetic rendering of this – the A of Delaney was formerly pronounced broad. An earlier anglicized form was O'Dulany e.g. Felix O'Dulany, Bishop of Ossory from 1178 to 1202, who built St. Canice's Cathedral in Kilkenny. Dubh means black and slainte is topographical – Slaney in English. If it refers to the river Slaney it suggests that this sept originally possessed a wider territory than that usually assigned to it, namely Coilluachtarach (now Upperwoods) at the foot of Slieve Bloom near the source of the rivers Nore and Barrow in Co. Leix. At the present time the name is chiefly associated with Counties Leix and Kilkenny and in 1659, when Petty's census was made, it appears as a principal Irish name in four baronies of Queen's County (now Leix) and in five of Co. Kilkenny. It is sometimes abbreviated to Delane in Co.

Mayo, and this was the form used by Dennis Delane (d. 1750), the celebrated Dublin and London actor. Dillane, however, is not a synonym of Delany, but the anglicized form of O'Duilleain, a Co. Limerick surname, sometimes disguised as Dillin. Dean Patrick Delany (1684-1768), the friend of Dean Swift, was a Leix man. His wife, the famous Mary Delany (1700-1788), was also prominent in the Swift circle. Michael Roland ("Ronny") Delaney, champion athlete who brought honours to Ireland in the 1956 Olympic Games, is a Dubliner. The 1659 census notes Dulany as a principal Irish name in the Co. Kilkenny baronies of Crannagh, Skillellogher, Fassagh Deinin, Galmoy, and Gowran. The 1890 census for Kilkenny noted 14 births in that year for the surname Delaney.

If you are unfamiliar with Irish history, as I was, I can recommend several sources that I found to be excellent. Check out the short bibliography in Appendix E. The Irish were one put upon bunch of people; I am here to tell you. Things started going South in earnest at the Battle of the Boyne when the Protestant forces of William of Orange caused the Boyne River to run red with the blood of Irish Kings and tribes loyal to exiled Catholic King James II.

When my wife and I visited Ireland in October, 2007, we stayed for a few days with a family in the countryside. The lady of the house told us, with some shame, that the family had been "soupers". Soupers were those Irish who, in order to receive the soup from the soup kitchens, agreed to drop the "O'" from their surname and to swear allegiance to the English. Those who did not bow to the demands were allowed to continue to starve. Ireland was the first of many countries to be conquered, subjugated, and occupied by the British Empire, and the Irish were the most vilified. Dehumanizing the Irish was a policy decision originating with the animosity toward the Catholics and orchestrated in part for the church's failing to grant a divorce to King Henry VIII.

Illumination of the extraordinary attitude adopted by Britain toward Ireland is perhaps best illustrated by the great Englishman Carlyle when he described Oliver Cromwell as "a soldier of God the Just, terrible as Death, relentless as Doom doing God's judgments on the enemies of God." Of all the many butchers by whom Ireland was visited over the eight centuries of oppressive English occupation and subjugation, Cromwell was the coldest-blooded butcher of them all. The first taste of the qualities of this agent of God the Just was given to the people of Drogheda. When he took the city he unleashed his men to a three-day and three-night unending orgy of slaughter. Ninety-nine percent of the Irish garrisons were put to the sword in a take-no-prisoners blood bath. The streets literally ran red with the blood of non-combatants, too. Men, women, and children were tortured, raped, and butchered in an unprecedented maniacal rampage. Young mothers were disemboweled and hung from trees with their infant children hanged by the neck from their mother's long hair. This trademark was to be repeated throughout the countryside. On October 2, 1649, the English Parliament appointed a national Thanksgiving Day in celebration of the dreadful slaughter. Town after town each showed thousands more slaughtered as Cromwell advanced his garrisons across the country. Priests were dragged, tied to a wild horse's tail, to the next town where they were hanged. He considered it to be simple justice that "the Saints" (his soldiers) indulge themselves in the little joy of slaughtering the Canaanites. Cromwell wrote, "I thought it not right or good to restrain off the soldiers from their right of pillage, or from doing execution on the enemy." The most appallingly dreadful and inhumane, the most exhausting and ruinous war with which unfortunate Ireland was ever visited was only the beginning of the destruction of a people. The surviving young men – perhaps as many as 30, 000 – were shackled and shipped as slaves to America and the West Indies. Countless thousands of weak and starving old men, women, and weakling babies were driven from their homes to plod west toward deeper misery. More painful starvation, and slow and painful death, awaited many. The fearful winter of 1653-1654 ended the suffering of thousands. The few survivors collected in Claire where it was popularly said to have not wood enough on which to hang a man, water enough to drown him, nor earth enough to bury him. Left with meager resources to complete the extermination of a people, the English were not content to allow Mother Nature to finish the job. Five-sixths of the Irish people had perished and still it was not enough. Upon penalty of death no Irish person was to be found east of the River Shannon (in the west of Ireland) after May 1st, 1654. Waves of conscription and wars followed.

No Irish battle is more famous than William III's July 1, 1690, victory over James II at the River Boyne, a few miles west of Drogheda. James, a Roman Catholic, had lost the throne of England in the bloodless "Glorious Revolution" of 1688. William was Prince of Orange. Religious genocide became *de rigueur*. The Orangemen (of the Orange Order) celebrate with parades in Northern Ireland to this day, but on July 12th thanks to eleven days being lost with the change from the Julian to the Gregorian calendar in 1752. The formal Irish surrender after the siege of Limerick in 1691 meant the Irish were soon to suffer from penal laws designed to reinforce Protestant ascendancy throughout Irish life.

When fire and sword failed to suppress the Irish, the conqueror invented the Penal Laws. The object of these was to deprive Catholics of all civil life, to reduce them to extreme and brutal ignorance, and to dissociate them from the soil. By the 18$^{th}$ century, Irish Catholics were legally forbidden to receive education, enter a profession, hold public office, engage in trade or commerce, live within five miles of a corporate town, own a horse worth more than five pounds, purchase or lease land, vote, keep any arms for his protection, inherit anything from a protestant, be guardian to a child, attend Catholic worship, educate his child (even at home), and many more prohibitions aimed at the destruction of not only a people, but their spirit and will to survive.

After the Cromwellian atrocities, the Irish were driven to the west when the rocky terrain would not support crops other than the potato. The potato blight of the 1840s would not have been so devastating except for the fact that deliberate British policy exported grains and meat from Ireland to England during the same time period. The Irish exported far more food during the famine than was required to feed her people. The English laissez-faire economic policy was a thinly disguised attempt to again wage genocide on a conquered and occupied people. The first recorded use of the 'laissez faire' maxim was by French minister René de Voyer, Marquis d'Argenson, another champion of free trade, in his famous 1736 *Memoires*. *Laissez faire, telle devrait être la devise de toute puissance publique, depuis que le monde est civilisé.... Détestable principe que celui de ne vouloir grandir que par l'abaissement de nos voisins! Il n'y a que la méchanceté et la malignité du coeur de satisfaites*

## I Am Becoming Hibernicis Ipsis Hiberniores

*dans ce principe, et l'intérêt y est opposé. Laissez faire, morbleu! Laissez faire!!* Translated this becomes: Leave them be, that should be the motto of every public authority, according to which the world is civilized..... A detestable principle that which would not wish us to grow except by lowering our neighbors! There is nothing but mischief and malignity of heart in those satisfied with that principle, and interest is opposed to it. Leave them be, damn it! Leave them be! There was never a more detestable application of this "detestable principle" than the passive aggressive English of the 1840s, while they watched the Irish starve to death and cheered for the famine to prevail.

But the Irish spirit would not break. In the last quarter of the eighteenth century, the English-ruled aristocracy of half a million may have found joy in having two million Irish slaves. The gentry, with legal impunity could lash with the horsewhip or cane, break the bones or even kill. The blood-hounds and wolf-hounds could be set against the teachers and priests. But the Irish spirit would not break. Latin and Greek were taught to ragged hunted ones under shelter of the hedges by "hedge schoolmasters". The hunted priest lurked like a thief among the hills and often ate and slept in holes in the ground, but on Sundays and feast days he celebrated Mass at a rock, on a remote mountainside. Lookouts would warn of approaching British soldiers, and if they failed, the troops would splatter the priest's blood on Mass Rock. The marvelous spirit that inspired young Irishmen who gave their lives for the preserving of their people's faith and education is further illustrated by those Irish who penetrated every corner of Europe, America, and indeed the world, in search of education and ordination. The Irish Diaspora were a scattering of a people unprecedented in human history. This phenomenon was brought about by a combination of harsh imperial British policies and the *An Gorta Mór* or "Great Hunger" of the Irish famine. Estimates are that beginning mid-19th century 45% and 85% of Ireland's population emigrated to countries including Britain, the United States, Canada, Argentina, Australia and New Zealand. The size of the Diaspora is demonstrated by the number of people around the world who claim Irish ancestry; some sources put the figure at 80-100 million.

Historic conquests and oppressive English rule do not begin to recount the bloody slaughter, poverty, Penal laws, and famine visited on the people who now are widely acknowledged as having saved civilization. When the Roman Empire was visited by wave after wave of barbarians, libraries were burned and institutions of learning disappeared. The ancient Greek and Roman literature, even the Bible, would have been lost but for intrepid journeymen, possibly Greek, who transported the ancient history of Western civilization through the Middle East, across Africa to the Iberian Peninsula, and eventually to Ireland. There monks living in tiny huts of stone, shaped like a beehive, dedicated their lives to faithfully transcribing the texts. When relative security returned to Europe, the holy men of Ireland began a pilgrimage to Rome and reintroduced a continent to its ancient literature, thus saving civilization. The Irish held on to one of the more richly illustrated tomes – the Book of Kells. The Book of Kells (*Leabhar Cheanannais*) is an illuminated manuscript in Latin, containing the four Gospels of the New Testament and transcribed by Celtic monks *ca.* 800. The illustrations and ornamentation of the Book of Kells surpass that of other Insular Gospels in extravagance and complexity. Kells Abbey was plundered and pillaged by Vikings many

# I Am Becoming Hibernicis Ipsis Hiberniores

times in the 10th century, and how the book survived there is not known.

The Irish were also scholarly and highly literate from the mid-fifth century days of St. Patrick. The ancient Irish virtues of lifelong loyalty, courage, and generosity evolved into the familiar Christian values of faith, hope, and charity.

Speaking of St. Patrick, I was reminded of Jeff when I read Thomas Cahill's description of that venerable Irish saint:

> He had a temper that could flare dangerously when he perceived an injustice – not against himself but against another, particularly against someone defenseless. But he had the cheerfulness and good humor that humble people often have. He enjoyed this world and its variety of human beings – and he didn't take himself too seriously. He was, in spirit, an Irishman.

Another insight concerning the nature of what it is to be Irish comes from the pen of William V. Shannon. Here again the Irish character reminds me of my brother Jeff and possibly helps to explain a pattern that seemed to run through his life. Shannon wrote:

> Supreme egotism and utter seriousness are necessary for the greatest accomplishment, and these the Irish find hard to sustain: at some point, the instinct to see life in a comic light becomes irresistible, and ambition falls before it.

More insights are found in the writings of Edmund Campion, the sixteenth century Elizabethan Jesuit martyr:

The people are thus inclined: religious, franke, amorous, irefull, sufferable of paines infinite, very glorious, many sorcerers, excellent horsemen, delighted with warres, great almes-givers, [sur]passing in hospitalitie....They are sharp-witted, lovers of learning, capable of any studie whereunto they bend themselves, constant in travaile, adventurous, intractable, kinde-hearted, secret in displeasure.

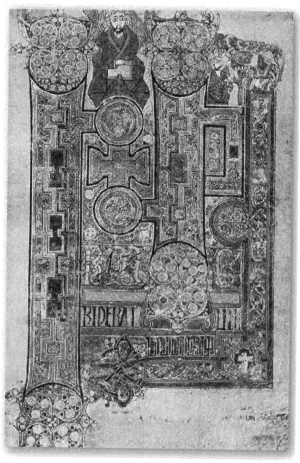

*Illustration from the Book of Kells*

# I Am Becoming Hibernicis Ipsis Hiberniores

I can identify with the Irish personality, the traits, and the romanticized myth of the people. I can embrace the history and persona of the Irish. I can laugh at Sigmund Freud when he muttered in exasperation that the Irish were the only people who could not be helped by psychoanalysis.

In addition to reading Irish history and wearing symbols of an Irish heritage, more that any of this is the mindset, the secure knowledge that I am of Ireland. *Is D'Eirinn Mé.* My genealogic confusion has dissolved and I am thankful for my identity. My genealogic identity is not all that I am thankful for. My brother and sister provided me with my Delaney heritage, but my identity and self awareness has been forged and hewn much sharper than that, thanks to my beloved siblings.

Writing the book, defining for myself what is real and important about the three of us, analyzing the roles of heredity and fate and circumstance, trying to make sense of it all has had its effect on me. I have long held an existential view of things – my place in the grand scheme of things and all that. I have often dabbled in notions of what it means to be part of humanity, and with human history the way it is, I have had to deal with concepts of good and evil. I have managed to muddle through life seeing and appreciating God in the wonders of nature and in the vastness of the universe and in the complexity of everything. My Judeo-Christian heritage led me to baptism, joining a church, and, more importantly, trying to emulate Christ in spite of the religious pomposity that abounds. Paula was raised as a Quaker. Jeff was brought up in the Hebrew faith but found comfort ultimately at the Clear View Worship Center. I was raised Methodist, but since our days in college Lynna Ruth and I have been devout Unitarian-Universalists. I have been unabashedly intellectual, scholarly, and proud of it. I know better now and I have been able to put a dull edge on that foolish pride, thanks primarily to Paula, who looked for me and found me, and to Jeff who found us both and taught me more about the meaning of life.

Jeff was a good man. He never had the support that I did and there is no telling what he could have done if he had. Nevertheless, he did what he did and took life as it came, but he lived it on his own terms. *My Way* was his fitting song. Like Job who remained faithful and feared God even when he was not protected or favored with His blessings, Jeff was upbeat, good hearted, and happy with what life brought his way. When I compare how our lives turned out to be so different, what is most clear to me is that my life has not been *better* than Jeff's life. Having had different experiences in life does not make one of us better than the other, and definitely does not make one's life richer or more meaningful than the other. The primary lesson for me is that accomplishments are not a critical component of life. It can be argued that the time spent away from family and pursuing "success" is actually a net negative even after one has reached some defined goals. I am not regretful or apologetic for having achieved, but neither am I proud. Knowing my worthy brother has allowed me to shed the sharp edges of my pride associated with my accomplishments. It is what it is. What does matter is *being that good person* – like Jeff and Paula definitely were, like I think I am. I thank my brother and my sister for showing me the way. I will hang on to this bit of personal truth and mix it with some Jungian collective Irish consciousness. I may just turn out alright after all. *Is D'Eirinn Mé.*

CHAPTER 14
# Thoughts on God, Art, Music, and Enlightenment

I conclude this story with an effort to show where these recent life experiences have landed me in an existential sense. The extreme introspection that is a necessary part of writing non-fiction about oneself and one's family creates a vision of one's inner space, analogous to how an erudite reporter of geopolitical current events might hone his or her own world view. To illuminate my current existential and spiritual place in the world, I shall share parts of a sermon that I gave in 2008 to the congregation of my Unitarian Universalist church. The title is "Got GAME? Thoughts on God, Art, Music, and Enlightenment."

## Got GAME?

This morning I want to take us on a journey to visit how some have envisioned God; how God has been represented in literature, art, and music; and how these near-visits with God might enlighten us.

The late great Joseph Campbell was a professor, writer, and lecturer best known for his work in the fields of comparative mythology and comparative religion. His work is vast and covers many aspects of the human experience, and his philosophy is often identified with the phrase he coined: "Follow Your Bliss".

A fundamental belief of Campbell's was that all spirituality is a search for the same basic, unknown force from which everything came, within which everything currently exists, and into which everything will return. This elemental force is ultimately "unknowable" because it exists before words and before knowledge. Although this basic driving force cannot be expressed in words, spiritual rituals and stories refer to the force through the use of "metaphors" – these metaphors being the various stories, deities, and objects of spirituality we see in the world. Campbell believed the religions of the world to be the various, culturally influenced "masks" of the same fundamental, transcendent truths. All religions, including Christianity and Buddhism, can bring one to an elevated awareness above and beyond a dualistic conception of reality, or idea of "pairs of opposites," such as being and non-being, or right and wrong. Indeed, he quotes in the preface of *The Hero with a Thousand Faces*: "Truth is one, the sages speak of it by many names."

In the interest of full disclosure, I should reveal that I choose to believe in God, therefore I am not an atheist; but I respect and I am fine with those who choose not to believe in God. I also choose to deal with the subject of the existance of God, therefore I am not agnostic; and of the many names I could use to reference the unknowable and indescribable force, the name I choose to use is "God".

I choose to believe in God because it is unacceptable to me to believe that mankind represents the ultimate truth and highest intelligence of our universe. I prefer to believe that truth is universal and that we humans have some capacity to glimpse this larger truth on occasion, and the capacity to tap into some mystical reservoir of a higher intelligence and, indeed, morality. Upon some inner reflection, it appears that I can no longer deny the existance of good and evil, although linking God to morality is tricky and unessential for me. My God is the life force of a complex nature and all that that implies.

If our earliest preserved art is cave drawings of scenes found in nature, is this not a reflection of our sense of the *integrated nature of creation and of its divine spirit*, and of both our appreciation of and participation in God's creation? Our earliest literature, our *written* art, finds *words* to describe God. An ancient Celtic poetic myth, "Song of Amergin", is found in the earliest existing Irish texts and represents an attempt by early poets to come to terms with the nature of God (or rather Goddess, as the earliest deities were female). Here the poet and the worshipper are one and the same. The language of true poetry is the language of the divine. I would love to hear the music of the Gaelic language repeating "Song of Amergin", but here at least is the translation.

# Song of Amergin

I am a stag: of seven tines,
I am a flood: across a plain,
I am a wind: on a deep lake,
I am a tear: the Sun lets fall,
I am a hawk: above the cliff,
I am a thorn: beneath the nail,
I am a wonder: among flowers,
I am a wizard: who but I
Sets the cool head aflame with smoke?
I am a spear: that roars for blood,
I am a salmon: in a pool,
I am a lure: from paradise,
I am a hill: where poets walk,
I am a boar: ruthless and red,
I am a breaker: threatening doom,
I am a tide that drags to death,
I am an infant: who but I
Peeps from the unhewn dolmen arch?
I am the womb: of every holt,
I am the blaze: on every hill,
I am the queen: of every hive,
I am the shield: for every head,
I am the tomb: of every hope.

# Thoughts on God, Art, Music, and Enlightenment

Art and music can be seen as metaphoric displays of the main spiritual threads common throughout the world. In "Song of Amergin", the image of the divine is woven with potent images of the natural world. There is fear, but also wonder and safety; there is life and death. The four elements; the animals, birds, insects, and fish; male and female; abstract and concrete are invoked to give a sense of the integrated nature of creation and its spirit.

Bruce Southworth, minister of UU church in Roanoke, Virginia, when Lynna Ruth and I were there in the early 1970s, gave a sermon titled, "One God at Most". Bruce is now minister of The Community Church of New York, and describes the events associated with Jesus' life and death thusly: Following Jesus' death, something happened to the small group of women and men who had chosen to join him. A contagion of love – some transforming, creative event bound them together into a fellowship. They told stories to heal their grief and celebrate their newly found joy and sense of liberation in a world that oppressed and despised so many of them. One Roman Catholic New Testament scholar calls the stories "creative fictions" yet affirms their continuing power.

I find spiritual wisdom in Jesus' affirmation, especially to the marginalized and oppressed of the world. Jesus taught, "You are the light of the world." Everyone, each one of us, is precious. We Unitarians call it, "Affirming the Inherent Worth and Dignity of Every Person." I know this because I have the T-shirt. The broad tent of Unitarian Universalism reflects the widest possible view of the plurality that is welcome in our movement.

I don't mean this to be a history lesson, but by the third century, Christianity had reinvented God as an all powerful male creator and destroyer; a bringer of order to chaos; a bringer of favor or disfavor to individuals and to whole races; quick to anger and ready to reward; exclusive rather than inclusive. The partisan and the political replaced the wondrous and the universal. Still in the *poetry* found in the Old Testament, and in the *songs*, the universal deity and the wonder are to be found. The art saves the essence of God from the political machinations of man's ways.

The Old Testament judgmental God dominates the Middle Ages, as seen in Milton's "Paradise Lost." The Cromwellian Old Testament God was harsh and repressive. Henry VIII considered representations of Christ to reflect Catholic idolatry and there was scant religious art produced until the arrival of William Blake, an artist whose attacks on conventional religion were shocking in his own day. Blake believed that the only true artists were those who were inspired by the spiritual. Blake's prophetic poetry has been said to form "what is in proportion to its merits the least read body of poetry in the English language". His visual artistry has led one modern critic to proclaim him "far and away the greatest artist Britain has ever produced". Blake challenged the 18th century religious order with his *poetry* that reflects a belief in a universal inclusive divinity. At age 30 he published a book titled "All Religions Are One". About Jesus Christ he said, "He is the only God ... and so am I, and so are you." Blake presents Jesus as a supremely creative being, above dogma, logic and even morality. Jesus, for Blake, symbolizes the unity between divinity and humanity: "Antiquity preaches the Gospel of Jesus." Blake designed his own mythology, as ultimately must we all.

Today *much* art has found its pre-Christian roots to transform the natural into the mysterious and supernatural. Many artists experiment with imaginative visions of nature.

# Thoughts on God, Art, Music, and Enlightenment

For example an ancient image of a tree is suffused with light and power as a symbol of regeneration, leaving no requirement for images of crosses or death.

It is common in the 21$^{st}$ century for artists to choose images beyond the confines of established faith. Recurrent motifs present images of God as light. German artist Rebecca Horn, in *Following the Light*, emphasizes God's immanence and the connectedness between the sacred and the everyday. She writes:

*What can you say about God?*

*He's everywhere, in such a special frequency,*

*That our world can hardly recognize him.*

*We just have to train a bit more.*

Perhaps it is the lack of certainty that works to produce such rich considerations of the nature of God in our art and our literature. Perhaps it is in the face of change and doubt that we are at our most spiritually aware. If religion is the everlasting dialogue between humanity and God, perhaps *Art is its soliloquy*. Perhaps God is at the center of all creativity.

I am an amateur musician, and rightfully a quite humble one. I wrote a song once and recorded it using a synthesizer, an electronic keyboard with many voices. I recorded one voice, then while listening to that recording through headphones, I recorded another part, and so on, and so on. It was difficult because it was a very long piece of music and it did not have the normal meter or rhythm and it did not have what many people would call a melody, so I had to keep the many parts in my head at the same time to make them fit. The genre of music that describes this is called ambient music. Without the normal meter there is no "rhythm entrainment" and without a predictable melody there is no "anticipation response". The body and the mind can "turn off" and relax even that much more than if they had to respond in kind to the music. To some, ambient music is very soothing and relaxing as it flows around you: to others I am sure it is just noise. You could say the same for the ambient wind; and the analogy holds for God. The song I wrote and recorded that day had a spiritual feel to it and I titled it "Agape".

I sometimes use words because of how I like the way they sound without full appreciation of their meaning. *Agape* is one of several Greek words translated into English as *love*. The word has been used in different ways by a variety of contemporary and ancient sources, including Biblical authors. Many have thought that this word represents divine, unconditional, self-sacrificing, active, volitional, and thoughtful love.

I played this song for an artist friend soon after I had recorded it. He said, "You didn't write this." Thinking he was trying to complement me, I smiled and said, "Yes, I did!" But his face became serious and he said, "No, you didn't." Thinking now that he was trying to challenge me, I looked sincere and convincingly earnest and said, "Yes, I did." And with direct eye contact he said, "No, you didn't. You were just the vessel." Then I understood, and thought, "What a compliment!" Later I understood that all artists are vessels and that God is the wellspring of all creativity.

From Gregorian chants to Handel's *Messiah* to Verdi's *Requiem* to Jesus Christ Superstar, there are abundant representations of God in music, just as in art and literature. The larger point to be made is that it is *all* art – not just paintings and poetry, literature and music. Quietly sitting

# Thoughts on God, Art, Music, and Enlightenment

together with a friend, holding a conversation over coffee, engaging the body politic, cleaning up the environment, driving defensively, gardening, almost any act, thought, or expression imaginable is art: it is *all* art. Therefore we are all artists... engaging in our own performance art, the art of living, the art of being. We are all vessels. God is in us and works through us and we express that same basic, unknown, creative life force in individualistic ways. We each are unique expressions of the same God – each one different – that is what makes it art. What a happy canvas we are. What a bold use for dust are we!

But time is waning and I wanted to touch on enlightenment. I mentioned previously that, in art, recurrent motifs present images of God as light. Should en*light*enment not follow?

To question is the answer. In other words, it is the journey, not the destination, which is important. It is who we are in terms of what we believe and hold dear, how we respect and treat others, and how we affirm our lives that gives our time on earth meaning and worth – not where we *plan* to be someday or even eternally. Among our most familiar and revered Unitarian ministers is Ralph Waldo Emerson. He once wrote:

> A person will worship something – have no doubt about that. We may think our tribute is paid in secret in the dark recesses of our hearts – but it will out. That which dominates our thoughts will determine our lives, our character. Therefore it behooves us to be careful what we worship, for what we are worshipping we are becoming.

As artists, as vessels, it is who we are in terms of what we believe and hold dear, how we respect and treat others, how we affirm our lives that gives our time on earth meaning and worth, and how we give expression to our art of living and of being.

Clearly to question is the answer, but it gives our lives sharper focus at times to give *answers* to the big *questions*. Immanuel Kant's essay "Answering the Question: What is Enlightenment?" held it necessary that all church and state paternalism be abolished and people be given the freedom to use their own intellect. Well, there is a defined starting point – intellectual freedom is the *sine qua non*, the without which none. But then where does one go with one's life to achieve enlightenment? I would hold that all roads can lead there! It's not as if that one has it and the other one doesn't. Rather it *is* the quest, the journey itself, the path one travels in the good company of God and nature, the way one *is* in thought and spirit – the way one *is* in brotherhood or sisterhood. One may *follow* one's bliss, but one must *travel* with one's true self and the good companions of God and nature. To Question *is* the Answer. To Search with intellectual honesty and freedom *is* the Answer. Go with Truth, and go with the creative life force of a complex nature, and go with Love.

*Dona Nobis Pacem.* Give Us Peace. *Dona Nobis Pacem.*

CHAPTER 15
# Closure

*Dateline: August 24, 2009*

I had already finished this book. I had actually first written it in November of 2006, the month after Paula died. It was in me and it had to come out. I let the book sit a few months then I rewrote parts of it. A year later I proofread it and wrote it again. And again; it never seemed just right. A few weeks ago I became interested in finishing the rewrite and publishing. I actually reorganized the book, removing one chapter entirely and inserting two other chapters that were not connected to the one I removed. Trust me: it is better now. As my chairman, Dr. J. Mack Worthington, has told me on multiple occasions, "The best writing is rewriting."

With the new work on the book, I had been thinking about my Delaney family rather intently. It was in this context that Brenda, Jeff's widow, called me yesterday. It was a fine, relatively cool, Sunday afternoon. Lynna Ruth was driving because I was between surgeries for cataracts; left one done, right one pending. My depth perception was poor and Lynna Ruth was my cheerful chauffer. We had been to church and to lunch afterward when Brenda called my cell phone.

"Hello", I answered.

"Hello, John." said Brenda. After some brief pleasantries, she said, "I didn't know if you would be interested, but your mother died this weekend."

What a bazaar phrase that is, but I fully understood what she was saying. I took me a second for that to sink in, partly because I had resisted thinking of my birth mother as my real mother. The woman who nurtured and raised me is my mother. Still there was this lady who 60 years ago had carried me in her womb, labored and birthed me. And she was, after all, my flesh and blood mother. Also, to be honest and to add to the irony, I had called in an effort to talk, then visit, with her about a month ago. The number listed in the telephone directory no longer worked. I could not have known she was in a local nursing home. I thought she was alive because she was mentioned in a magazine article. Memorial hospital has a local publication called Chicken Soup. Imogene Aslinger was featured in an article about the hospital's home health services. Mrs. Aslinger said she was very grateful to the nurses and home health aides for their kind attention.

# Closure

I reminded Brenda that Paula had visited with our birth mother in the early 1990s, and Mrs. Aslinger was disengaged and disinterested. Paula advised me that I might not want to contact her. I too thought that I would not stir what for her might be painful memories of a difficult time in her life. I thought too that the family had their chance to have me in their lives, but I was placed for adoption. I too was resentful for how Jeff was treated by the family. He found his way back "home" as a young man and was sent away again. Brenda shared with me yesterday that Jeff did call our birth mother, maybe 10 or 15 years ago. They talked briefly and she said she would call him back, but she never did.

## Obituaries
### Aslinger, Imogene Clark
posted August 22, 2009

Imogene Clark Aslinger, 87, of Hixson, Tennessee, died on Friday, Aug. 21, in a local hospital.

Mrs. Aslinger was preceded in death by her husband, Ronald C. Aslinger.

She is survived by her children, William C. Aslinger, Donna L. Croft, both of Chattanooga, and Audie R. Aslinger of Ringgold; her grandchildren, Audrey Lacy, Samuel Leon Carr, Timothy R. Aslinger and Christina Aslinger; and four great-grandchildren.

Funeral services will be held at 1 p.m. on Tuesday, Aug. 25, at Heritage Funeral Home Chapel with Rev. Billy Dean officiating. Interment will follow in the Chattanooga National Cemetery.

The family will receive friends from 2-4 and 6-8 p.m. on Monday, Aug. 24, at Heritage Funeral Home, 7454 E. Brainerd Road, Chattanooga, Tn. 37421.

On this day of August 24, 2009, I am thinking that this cannot be what it is like to write a "real" book. Apart from the mindful musings about life and death, fortune and fate, and the existential contemplations of the "big" questions – our relationship to one another as people, what life is all about, why are we here, who is your mother – aside from all of that nonsense, there is the "real time" aspect of these current words. It is surreal. It must be what it would be like to blog or twitter, if I were ever to do that. In three hours I plan to act on the above opportunity and go to my mother's funeral home where my genetic family is holding a reception. How do I feel about meeting my half-brothers and half-sister? News at eleven. Press pause. Page break.

So, I just got back from the funeral home…

It is across the road from East Brainerd Elementary School where I attended the 6$^{th}$ grade.

Curious aren't you?

My birth mother looked peaceful lying in her casket, and Lynna Ruth was amazed at how much she resembled Paula. There was a digital slide show of her and Ronald Aslinger and their family. Everyone was very nice to us. Bill, Donna, and Audie and their families were wonderful to meet. They were genuinely pleased that Lynna Ruth and I came. We hugged. We planned to meet for dinner soon.

Bill and Donna were *Aslingers* because Ronald Aslinger had legally adopted them. Audie was Ronald's son. We talked about the family. They had known about me but knew nothing about where I might be living. They certainly did not know I lived locally. They were all very interested to meet Lynna Ruth and me, and each was also very interesting to us. I could have learned more about my birth mother's family but I had come to pay my respects. This reception was not about me and I did not want to impose my story. I am very glad that I went. I am glad to have seen my birth mother and met her other children.

Here is the neat part. While Bill, Donna, Audie, and I all have the same mother, we each have different biologic fathers – Boyd, Allen, Aslinger, and of course, Delaney. We are equals that way.

I have two new brothers and a new sister. And this time, I am the oldest.

When God closes one door, He opens another.

# Appendix A –
# First Contact: Letter and Emails

## Paula A. Cope

January 3, 1996

Dear Mr. Standridge,

I am searching for a brother who was given up for adoption at the age of three months. He was born in 11/21/48 in Chattanooga, Tennessee. He was adopted by John and Juanita "Annie" Standridge, and they named him John Brendle Standridge, II or (Jr.) The Standridges lived in Benton, Tennessee at the time of the adoption.

I am 14 months older than John, and we are natural siblings (same birth mother and father). I was adopted through the Tennessee Children's Home Society, as John was, but was sent to a family in California.

If you have any information that would help me locate him, I can be reached at the address and phone number listed above. I do not want to disrupt anyone's life, nor do I want anything from him other than to locate him. If you know my brother, I would appreciate it if you would forward this information on to him. If he does not wish to have any contact with me, and lets me know that, I will discontinue my search immediately.

Sincerely,

**Paula A. Cope**

Paula A. Cope

# APPENDIX A – First Contact: Letter and Emails

## John and Lynna Ruth Standridge

Paula Cope

January 10, 1996

Dear Sis,

You will forgive me if I am only occasionally coherent, I didn't have a sister 24 hours ago. It has taken some time to sink in.

Hi, sis. This is something. I had never thought in terms of my – what do you call it? – other family. I think I thought that it was not possible to find out about family so I dismissed the idea of ever finding out.

It was really good talking with you. I have been trying to let the idea of another family sink in, but so far I have not been able to make it feel exactly right. I have a lifetime in, you know, *my* family. But it feels good to have a sister.

I have given some thought as to what impact this should have on my sons and their families. I would like to meet your daughter and, of course, Jacob Daniel. How Adam and Aaron want to do sounds like their call. We have a small guest bedroom and would be happy to put you up. You would be welcome anytime.

You are my flesh and blood sister. Welcome, I look forward to getting to know you. I have enclosed some pictures of our family, yours and mine. Notice how adorable Addison is. Also here is the newspaper article that came out about 15 months ago.

Keep in touch and we'll get together soon. I have some vacation time coming. I look forward to getting to know you. Affectionately,

Your brother,

John

p.s. I can cook.

*January 13, 1996*

**Dear Sister Paula,**

Hi! I still can't get over it.

We spoke on the phone last night for just the second time ever, and I feel like I know you. Something else I thought of is that it's not that we've never met. We were just very young those 3 months. It's more like a Reunion almost.

Also found it strange or way co-incidental that your husband and my wife are both from around Oneida. Which…by the way is between you and me on I-75. I am headed up to Knoxville to see Aaron's band play. Adam, Betty and Addison will be there, and maybe their cousin Marejka will be there.

Well. Gotta go. See you soon. Get out your camera and take some pictures.

John

# Appendix A – First Contact: Letter and Emails

*January 16, 1996*

Dear John,

 I just wanted to drop you a quick note before I run this package of photos over to the post office. I got your first two letters today and just wanted to let you know how **proud** I am to call you brother! And what a nice looking family! Addison is a **doll** and I can see why you are so taken with him! In fact, I am proud to call all of them family — they are my family now, too, you know!

 I think you look a lot like our father through the eyes and nose, but Larry says it's hard for him to tell... he wants to reserve judgment on who you look like until he meets you.

 Did you get the first batch of pictures I sent? I am really anxious to meet you. I have to admit, however, that I am a little afraid that the anticipation of meeting may result in some kind of a letdown for you when we are finally re-united... I just don't want you to be disappointed in your new sister! I am what I am...as Popeye used to say. I haven't always had it easy, but I am a fighter! And somehow I think you are too.

Talk to you again soon,

       Love

       Sis

Date: Fro. 19 Jan 1996 22:09:06 –0500

From: PACope

Subject: 8 days and counting...

I forgot to tell you how much I enjoyed the Irish touch to your last letter... real cute, but no one will mistake you for a leprechaun (you are too tall)! The cottage sounds great! Do we need to bring anything...? With the kind of frigid weather we are having today (it has dropped 50 degrees in the last 24 hours), that fireplace sure sounds good about now! What time of day do you think you will be arriving at the Lodge? I know you said you were going to stop off in Oneida.

So the office crowd thinks we look alike, huh? Well, we will just have to take lots of pictures of the two of us together so we can see for ourselves! I grew up thinking I didn't look like anybody, so it's really hard for me to see myself in others... even my own daughter! People tell us we look alike all the time, but I can't see it.

What does your wife prefer to be called? Lynna Ruth or Ruth? Larry says "hi" right back at ya... I think he's as anxious to meet the two of you as I am... he has been with me every step of the way in my quest for roots.

Well, Doc... I will talk to you soon.... Love, Sis.

---

Date: Sun, 21 Jan 1996 19:31:04-0500

From: PACope

Subject: Okay, you beat me this time...

It may only be 6 days now, but I have a feeling this will be the longest week! I am glad to hear that you're not a stuffed-shirt.... But I could tell that just by talking to you! You have a warm heart and a way of putting people completely at ease, and your sweet note the other night (the one you say you wrote just before getting beeped) touched me to the point of

## Appendix A – First Contact: Letter and Emails

tears... I feel truly blessed that my 'missing brother' turned out to be YOU. As for you being a 'strange duck'.... I would be worried that we weren't really related after all if you weren't but now I KNOW we're kin!

You mentioned in one of your letters that you like to cook... do you have a specialty? Larry hasn't done too much of it lately, but for years he tried to perfect the perfect barbecue sauce for ribs. He also makes a mean spaghetti sauce. I am, on the other hand, a lousy cook.... A great eater, but a lousy cook!

You have never mentioned what Lynna Ruth's profession is?

Well, Doc, I am going to wrap this up and go give my California Mom a call, and then get ready to go back to work tomorrow. Before I forget, let me know how much our share of the cottage comes to so we can split the expenses...... Take care... we'll talk again soon!

Love, Sis

---

Date: Thu, 25 Jan 1996 01:34:38 – 0500

From: PACope

Subject: Won't be long now!

John and Lynna Ruth,

What is the weather like down there? We had rain yesterday, but today it turned to snow... not a lot of accumulation, but snow just the same (as if the current flooding up here isn't bad enough....worst in 20 years... I think Mother Nature must have PMS, or something!) The weather for this weekend looks like it will be cold and maybe a little snow in the morning on Saturday, but nothing drastic as far as I can tell... not drastic enough to keep me from getting to

Cumberland Falls State Park, at least!... See you soon! Love, Sis.

---

Date: Mon, 29 Jan 1996 18:26:44 – 0500

From: PACope

Subject: Re: Seems just like yesterday....

You were right on all accounts... it DOES seem like just yesterday, it WAS a great weekend, and Larry and I ARE terrific people! And so are you and Lynna Ruth! I meant what I said about how I could not have gotten a better brother if I had hand picked him myself! And I REALLY like Lynna Ruth.... Getting her as a sister-in-law is an added bonus! I look forward to getting to know both of you a lot better in the lifetime we have ahead of us!

Okay, so much for the mushy stuff. I took the picture you wanted from Beth's wedding up to have a copy made, and they said it would take a week. It was really hard to go back to work today, but I enjoyed showing off the charm you gave me (I put it on a gold chain I had), and showing everyone that picture of you and Lynna Ruth (the votes are split as to whether or not we look alike).

The bread you sent home with us was good... I had a chicken sandwich on a couple of slices of it for lunch today. We have a bread machine, too, but ours makes smaller loaves than that.

Well, I'll be thinking about when we can get together again, and you be doing the same... in the meantime, just know that someone in Cincinnati loves you!

Sis

---

## Appendix A – First Contact: Letter and Emails

*Date: Mon, 26 Feb 96 12:45:45 EST*
*From: Paula Cope*
*Subject: Four days and counting*
*Hey Doc,*

*So you are on your own for a couple of days, huh? Something tells me you are pretty self-sufficient, though I am sure Lynna Ruth will be greatly missed. Do you have a crib or playpen or something we can use for Jake to nap in while we are down there, or should we pack a portable crib? The Holiday Inn has a crib for us to use at night, so all we need to worry about is naps away from the hotel. The car will be pretty loaded down, so I don't want to bring one if you have one we can use.*

*Has it really only been a month since we've seen each other?... it seems like FOREVER!!! I am REALLY looking forward to this weekend! Do you think your boys and their loved ones will make an appearance some time Saturday? I hope so, I am looking forward to getting to know them as well. 4 days and counting... Sis*

---

Date: 5/4/96 09:19

To: PACope

Subject: Hi Sis....

    It's Saturday morning and Ruth is still catching up on her sleep, so it's a good time to write.

    So, you got the coffee mugs... You can drink hot chocolate out of them if you want, but we use ours every day. We really like the stuff from Sanibel Pottery and have been getting stuff a little at a time from them for years. This year we got cups for the boat: kind of greenish with sea gull designs, like ours at home.

We tried to mow the lawn when we got back (honest) but the mower tire was flat. Fixed that then couldn't find the key. Found that then grass was so high and wet it clogged the bagger tube and caused bad vibration. Fixed that then battery terminal wire broke in two. Now have to go to Snapper store and get another (wire, not mower). Fortunately it's near the Waffle House (breakfast...yes). We have plans to go to the boat this weekend if we can get everything else done. Sounds like a setup for disappointment to me.

We rode bikes in Sanibel and it was so much fun, and the exercise was good for us and not too much. And then I saw this ad (30 minute infomercial) on TV for those nice looking bikes that are 6-speed but shift automatically to make it easier riding. I just don't know if it would be easy enough for us with all these hills around here. Sanibel is flat you know. Anyway I want to get them. We have to find some exercise that is fun enough to stay with. I just don't know if we really will make the time. You know?

Essay on southern women during the Civil War? Growing the corn, plowing with the mule, trying to raise bunches of kids while the menfolk are off getting slaughtered, waiting for the damnyankees to come rape and pillage? I don't know... sounds like a touch subject to sell in Cincinnati. Why can't y'all forget that war? Ha!

It was a tough week at the office. It always is the first week back after being gone for vacation or conference. Lots of patients, tough causes, nursing home... the free clinic was good though. I volunteer there some evenings.

Cindy, my nurse, got married while I was gone. Big surprised, but cool... 'cept now I need to find her a nice wedding present. I don't know if this is her 4th or 5th marriage or what. But it was casual enough... blue jeans and margaritas. She's a Harley-riding grandma to boot. Takes all kinds. She's a good nurse though.

## Appendix A – First Contact: Letter and Emails

Y'all take care. Sorry about your car. Bent frames are bad news. I hope the guy that hit you has insurance and will cover this. You ought to consider trading though. Sure you were not hurt? Sounds like a hard impact.

Guess I'll sign off. Yes the Loft is excellent. Come on down. Stay in our guest bedroom (That's what it is for.) and we'll take you there.
Love you. John

---

*Date: Mon, 13 May 1996 18:12:14 –0400*

*From: PACope*

*Subject: I'm so glad you're out there, too!!*

*Thanks for the Mother's Day wish... I hope my newest sister-in-law had a happy Mother's Day too... I meant to write to you yesterday, but you know how weekends can get away from you! Did you get to take Addison out on your boat? I hope so... Beth & Paul gave me some new pictures of Jake for Mother's Day... 3 very good 5x7s.. took two of them in to work to put on my desk and left one at home.*

*I feel so blessed to have you and your family in my life! Gotta finish the final draft of my "Dr. John" essay... teacher read the first draft last week and said you sounded like a pretty neat guy... hey, I knew that!*

*Hope everything gets straightened out at work... I'd hate to see you have to quit. What will happen with the contract you've signed... won't that significantly limit your options?... Well, I'd better get busy finishing up on my essay... I've got to turn it in tomorrow night... Love, Sis*

---

*Date: Tue, 4 Jun 1996 23:28:04 –0400*

*From: PACope*

*Subject: Hello... How are you?*

Glad you liked the essay. I just got home from taking my final exam.... 2 ½ hours of writing a persuasive essay on no-fault divorce in class.... I had writer's cramp so bad by the time I finished! I didn't do as well on it as I would have liked, but I have gotten A's on all of my other papers, so I don't think this one will hurt me. I am really glad it is over with, however. I am not taking any classes this summer because they have divided the summer into two halves – each one is half as many weeks as a normal quarter, but each class is 2 nights a week instead of one. I'm not ready for classes more often than once a week.

Both Larry and I were on vacation last week and we babysat for Jake 4 days... spent some quality time with him at the part, etc. Yeah, I really dig this grand parenting stuff! We also got to spend some quality time with each other. Finally made it to the OmniMax Theater (that I wanted us to go to when you were here, (but you wanted to go sit in the rain at the ballpark, remember?)... saw a documentary called "Storm Chasers," about people who oddly enough, chase after storms! Movie was just okay, but the theater itself is quite an experience.... 5-story high dome shaped movie screen, seats sloped sharply up-hill, massive speakers and swirling camera effects... all left me feeling like I needed a seat-belt and some Dramamine for motion sickness!

My new printer is a Cannon bubble-jet, and it came with a CD-rom (Cannon Creative) which contained all kinds of neat software, including one that creates Hallmark Create-a-Care (kinda like the ones they have in those machines in the Hallmark shops. I'm having a lot of fun with it. Sorry to hear about your nurse... that's really a shame!

## Appendix A – First Contact: Letter and Emails

*I have a week of vacation on the 4th of July week, and I will be in Chattanooga all that week, but I will be staying with our cousin, Sharon (this is my annual get-together with her that I told you about). Larry will drive me down, drop me off, and come back to get me the following weekend, and Sharon and I will hit every store in Chattanooga. I would love to see you while I'm there, and I know Sharon would LOVE to meet you, but that will have to be your decision. Tell Lynna Ruth that we will be doing some "power shopping" while I'm there, and we'd love to have her join us, if she'd like. Then sometime shortly after I return from Chattanooga, we have to drive to the northeastern corner of the Ohio and bring Larry's youngest daughter (and maybe a friend) down to stay with us for two weeks, and then drive them back home (5 ½ hour drive each way so we spend the night in a hotel and do it in 2 days).*

*Between the new printer, my week with Sharon, and Larry's daughter coming to stay with us, quite honestly, my finances are stretched way past their limit!!! I miss you very much… I really wish we lived closer! I appreciate your offer to let Larry and I stay with you any time, which would save some money, but Larry does not like to stay with ANYONE. He just doesn't feel comfortable staying at anybody's house – he won't even stay with his oldest daughter when we go up to see his kids. If we can't stay in a motel he won't go… simple as that. I, on the other hand, as evidenced by my up-coming week with Sharon, do not have a problem with free-loading off my relatives!*

*I guess having said all that.. the bottom line is I really can't afford to make any get-away plans any time soon…. So I hope you'll consider letting Sharon and me visit while I'm down there the first week in July!! At least think about it!*

*Love, Paula*

Date: Sat, 8 Jun 1996 21:30:25 – 0400

From: PACope

Subject: Re: Hi Sis.

 Cool... I'm looking forward to seeing you, too! We'll drive down Saturday, the 29$^{th}$, spend the night in the Holiday Inn & then Sharon will pick me up Sunday and take me to her house.... Larry will drive back down the following Saturday, we'll spend that night in the Holiday Inn again, and head back to Cincinnati Sunday morning. Don't make specific plans... like buying tickets to anything for a specific date and time... until I get a chance to talk to Sharon and see if she has anything in particular planned... me, I'm just going along for the ride and looking forward to seeing my loved ones!

 Sharon is our first cousin on our father's side... her mother was our dad's sister. She is a year older than I am, and has two younger brothers, but they don't' live in Chattanooga and I have never met either one of them. You're going to have to let me know how much you want to know, etc., so I don't push you into anything you're not ready for. Okay?

 Yeah I have kept all our letters... that's where I got most of the quotes for my Dr. John essay... my memory isn't THAT good! Who knows, it might be kinda fun collaborating on a best seller... but it probably wouldn't buy me any extra credit for Freshman English! And I am like you in that I think it's a great idea for a day or so and then nobody but us would read it... oh well, maybe that's the key... we write it four ourselves, and our families.

 I love you, and am really looking forward to seeing Ya'll.... Love, Sis.

---

# APPENDIX A – First Contact: Letter and Emails

Date: Wed, 12 June 1996 23:11:12 –0400

From: PACope

Subject: You've got mail!

Just a really quick note... talked to Sharon last night, she says "Yes" she would like to meet you. I told her you suggested maybe going out on your boat, but she says she can't swim and is pretty nervous around boats, so maybe that's not such a good idea. Told her another suggestion you had was the IMAX Theater & she said she had been wanting to go there, so that is a possible option. We can talk more about all that later, though. What we do isn't the important thing.... Just being together is what's important! Did you manage to get someone to cover for you so that you can take a few days off? Hope so! I'll talk to you later, Little Brother... I love you...... Paula

---

Date: Sat, 15 Jun 1996 13:56:18 –0700

From: Paula A. Cope

Subject: Hey Little Brother, I'm trying out a new Online Service

I have just signed up on a new online service called NETCOM (well, new to me anyway), so please let me know if you get this message! The service is $5.00 the first month, $20 a month after that, but you have unlimited access hours... and with school, now, I really can rack up the hours doing research for papers. So anyway, thought I would give it a try. I still belong to America Online, but if this works out I will probably drop it... so let me know when, and if you receive this. I am sure you will be able to tell what my email address is here, but I'll give it to you anyway... Talk to you soon!

Sis

From: PACope

Subject: Eleven more days!

Date: 06/18 07:16 PM ET

Hey, there! Did you have a nice Father's Day? We had a couple of really hot days last week, and a dry weekend, for a change, but rain and thunderstorms have returned again today ( and I think are expected to continue on and off all week). I am soooo sick of rain! Sure hope the weather is a whole lot better where you are.

I wasn't feeling well today so I played hooky from work and laid around on the couch all day. My upper back has been bothering me for the last few days, and I have a bunch of fibroid tumors that make the monthly cycle rather painful, so I decided to feel sorry for myself and vegetate for the day... I'm feeling better now. Won't be long now... the countdown is on......

Love, Sis

---

Date: Sun, 23 June 1996 20:34:07 – 0400

From: PACope

Subject: 5 more days....

Hi!

How is everybody? Nothing new going on here... just starting to get things ready for vacation. The weather here has been one extreme or the other.... Either rain and thunderstorms, or sweltering heat!

We both had a good weekend with Jacob, we watched him both Friday and Saturday nights while Beth and Paul went out. He is just starting to say words now... he calls Larry "Pah Pah" and mumbles something that sorta sounds like "ma" at the end... it's close enough for me, anyway. He says "apple" and "clock" very plainly (but can't say Grandma!... go figure) ... and he's come up with his own version of banana which sounds more like "banamina", but he is trying! He wants you to read to him ALL the time... he would rather look at books than play with his toys.... Sure hope he feels that way about 15 years from now!

I dread next week....you know what work can be like when you are trying to get all the loose ends wrapped up so that you can go on vacation! Tell Lynna Ruth I said "Hi"... looking forward to seeing Y'all (see I spelled it right this time... last time was just a typo)...... Love, Paula

---

Date: Sun, 7 Jul 1996 22:07:26 –0400

From: PACope

Subject: I'm back home again....

Just a quick note to let you know we made it home okay.... Really rough trip, thought... REALLY heavy stop-n-go traffic all the way, and got tied up in a VERY serious accident on I-75 somewhere between Knoxville and Jellico.... 4 cars involved (we heard a car going southbound jumped over and across the median and hit northbound cars head-on) ... many, many emergency vehicles and they shout the highway down altogether to land a helicopter to air-care someone out. Everyone just shut their cars off and got out and walked around on the freeway. We just took our time after that, because even after we finally got around the accident, traffic was just too heavy. We left Chattanooga a little after 9:00am and pulled in here at almost 6:00pm!!!!!

I am very thankful to be home safely, but I'm sure going to hate going back to work tomorrow! Thank you again for EVERYTHING this past week! I really enjoyed spending the time alone with you! Like I told you the other night... you really spoiled me... but I LOVE being spoiled!.... I love you and I miss you already! Paula

---

Date: Sun, 14 Jul 1996 07:48:31 –0700

From: Paula A. Cope

Subject: Hidee Ho, Little Brother!

Whole bunch! Not much going on here. Larry's daughter isn't coming down after all.... I wish I could say I was sorry about that, but...!

I am cleaning closets out today to make room for all the new clothes I bought while I was down there. What a chore! Long overdue, though, believe me.

I am going to start trying to use my new service, NetCom, for mail now, too, so please start using this e-mail address from now on. I have been using AOL for e-mail and NetCom for everything else.... Doesn't make sense to keep paying for AOL if I'm not going to use it!

Babysat for Jake last night. He's just discovered his independence and likes to say "NO" to everything now. The kid is developing a bit of a temper too.... I can't imagine where he inherited THAT from! But he's still the cutest kid this side of Tennessee!

Tell Lynna Ruth I said 'Hi', and give yourself a hug for me.... Love, Sis

---

Date: Sun, 4 Aug 1996 16:3508 – 0700

From: Paula A. Cope

Subject: Hey, Bro

# Appendix A – First Contact: Letter and Emails

*Pick up the phone once in a while... will try to do just that occasionally. Did you and Lynna Ruth sleep in this morning to take advantage of your last day of vacation?*

*Larry and I watched Jake for a few hours today while his parents went to the toy store to get him a backyard playset (a combination sandbox & pool in the shape of a dump truck). Then we delivered him back hope and watched him 'dig' into his new sandbox! We had a good time!*

*What are micro-calcifications in the breast? Are they anything like fibroid tumors? It seems I have a lot of them, and had to go have some special views of my right breast done last week as a follow-up to the mammogram a few weeks back. All they told me was that there are two patches of these calcifications and a very small 'benign-looking' tumor in the right breast (and some calcification in the left breast that they didn't seem to think was a problem). I won't know the results of those until the end of the week sometime, but I assume that there must be a reason that they wanted all these special views.... Doesn't sound like a good thing, but I don't want to go looking for things to worry about either.*

*Well, Little Brother... until next time...*

*Love Ya!*

---

## Typical email from Paula

*Subject: Hey there, Little Brother..*

*Date: Sat, 13 Nov 1999 10:37:24 EST*

*From: Pacope@aol.com*

*To: ridgeway@chattanooga.net*

I was so great to see all of you last month! I tried to call you before we left, but whoever it was that answered the phone said you weren't there. Did you tell you I called?

Not much is new here. I think we're going to do a little Christmas shopping today for Larry's grandkids. This is the first time I've logged on to my computer in a couple of weeks. I was browsing for some good low-cal, low-fat recipes. I joined Weight Watcher's last week and am currently obsessed with food (what can I eat, when can I eat... ). I know that will pass, but right now that seems to be all I can think about! Joining just before the holidays probably wasn't one of the smarter things I've done!

I chatted with Beth online this morning. She said she was looking for craft projects for Jake. He has decided this week that he wants to be an artist instead of a policeman.

Would love to hear from you.

Love, Paula.

---

### Typical email from John:

Subject: Try again...

Date: Mon, 17 Jan 2000 17:25:48 -0500

From: John & Lynna Ruth Standridge <ridgeway@chattanooga.net>

To: Ridgeway@chattanooga.net

I never got a reply to my last email, so I'm still not sure I have the address correct, but I thought I would try again anyway. I got a new computer (my old one died), and I lost all my email addresses. I've also switched from America Online to CompuServe, so my new email address is pacope439@cs.com.

# Appendix A – First Contact: Letter and Emails

---

*Please drop me a line to let me know that you got this note. Hope everyone is well and that the new year is treating you right!*

*Love, Paula*

---

Right address. I typed a long letter and the thing terminated, crashed, and in general wouldn't co-operate. Luckily I saved it the second time so I'm sending it as an attachment. Let me know if you get it or not.

John

---

Will wonders never cease? It lives.

I'm referring sarcastically to my own self and simultaneously wondering if I can make that claim if I don't have a life.

I just seem to be so busy these days. First there is work, of course. I am on hospital service this month and we are maintaining record numbers of patients – half of them so sick they are in ICUs on ventilators with multi-system organ failure. Also I'm seeing large numbers of office patients and precepting residents in the office as well as rounding with them in the hospital. I have two talks to give this week – one at Women's East to a group of ob-gyns and the other to an Indian (as in Hindu) Medical Group. Plus I'm reviewing and writing articles for medical journals and textbooks. Plus we are recruiting for next year's crop of residents, which means interviewing medical students. Plus administrating a medical office and a residency program. Plus I'm medical director at a nursing home and physician to about 40 of the patients there. Plus tons of paperwork. etc… and that's just work.

Lynna Ruth has resigned her old job and is full time with her new business enterprise – Liberty Tax Service. She has opened 3 new offices: 2 in Cleveland and one in Athens, TN. We are way in debt getting these up and running, but this has potential and could secure a future for Adam and Betty (who really know taxes after 6 years with H& R Block, supervising and becoming IRS Enrolled Agents). Aaron left school this semester to help out and learn the business. I hope he will go back to UT and finish up starting this summer. We bought 10 franchises, and 5 of them are in Knoxville. If Aaron goes back to UT, he could help with the start-up of these.

So, that's work. We are also trying to maintain a social life with our friends, dinners and so forth. And we still do the Suck Creek Wine and Country Club. I'm also trying to find time for my music. It has evolved over the last few years and I now have the framework for a CD. Still mostly Tommy Cotter and myself. I've written the majority of the songs and play piano, synthesizer, trumpet and sax. My vocals have improved, too. We still call it ConceptPeace, and label it as eclectic folk music for the 21st century. So anyway, let me know if you want a CD and I'll send you one. They're just homemade CDs at this point.

Happy new millennium, btw. I know.. they didn't have a year "zero" so technically it's next year, but that's just an excuse for two parties if you ask me.

Well, my stupid internet provider couldn't tell I was online, so it terminated my connection. High tech needs to get just a little bit higher to suit me. They cannot conceive of a "long" letter. Seems like people's attention spans are not too impressive, anyway. Stock market looks like a bit of a mania to me... unreasonable valuation. Of course that's just sour grapes since I have no "investments". Nevertheless, I would love to short it at the top and get some positive cash flow in our family's picture.

# Appendix A – First Contact: Letter and Emails

This is MLK day. I'm a state employee. That means I got to work at home today instead of going in. Nice.

LRS is interviewing receptionists tonight so I do not look for her to get home until 9:30 or so.

We had a good Christmas. I was on call and doing hospital rounds, but kids came in Sunday afternoon and we had family time.

I have been following the Tennessee Titans this season, even went to two games – Atlanta (pre-season) and the Rams. They have done well. Now, can they beat Jacksonville for the 3rd time this year and go to the superbowl?

Well, I'm going to go to the supper bowl, or at least go fix myself something.

Write and catch me up on everybody up there, and say "hi" to everyone and give them my love. And yourself. I think of you often, even though I've turned into a poor correspondent.

Take care.

Love, John

---

## Typical emails from Jeff

### This one from 11/17/03:

wow guys this year we doubled last year and raised 2800.00 for the kids for christmas gifts for the kids who would not get one otherwise...and it all stays in this county...had a chance to buy a 1967 pickup for 950, but passed it up, to pull my trailer for the car shows, water pump went out while i was test driving it, figured it was gonna be more trouble then i needed... carl not doing much better, but still holding his own for now, i think a fellow here in town is going to ask me to do karaoke in his

resturant on saturday nights and i think i will for a while....sorry i missed you this weekend sis, couldn't get away from work long enough to call, and your right that is BUSY, LOVE YOU ANYWAY, WILL MAKE IT UP NEXT WEEKEND I PROMISE..., J
I HAVE NO DOUBT YOU DID WELL ON YOU RECERT, JOHN , I THINK YOUR A SHARP COOKIE AND I'M HARD TO IMPRESS, BUT YOU DO WELLLLLLLLL...LOVE J

And this one from 10/11/04, titled "I am glad you finally redeemed your part of the family":

Brenda felt that Paula and I were the only nuts that had that type of humor and I tried to assure her that that was not the case...well you have now proved my point.... She did like the one about "they blow up so fast"... we are fine, but really strapped for money as Jr. still has the estate tied up, but it will come to pass, i hope. I have amassed 1100 pages of evidence that proves that Jr. has been stealing from his dad since 1985 and a lot more than 40, 000.00... There is no telling exactly how much he did get away with, but i feel somewhere in the neighborhood of 150, 000.00....

I was just reading what i wrote and i mentioned the money to explain why we were not traveling around like we want to and going to see y'all and spending time with Paula and you guys... when it rains it pours and as if the price of gas is not bad enough they sent property taxes of double what they told me they would be and the ones for KY. as well. Now i find that propane is going to be about 60% above what it was last year.... we had some friends from Mich. here for two weeks and that was nice, they travel full time and it was nice to see them again. we washed his motor home and car and when he left he was as proud as if it was a new one... i was glad to see them that happy...

Other that that there is still alot more, I had my last car show for the year and played "MY" song you know my way in

## Appendix A – First Contact: Letter and Emails

spanish. i liked it and did not care if anyone else did , but they did. the only show i have left this year is the Christmas parade, but i do that for free, so we just enjoy that....

I'm glad that John is doing well and keeping busy and if my Gene's are working on him as they worked on me, he should be slowing down at about 55, but will push himself to his total capacity till, don't know when i haven't reached it yep....my capacity is less than it used to be but i still work at whatever it is, getting less all the time... i now have two lawyers who want me to do p. i. work for them, and i like it.... ok enough for now..., love to all j

APPENDIX B –

# The Adoption Records and Other Documents

## CHILD'S OWN FAMILY

Child's Name <u>Marion Richard Delaney</u>   Birthdate <u>October 27, 1943</u>
Birthplace <u>Chatt., Tenn.</u>

Child's Name <u>Mary Elizabeth Delaney</u>   Birthdate <u>September 18, 1947</u> Birthplace <u>Chatt., Tenn</u>

Mother's Name <u>Imogene Mathis</u>   Age <u>29</u> Address <u>West 5th St., Chattanooga Tennessee</u>

Father's Name <u>Marion Delaney</u>   Age <u>27</u> Address <u>Overman Apts., West 6th St., Chatt.,</u>

Surrendered <u>March 21st, 1950</u>   Worker <u>Margaret Hall, TCHS Field Secretary</u>

<u>Referral:</u> On 3-15-50, Mrs. Imogene Mathis in office without appointment. As she walked in

The office unannounced she asked, "Do you remember me?" I did remember that in February of 1949, she and her husband released Jerri Wayne Delaney, age 3 months for adoption. She then stated that she had 2 more children she would like to release for adoption. She explained that he was given temporary custody of Marion Richard, age 7 and Mary Elizabeth, age 2. It seems that he placed them in Vine Street Orphanage for a period of three months. After she was remarried to Mr. Mathis the Court modified the Decree December 19th 1949, so as to give her custody and $6.00 a week alimony. She said she thought her husband would make a good home for them, but this marriage had failed too and she is now unable to make a home for the children. Her children, and her mother an OOA recipient, are living in a basement apartment on West 5th Street. Mrs. Mathis said she was working part time at a dress shop but that her earnings together with the alimony was not adequate to provide a decent home for the children. She was moved about so often that Dickie has had to repeat the first grade.

Mrs. Mathis indicated that her husband probably would not consent to releasing the children although; he shows very little interest in them outside of paying the alimony. I agreed to contact him and to review the Court record to see what could be worked out. She said she would like placement as soon as possible because the children were both unhappy and emotionally disturbed.

I later reviewed the Circuit Court divorce record and verified the facts as presented by the mother. I also contacted the father, who at first said he would never consent to releasing the children for adoption. He said he knew they were not being properly cared for and that it was impossible for him to assume the responsibility of them at this time. He said that he was very happily remarried, his wife works, and he is earning $30.00 per week driving a truck for Merten's Dry Cleaners. If he accepted custody of the children again he felt they would have to place them in Vine Street Orphanage again (the mother told me she would never consent for him to have custody of the children again because she knew he would place them in the Orphanage). Mr. Delaney said his former wife had cost him his good job at the Southern Coach Lines, kept him upset all the time, and forced him to pay attorney's fees and Court costs numerous times. He seemed to think that if he took the children and employed someone to look after them during the day their mother would never cease to interfering. He went on to say that she was emotionally and morally immature, and actually not fit to have the care of the children. He said the baby they released in 1949 was not his child; therefore he had no hesitancy in releasing it. He said he would think the matter over and get in touch with me later.

The following day he called and said he had reached the conclusion that if the children were to have a chance in life they would be better off in an adoptive home. He consented to a Hearing in the Circuit Court.

On March 23$^{rd}$, 1950, Mrs. Mathis and Mr. Delaney were present at a Hearing before Judge L.D. Miller. An Order (#83617) awarded custody of the two children to the Tennessee Children's Home Society to place said children for adoption into proper homes. The mother and father also signed a surrender, which became part of the Court record.

Pending relinquishment of the children we paid the mother board for their care. The date the Court released them they were transferred to the Memphis Receiving Home for placement. The parents were told that they would not be placed in this community.

The following is a copy of the social history on Jerri Wayne Delaney:

C O P Y

2-21-49: Mrs. Delaney, a tiny, delicate young woman in office by appointment. She wore rather heavy make-up and her hair was rather heavily dressed - curls and heavy bangs. Her hair and eyes are dark brown, her features even and her teeth badly in need of dental care. She is 5'1" tall and weighs 92 pounds. She said she had had her three children so close together she had lost her health and suffered an almost complete nervous breakdown just before the baby was born. Dr. Richard Fancher, her private physician had delivered Jerri, and advised her against another pregnancy, soon. She went on to say that they had practiced birth control but that nothing worked satisfactorily and that it looked like each intercourse meant a baby. When Jerri was born her husband came to the hospital to see her and she refused to see him. She said she knew it hurt him terribly but that her mental attitude was such that she could not bear the sight of him.

She and her husband, Marion H. Delaney, were married 11-24-41 At Ringgold, Ga. and divorced 5-26-43 in Chattanooga. They were remarried 9-29-43 at Rossville, Ga. She said her husband drank and did not provide for her and the children like he should have. He became so involved in debt that it became necessary for him to bankrupt. He has been employed for the last 16 months as a bus driver for the Southern Coach Lines. She says he had a good job and while he makes a fairly good salary he cannot keep up two homes. Her physical and mental condition made it necessary for him to take the two older children, Marion Richard, born 10-27-43 and Mary Elizabeth, born 1-18-47 to his mother's. She says she is planning to get a divorce again; that her doctor says that she should not have sexual relationship any time soon. She says she has such a fear of pregnancy that she does not believe she could ever be a wife again. She was fitted with a diaphragm by her doctor but it was not successful.

For the past few months Mrs. Delaney, her mother and Jerri have been living in one room at 815 McCallie Avenue. a rooming house. Her husband gives her $15 per week. She has not had the money to take Jerri to the doctor, nor to buy cod-liver oil, baby good, etc. that he should be having now. She says it will always be that way. She knows that it will be impossible for them to adequately support Jerri and give him the things every child needs. "We could not give up the older children because they already know us but the baby will not know the difference," she said seriously. What she was saying seemed to be painful to her and yet we recognized that she had deliberately arrived at this decision.

I interpreted the meaning of adoption and she said she fully understood that it meant final separation and that while she regretted this action it was the only solution to the problem. I went into temporary foster care with her and asked if the Family Agency could provide this care until she and her husband worked through some of their problems, she would accept their help. She said no, that temporary care would not solve their problems; that her husband would probably never make any more money than he does now and that it is not sufficient to support his dependents. I asked what her husband thought about the adoptive plan and she said they had talked it over numerous times before, she never got in touch with me and that he had sent her to talk with me about is. She said she would come too when I needed him.

I asked Mrs. Delaney what she planned to do if we took Jerri. She said she had a job to go to on the 24$^{th}$ - a new orange drink stand is opening on Market St. and she has promise of employment there. She feels that if she does not have the responsibility of the baby and can get out and meet new people she will regain her health more quickly. Staying at home and looking after Jerri has apparently made her very unhappy and her mother is too old to care for the child while she works.

Mrs. Delaney said she was so mentally and physically run down she could not be a good mother to her children. In time, if she gets to feeling better she may ask for custody of her two older children when she gets a divorce, otherwise she will leave them with her husband and his people. She also mentioned

## Appendix B – The Adoption Records and Other Documents    219

that part of her marital difficulty could be
blamed on "in-laws".

We suggested that she have her husband to come
and talk with us before a definite decision was
made. She asked if I didn't wish to come and
see Jerri before she and her husband signed
the surrender. I told her I might drop by
there later on during the day.

I did stop by and went on upstairs to the room
where I found Jerri lying on the bed. The
room with a bed, oil stove, small table and
an old refrigerator, was spotless. I met Mrs.
Delaney's mother, Mrs. Mary (McJunkin) Clark,
age 68. She was very clean and had little to
say except that Jerri was a fine baby but was
not getting certain things that he needed
because they did not have the money with which
to buy them. Jerri was kicking his feet in the
air and looked like a perfect specimen. Mrs.
Delaney remarked that anybody would love him
because he was such a sweet baby. He smiled
and cooed and all of his reactions appeared
normal. Mrs. Delaney said she had talked with
her husband over the phone since seeing me and
that he was coming to see her that night. He
would be off from work the next day and she
thought they might come together to sign the
papers. She said she would let me know.

2-22-49 Mrs. Delaney called first to say
that she and her husband would be in around
ten o'clock. When they arrived she remarked
that she had stopped at the Fountain in the
building lobby to have a Coca-cola with
ammonia in it since she had a dizzy feeling
and was pretty nervous. Mr. Delaney is a very
handsome young man, 26 years of age. He was
dressed in excellent tasted, was polite and
well mannered and quiet. He allowed his wife
to do most of the talking. He said he had seen
Jerri only one more time since he was born and
the way in which he said it led me to believe

that he had no feeling whatsoever for the child. He said he was doing the best he could for the two older children and that doctor bills had been mainly the cause of him having to bankrupt. Mr. Delaney is 6'1" tall and weighs 212 pounds. He has hazel eyes and light brown naturally curly hair. He wears glasses. He gave the impression of being a stable and intelligent individual and his employment indicates that he is. He completed high school. I interpreted adoption to Mr. Delaney and he said he fully understood what it meant and that they would never know where Jerri was again. He felt that his wife did. That they could not provide for this child and that both were ready to take the final step of release.

I had the feeling that this child should not be separated from his parents and that here were two parents not trying to adjust to circumstances. Mr. Delaney seemed kind and sympathetic toward his wife. Once she started to cry he pulled out a snow white handkerchief and handed it to her and looked as though he might like to comfort her if she would let him. I asked them if they did not wish to consider the matter for awhile longer and they said they did not; that they considered it long enough. Recognizing their determination in this plan I decided that if we did not accept the child they would make an independent plan and which would not be good for the child. At this point I gave support to this plan and explained how we went about selecting homes for babies like Jerri and that we would see to it that he had a home where all of his needs would be met. I said now that we are planning for Jerri perhaps they could work out things whereby they might re-establish a home for Marion and Mary Elizabeth.

Mrs. Delaney said she completed the 7$^{th}$ grade and that her only employment had been as

## Appendix B – The Adoption Records and Other Documents

a saleslady at the Betty Maid Dress Shop. She gives the impression as having had more education. She had a good vocabulary and uses words correctly. Her father, John L. Clark, died 1922 the result of a hernia operation. She has six sisters. One sister, Elizabeth Davis, age 47, has been in a mental institution (Silverdale) the past three months, the result of menopause. Her only brother, Bill Clark, age 49, works in an Alabama steel plant. She has a brother-in-law who is a salesman at the Goodyear Store and who has given her some financial assistance. She and members of her family belong to the Baptist denomination but are not active in church life.

Mr. Delaney was born September 23, 1922 in Chattanooga. He resides with his mother at 2809 East 47$^{th}$ St. in Chattanooga. For a long time he drove truck for the Atlanta Constitution and quit it for the Southern Coach Lines job, a better paying job. His father, Ralph Delaney, is an upholsterer. His mother is Elizabeth (Jones) Delaney. His parents are separated. I believe he is an only child. He is a Baptist.

<u>Additional Information:</u> Mary Elizabeth Delaney born 9-18-47 at Erlanger Hospital, Chattanooga, Tennessee, by Dr. Richard Fancher at 8:30 A.M. She weighed 8lbs 5oz, 50½ cms. Normal delivery, Baby diagnosed as normal. Mr. Jack Tepper, pediatrician, gave her diphtheria and tetanus shots 3-20-48 and 5-15-48. She was due a booster in May of 1949. The Vine Street Orphanage record shows she had 1 diphtheria shot 11-4-49. Dr. Tepper's record shows that she has had whooping cough. He has not seen her since 5-15-48. The mother could not remember which diseases this child has had. She kept saying, "She has had everything there is to have."

Marion Richard was born in Chattanooga on 10-27-42. The mother said he had completed immunizations and that Dr. Tepper had the record, however revealed that he saw Richard only 1 time on 1-2-48, at which time he had a bad cold. The record indicated that the child had no immunizations and none was given at this time. At Vine Street Orphanage the Health Department gave him 1 diphtheria shot on 11-4-49. The Health Department keeps these records and were of the opinion that these children had been vaccinated, although, they could not find any record for verification.

At the time Richard was released for adoption he was in the first grade of school at H. Clay Evans. His report card is herewith enclosed.

MJH: bm
3-29-50

### SUMMARY

Taken from the Records of the Hamilton County Branch and Shelby County Branch of the Tennessee Children's Home Society

August 6, 1951

THE CHILD: Mary Elizabeth Delaney, born 9-18-47 (verified) in Erlanger Hospital, Chattanooga, Tennessee.
Placed in the Shelby County Branch, Tennessee Children's Home Society Receiving Home 3-23-50.
Guardianship removed from the parents, Marion H. Delaney and Imogene Mathis, and placed with Tennessee Children's Home Society by court order #83617, Circuit Court, Hamilton County, Chattanooga, Tenn. On 3-23-50.

# APPENDIX B – The Adoption Records and Other Documents

Placed:  3-28-50 for adoption by Shelby County Branch of Tennessee Children's Home Society in home of Paul R. Crippen, age 41 in August 1949, of English descent, occupation sales engineer, no church affiliation, and Janet Allan Crippen, age 39 in August 1949 of Scotch descent, housewife, member of Quaker sect. 3941 Ridgelay Drive, Los Angeles Calif.

PREVIOUS APPLICATIONS: State Social Welfare placed boy 4 ½ years of age (in August 1949) Children's Home Finding (no address given) Native Daughters

New Name: Paula Allan Crippen

## CHILD'S HISTORY

Mary Elizabeth Delaney was born 9-18-47 (verified) in Chattanooga, Tenn. According to the Hamilton County Branch record, she was diagnosed as normal at birth in Erlanger Hospital. Nothing is known of her early development and little of her physical condition, except that a pediatrician gave her two immunization shots for diphtheria and tetanus in 1948 and recorded that she had whooping cough. Her mother gave the Hamilton County worker a vague history indicating numerous illnesses.

The extent to which Mary Elizabeth was affected by parental discord is not known, the mother described her prior to the time of surrender and emotionally upset. Apparently, when not with her parents, she lived with both grandmothers and was placed for three months in 1949 in Vine Street Orphanage. She lived with her mother and stepfather briefly after that. There were no dates given indicating when and how long she lived with various relatives. Her custody was removed from the parents by court order at the parents' request, March 23, 1950, and transferred to the Tennessee Children's Home Society.

One brother, Marion Richard, born 10-22-42 (verified) was placed by court order at the parents' request at the same time. This child was repeating the first grade. Another brother at the age of 3 months was released by the parents to Tennessee Children's Home Society for adoption on 2-22-49. He was considered normal by the Hamilton County Branch worker. Mr. Delaney denied paternity of this child.

The mother, Imogene Mae Clark Delaney Mathis, age 27 in March 1950, was described as 5'1" tall, weight 92 lbs., dark brown hair and eyes. She stated that she had completed the 7$^{th}$ grade and her occupation was that of saleswoman in a dress shop. She was a Baptist. She asserted that her health had been ruined by having her children too close together and that she had a nervous breakdown before the birth of her last child. She expressed antipathy to sexual contact with the father of her children. Her father, John L. Clark, was said to have died in 1922 following a hernia operation. Her mother, Mrs. Mary McJunkin Clark, age 68 in Feb. 1949, received an Old Age Assistance grant. Mrs. Mathis reported she had six sisters, one of whom, Elizabeth Davis, age 47 in Feb. 1949, was in a mental hospital at the time of menopause. Her only brother, Bill Clark, age 49 in Feb. 1949, worked in an Alabama steel plant.

The father, Marion Henry Delaney, was born 9-22-22 in Chattanooga (not verified). He was described as 6'1" tall, weight 212 lbs., light brown curly hair, brown eyes. He wore glasses. He was said to have completed high school. The Hamilton County worker for Tennessee Children's Home Society was impressed by his stability and intelligence. His occupation had been as bus and truck driver. He had gone bankrupt and gave as the reason medical bills and court costs which his wife had caused. He was thought to be an only child and a member of the Baptist Church. The recorded information about his family was brief. His father, Ralph Delaney, was an upholsterer. His mother was Elizabeth Jones Delaney. His parents were separated.

Imogene Clark Delaney Mathis first married Mr. Delaney on 11-21-41 at Ringgold, Ga., and divorced him on 6-26-43 in Chattanooga, Tenn. They were remarried 9-29-43 at Rossville, Ga. And were divorced on 4-21-49 in Chattanooga. The Hamilton County worker for Tennessee Children's Home Society verified this information through the Hamilton County Court records and learned that the mother married a Mr. Mathis, whom she left after a few months. The date of this marriage and the husband's first name were not recorded or verified.

---

CHILD'S DEVELOPMENT AND ADJUSTMENT
IN FOSTER HOME

Mrs. Crippen sent doctor's reports, attached, after the child's placement. Her letters were very brief with no indication of the child's development but stated in one that the child was happy and in other that she fitted well with the family. In a letter of June 21, 1951, Mrs. Crippen inquired about her final adoption.

VK:gm

(Mrs.) Virginia Kuhlman
Child Welfare Worker

RECEIVED
OCT 14, 1952
Tenn. Children's Home Society

Minor.

Paula, as the petitioners have named the minor, is a very vivacious, lively child who gives every evidence of being happy and well adjusted in this home. Although naturally fair complexioned, with blue eyes and blonde hair, she is now deeply sun tanned, the result of spending the greater part of the summer at Catalina Island where the petitioners own a beach cottage. She is of slender build and has fine, delicate, well-formed facial features. Not only is she physically attractive but her out-going, friendly personality adds to her appeal.

Placement.

Mr. And Mrs. Crippen learned of the Tennessee Children's home Society through a friend and reported that Paula's placement with them occurred approximately a year after they first applied. Prior to the minor's placement, they stated they had two telephone calls from miss Alma Walton offering infants for placement. In each instance, they rejected such placements feeling that a toddler would suit their ages and family better. They showed us photostatic copies of two checks, one for $168.72 and one in the amount of $202 made out to Miss Tann, which they stated they were informed were to cover transportation costs. They did not have a copy of the canceled check, but reported one further check had been made out to Miss Tann in approximately the same amount, i.e., $150 to $200.

Both Mr. and Mrs. Crippen were genuinely interested in the background information on the child, which we shared with them.

They were, however somewhat surprised at
the mother's statement that the child was
emotionally disturbed. On the contrary, they
reported that when she came to them she was a
most self-assured and independent youngster.
To illustrate the independence, Mrs. Crippen
told us that on the first night that Paula
was in their home, she put the child in the
tub to bathe her, whereupon Paula said "me
do," and proceeded to soap and scrub herself
in a very efficient fashion. They continued
that her adjustment in the home was quick and
easy and that they were pleasantly surprised
at the lack of any particular problems. She
reportedly accepted them readily in the role
of parents and Craig as brother. Relative to
Craig's reaction to the minor's entrance to
the home, the petitioners informed us that
he had been included in their discussions
concerning the adoption of another child
and had indicated a definite preference for
a sister. In this area, also, they reported
no particular adjustment problems and no
indications on Craig's part of resentment or
jealousy of Paula.

Education and Psychological.

The petitioners are aware that the minor is a
bright, alert youngster and feel certain that
she is college material. They stated that she
would certainly be encouraged to plan on a
college education, but would be free to choose
her own field of specialization or training and
her own school, with counseling and guidance
from them.

Study of the Home of
Dr. and Mrs. Paul R. Crippen

The impression of the writer that the minor
was of better-than-average intelligence is

confirmed by the report of the psychologist, of which a copy is attached hereto.

### Health.

Concerning Paula's health, they informed me that the child was extremely thin and underweight when placed with them. They immediately took the child to their physician for examination and check-up and he diagnosed the youngster as suffering from malnutrition and probable mild rickets. They reported that they have followed closely all the doctor's directions to bring about a weight gain but she is still somewhat underweight. However, aside from this, she is in good health and physical condition. Attached hereto are reports of recent medical examinations of the petitioners and the minor.

---

COPY        MAUD O'NEIL, PH.D.      4.
637 Laudfair
Los Angeles 24
Tel: Arizona 8-2580

Mrs. Harriet Ohmart
State Department of Social Welfare
145 South Spring Street
Los Angeles 12, California

Dear Mrs. Ohmart:

According to your request, I administered an intelligence test to Paula Allan Crippen on August 8, 1952. The Stanford Binet Scale (Form L) was used and the findings were as follows:

    Chronological Age:    4 years, 11 months
    Mental Age            6 years, 2 months
    Intelligence Quotient  125

This I.Q. places her in the superior intelligence group, and much above the average child. She was interested in the rest, and seemed to enjoy the challenge it gave.

She passed all tests on the five-year level, obtained a score of 8 months on the six-year level, 2 months on the seven-year level, and 4 months on the eight-year level. Her strong points were vocabulary and memory for stories. On the seven-year level, her comprehension was excellent.

She appeared well-adjusted, emotionally and socially, and showed no fear or hesitancy in accepting the test situation. She should be a pleasure to her teachers when she enters school.

                Very sincerely,
                /s/ Maud O'Neil

COPY
10-9-52
                              RECEIVED
                            OCT 14, 1952
            Tenn. Children's Home Society

| | | |
|---|---|---|
| AREA OFFICES | **Earl Warren** | STATE HEADQUARTERS |
| LOS ANGELES OFFICE | **Governor** | SACRAMENTO |
| MICHIGAN 8411 | | GILBERT 2-4711 |
| MIRROR BUILDING | | 616 K STREET |
| 143 SOUTH SPRING STREET | STATE OF CALIFORNIA | 14 |
| 12 | | |
| SACRAMENTO OFFICE | **Department of Social Welfare** | |
| GILBERT 2-4711 | | |
| 924 NINTH STREET | CHARLES I. SCHOTTLAND | RECIEVED |
| 14 | DIRECTOR | NOV 3, 1952 |
| SAN FRANCISCO OFFICE | Los Angeles | Tenn. Children's Home Society |
| EX BROOK 2-8751 | October 30, 1952 | |
| GRAYSTONE BUILDING | | |
| 948 MARKET STREET | | |
| 2 | | |

Miss Lena Martin, State Superintendent
Tennessee Children's Home Society
901 Acklen Avenue          ADDRESS REPLY TO:
Nashville, Tennessee       145 South Spring Street
                           Los Angeles 12

OSC "D"
Adoption of Mary Elizabeth Delaney
By Mr. And Mrs. Paul A. Crippen

Dear Miss Martin:

We are writing to ask your assistance in the clarification of some questions we have concerning the adequacy of the court order by which Mary Elizabeth Delaney was given into the custody of the Tennessee Children's Home Society for adoption placement. After careful review of the record we find that the following things apparently happened.

A. The natural mother, Mrs. Mathis, apparently brought some action against the natural father, Mr. Delaney, to affect the transfer of the minor and her older brother to the Tennessee Children's Home Society. Since we have no copy of her petition we do not know precisely what pleading was made.

B. Both parents reputedly signed some document approving the placing of the children with the Tennessee Children's Home Society for adoption placement. However, we have no copy of this document, which according to the chronological record of the Tennessee Children's Home Society was made a part of the court record.

C. In the findings as stated in the court order it is indicated that Mr. Delaney agreed to this placement.

D. The court, however, in making its order made reference only to the removal of custody from the petitioner, Imogene Mathis. It does not indicate in its order that custody of the children is also taken from Mr. Delaney. Hence, while there seems no doubt that Mr. Delaney approved of the plan, we do not seem to have eliminated his parental rights by actual court decree.

This action brought by the mother in the form of a petition is one that is unfamiliar to us in California, and in the absence of a copy of the actual petition we are a little at a loss to understand it. This would not bother us too much if the father had also been named in the court order removing custody. In a similar action herein California we are sure he would have been named.

Do you feel confident that the record is sufficiently clear on this point to remove any question of the Tennessee Children's Home Society's right to guardianship of this minor and the right of the agency to agree and consent to the minor's adoption? Your consideration of this matter will be appreciated.

      Very sincerely yours,
      RALPH L GOFF, Area Director
      By: *Harriett Ohmart*
      Mrs. Harriett Ohmart
      Adoptions Worker

Cc: Mrs. Valle S. Miller, Director
    Division of Field Service Consultant
    Department of Public Welfare
    State Office Building
    Nashville, 3, Tennessee

COPY

SUMMARY
taken from the records of the Hamilton County
Branch and Shelby County Branch
Tennessee Children's Home Society

THE CHILD: Marion Richard Delaney, born Oct. 27, 1942, in Chattanooga, Tenn. verified). Placed by Circuit Court, Hamilton County, Tennessee, Court Order No. 83617 under guardianship of Tennessee Children's Home Society for adoption placement, March 23, 1950.

Placed: 4-5-50 placed for adoption in home of Herbert M. Boyar, age 38 in 1950, Jewish, store owner, and Fannyetta Niederberger, age 37 in 1950, Jewish housewife, (old address 856 So. Montebello Blvd., Montebello, Calif.) now residing at 1758 Preuss Road, Los Angeles 35, Calif.

PREVIOUS
APPLICATIONS: Los Angeles County Bureau of Adoption

NEW NAME
OF CHILD: Jeffrey Dean Boyar

CHILD'S HISTORY

Marion Richard Delaney was born on October 27, 1942 (verified). Nothing is known of his early development. At the time his mother applied for help from the Hamilton County Branch of the Tennessee Children's Home Society she stated he was repeating first grade because she had moved their residence. His report card from Sunnyside School in Chattanooga for 1949-50 verifies his satisfactory progress in the first grade. His mother said he was emotionally disturbed. The extent to which he was affected by the constant parental discord is not known. Prior to his placement in California he had lived with both grandmothers and after his parent's second divorce in April 1949 he had been placed for three months in Vine Street Orphanage. He then lived with his mother and a stepfather briefly. The sequence and dates of his stay with relatives is not recorded.

On 3-15-50 his mother, Mrs. Mathis, who had custody of Marion Richard, sought help from the Hamilton County Branch of Tennessee Children's Home Society in releasing him and his sister for adoption. The father agreed to relinquish the children, and on March 23, 1950, Mrs. Mathis and Mr. Delaney went for a hearing before the Hamilton County Circuit Court. An order (#83617) awarded the custody of the two children to the Tennessee Children's Home Society to be placed for adoption.

His sister, Mary Elizabeth Delaney, born 9-18-47, was considered normal at birth. She was also place for adoption by Tennessee Children's Home Society through court order at the parent's request.

A brother, Jerri Wayne Delaney, was released at the age of 3 months to the Hamilton County Tennessee Children's Home Society for adoption on 2-22-49 by his parents. He was considered to be normal by the Hamilton County Tennessee Children's Home Society worker. Mr. Delaney denied paternity of this child.

The mother, Imogene Mae Clark, Delaney Mathis, age 27 in March 1950, was described as 5'1" tall, weight 92 lbs., dark brown hair and eyes. She claimed she had completed the $7^{th}$ grade and her occupation was saleswoman. She was a member of the Baptist Church. She claimed that her health had been ruined by having her children so close together and she had a nervous breakdown before the birth of her last child. She was unable to adjust sexually to a marriage with the father of her children. Her rejection of her children was obvious through her requests for their adoption.

Mrs. Mathis' father, John L. Clark, was said to have died in 1922 following a hernia operation, according to information she gave the Hamilton County Branch worker. Her mother, Mrs. Mary (McJunkin) Clark, age 68 in February 1949 received an old age assistance grant. Mrs. Mathis had six sisters, one of whom, Elizabeth Davis, age 47 in February 1949, was in a mental hospital at the time of menopause, according to Mrs. Mathis' statement to the Hamilton County worker. Her only brother, Bill Clark, age 49 in February 1949 worked in a steel plant.

The father, Marion H. Delaney, was born September 22, 1922, in Chattanooga (not verified). He was described at 6'1" tall, weight 212 lbs., light brown curly hair, and brown eyes. He wore glasses. He was said to have completed high school. The Hamilton County worker for Tennessee Children's Home Society was impressed by his stability and intelligence. His occupation had been bus and truck driver; although his earnings were good, he went bankrupt and gave as the cause high medical bills and court costs which his wife incurred. He was thought to be an only child. He was a Baptist. The recorded information about his family was brief. His father, Ralph Delaney was an upholsterer. His mother was Elizabeth Jones Delaney. His parents were separated.

Imogene Clark married Marion Delaney on 11-24-41 at Ringgold, Ga. And divorced him 6-26-43 in Chattanooga, Tenn. They were re-married on 9-29-43 at Rossville, Ga. and were divorced on 4-21-49 in Chattanooga. The Hamilton County worker of Tennessee Children's Home Society verified these statements through examination of the Court records. Mrs. Delaney then married a Mr. Mathis whom she had left by March 1950. The date of her marriage and the first name of Mr. Mathis were not given.

CHILD'S DEVELOPMENT AND ADJUSTMENT IN FOSTER HOME

Although the Boyars had requested to adopt a girl, the letters from Mrs. Boyar indicate and acceptance of this boy. Mrs. Boyar in several letters implied a close relationship between their natural daughter and this boy and expressed surprise in how well and quickly he adjusted to his new mode of living. She expressed pride in his good physical condition, in his interest in Sunday religious school, and his completion in June 1951 of the second grade with good comments from his teacher.

In February 1951 and subsequently they requested information regarding the completion of his adoption.

In the last letter mention was made of having taken him to an optometrist who prescribed glasses.

/s/ Virginia Kuhlman
(Mrs.) Virginia Kuhlman
Child Welfare Worker

VK: gm

TENNESSEE CHILDREN'S HOME SOCIETY
PLACEMENT AND SUPERVISION

4-5-50:
Marion Richard (Dickey) Delaney placed with Mr. and Mrs. Herbert M. Boyar, 856 So. Montebello Blvd., Montabello, Calif.
Mr. and Mrs. Boyar were delighted with their son; they could hardly believe their own eyes when they saw that Dickey had dimples just like they did! Their little daughter was so pleased with her new brother and told him she had an Easter surprise for him down in the car! All left looking very happy.
                        Alma Walton

4-18-50:
Letter from Mrs. Boyar giving a report on the child also had a picture. "It seems like yesterday we met our little Jeffrey for the first time: and yet, on the other h and, we feel as though he has always been with us. He certainly has made a rapid adjustment to his new mode of living. Jeffrey and Stephanie, our daughter, have become very fond of one another and are constant companions. He also enjoys playing with the other children on our block and gets along nicely with them. He started school out here, first grade and is doing very well. His reading is above average for his class and his teacher is pleased with his work. We are so grateful to you and your organization for the new richer and fuller life we are experiencing and enjoying."

7/18 AW visited (written insertion)

8-2-50:
Letter from Mr. and Mrs. Boyar, enclosing snapshots of the children. "The summer is passing much too quickly. We are trying to fill each week with outings that the children will enjoy and so far we have covered quite a bit. We have

purchased for Jeffrey an educational insurance policy with Prudential Life Insurance Co., same as we have for Stephanie. A complete examination and X-ray of his mouth was made recently and a report from the dentist is enclosed. The dentist remarked that Jeffrey's teeth were in unusually fine condition. He has now had the complete series of diphtheria-tetanus shots, and is looking very well with his additional few pounds and a coat of summer tan."

| | | |
|---|---|---|
| AREA OFFICES | **Earl Warren** | STATE HEADQUARTERS |
| LOS ANGELES OFFICE | **Governor** | SACRAMENTO |
| MICHIGAN 8411 | | GILBERT 2-4711 |
| MIRROR BUILDING | | 616 K STREET |
| 143 SOUTH SPRING STREET | STATE OF CALIFORNIA | 14 |
| 12 | | |
| SACRAMENTO OFFICE | **Department of Social Welfare** | |
| GILBERT 2-4711 | | |
| 924 NINTH STREET | CHARLES I. SCHOTTLAND | |
| 14 | DIRECTOR | December 15, 1952 |
| SAN FRANCISCO OFFICE | Los Angeles | |
| EX BROOK 2-8751 | December 11, 1952 | |
| GRAYSTONE BUILDING | | |
| 948 MARKET STREET | | |
| 2 | | |

Mr. J.O. McMahan, Commissioner   ADDRESS REPLY TO:
Department of Public Welfare     145 South Spring Street
State Office Building            Los Angeles 12
Nashville 3, Tennessee

                      OSC "D"
                      Adoption of Marion Richard Delaney
                      By Herbert M. And Fanny N. Boyar

Dear Mr. McMahan:

We have recently completed our investigation in the above-mentioned adoption case and are glad to be able to forward to you this report.

The child, whom Dr. and Mrs. Boyar call Jeffrey, has made a nice adjustment in this home. They report that when he first came they had some behavior problems, but appear to have given expert consideration and understanding of the factors of the child's background that might lead to this rather poor adjustment at first, and have been most successful in their handling of the problem.

When Jeffrey was placed in their home they were given a paper with a scant amount of information regarding his background, and on this it gave his birth date as October 27, 1943. They have been proceeding on this supposition, and were considerably surprised when agent informed them that the birth certificate gave his birth date as 1942. They had been told he was in the first grade when last in school in Tennessee, so had given no thought to it, and had no reason to question his age, as he progressed normally in the second and third grades in school, and is now in the fourth grade. Mr. and Mrs. Boyar's natural daughter, Stephanie, was born in 1942, and they state that in every way Jeff seems to be about a year younger. They realize, however that it is difficult to judge at this particular age. They have just had a psychometric test of Jeffrey, which has indicated that he has an intelligence of a very superior nature: that if at the age level of nine, he would have a full scale I.Q. of 146, and if at the age level of ten, he would have a full scale I.Q of 133, so there seems to be no question but that Jeffrey is a brilliant child.

In considering the question of the age, Mr. and Mrs. Boyar feel at this time that they will make no point of the age difference, and will not change his age in any records. They realize that his birth certificate will be the correct one. They think it very probable that between now and college age he may skip some classes, as he seems to do well in school, and in that way he will possibly make up for the year he lost earlier. It is interesting to note that the doctor making the psychometric test stated that Jeffrey is definitely college material and should experience little difficulty academically.

Mr. and Mrs. Boyar and Jeffrey have all had recent medical examinations, and in every instance were reported to be in good general health and physical condition. Mr. and Mrs. Boyar both had serological tests and chest x-rays, all having negative results.

=====  FLOOR COVERING =====
8512 East Artesia Boulevard, Bellflower, California
Metcalf 3-4496

October 3, 1952
Received Oct 7, 1952
Tennessee Children's Home Society

Tennessee Children's Home Society,
901 Acklen Ave.,
Nashville, 4, Tennessee

**Att: Miss Lena Martin**

Dear Miss Martin,

    It has been a few months since we have written to you, but now want to report that we received the application from the California Department of Social Welfare for the adoption of Jeffrey, which we have filled out and returned, and are now awaiting the home interview. After that, we do hope the final paper will come through in short time.

    We had a wonderful summer with the children. Spent three weeks on a Dude Ranch in Colorado, with Horse Back Riding, Fishing, Mountain Climbing, etc. It was a new and delightful experience for all of us. When we returned, Jeffrey took swimming lessons, and by the end of the summer, he was swimming the length of the pool in good form, also diving off the board fairly well. Now he is back at school in 4$^{th}$ grade and trying hard to settle down to his school work after a very active vacation.

    We shall keep you informed of Jeffrey's progress, and let you know when we have our home interview. Our thanks for your close cooperation.

                  Sincerely,
                  *Mr. & Mrs. Herbert M Boyar*

*Appendix B – The Adoption Records and Other Documents*

G-2   TCHS   **TENNESSEE DEPARTMENT OF PUBLIC WELFARE**
4-59  #7779  INTER-OFFICE CORRESPONDENCE

March 13, 1962<br>DATE

MAR 14, 1962

TO:      Miss Sarah C. Justice, Supervisor,
         Adoption Services Unit, State Office

From:    Mrs. Anne Griffitts, Child Welfare
         Consultant, Hamilton County

SUBJECT: Jeffrey Dean Boyar, B. 10-27-43 (42),
         adopted name
         Merion Richard Delaney, original name

Jeffrey Dean Boyar came to my office 3-9-62 seeking information about his younger sister, Mary Elizabeth Delaney, commonly called Betty, born 1946, and believed to have been adopted just as Jeffrey Dean was.

At first, this boy indicated concern that his 15 year old girl friend here might be his sister because he suspected she had been adopted, too, and since they have similar looks he wondered if she might be his real sister. The more he talked on 3-9-62 and again 3-12-62 the less worried he seemed about the relationship between him and the girl friend. He had sought her records in the Courthouse and believes now he knows the girl is really her father's natural child by another woman.

Jeffrey Dean seems quite intent on seeking this sister, Betty. He sets his question out as:

   1. Has she been adopted?
   2. Did her adoption occur in Tennessee? In another state?
   3. If in Tennessee, could it be in Chattanooga?
   4. How is she?

## Appendix B – The Adoption Records and Other Documents

5. If she hasn't been adopted, could she return to her family?

I have explained to him that we may be unable to answer his question. I pointed out he is a sibling asking, not a parent, or Betty herself. He is only 18, his sister 15. In view of his experiences he will naturally find it hard to believe she has achieved a happy adoptive home placement.

His story to me began with the more recent events - his location of natural relatives - but in relating it to you I will reverse the story.

Jeffrey Dean Boyar was adopted in California in April 1950, by

Herbert Matthew Boyar
Fannie Etta Nederberger Boyar
157 N. Stanley Drive
Beverly Hills, California

The Boyars obtained him through TCHS in Memphis but never saw the boy until he arrived by plane accompanied by a woman delivering him. He remembers vividly this first plane ride. He wonders if the little girl he remembers playing with before his placement wasn't his sister, Betty.

He remembered his name and with facts the Boyars had he has been able to relocate his own relatives. His adoptive parents are Jewish, the father a contractor. TCHS had presented him as a Jewish child in need of placement. "Nothing on his papers are correct," said Jeffrey Dean to me. He was confirmed in the Jewish faith, attended Hebrew School.

In the adoptive home where he felt unrest since age 13, he felt unloved, unwanted and if he questioned their love the father would remind him he was bought and paid for, once saying he paid "ten grand".

Jeffrey Dean hasn't lived in the Boyar home since before November, 1960. He hasn't finished high school but indicated he reached the 12th grade. He joined the Navy to get away from home on November 9, 1960, and was medically discharged January 27, 1961, before boot training was completed, thereby disallowing him Navy benefits. Since leaving the Navy he worked at various places and came to Chattanooga September 6, 1961.

Seemingly he may have located his father's old address through voter's registration here. He found his grandmother, Mrs. Elizabeth Jones Delaney. His father is in the Navy in California and he, Marion Henry Delaney, rushed to visit his son, Marion Richard Delaney, the real name, but once Jeffery Dean met his real parents he felt "they couldn't care less."

His mother, now Imogene May Clark Delaney Aslinger, lives in East Lake Court Housing Project and we may have known her in an ADC case as Imogene Clark Allen (33-C-9030) and more recently in two independent adoptions (no orders of reference) where Aslinger as a stepparent seeks to adopt two of her children. (This was learned after the boy's second office visit.)

TCHS  This adopted son understands his and the sister's release for adoption came

7468  about when the Delaneys divorced and a third child, Jerri, was placed also but little is known about this. Mr. Delaney accused his wife of running around and said Jerri wasn't his.

Jeffrey Dean puts little concern on his own parents now they are located, their lack of interest detected. His prime aim is to see what he can find out about Betty.

## Appendix B – The Adoption Records and Other Documents

He lives with a paternal aunt and uncle:
Anna Lee Delaney Deitch
Ike Deitch
3111 Idewild Drive
Chattanooga, Tennessee

He has worked at Kroger's, quit recently to find a better job because he wants to marry as soon as he can support a wife. (I wonder if he isn't already married.)

This bespectacled, thin body is another good example of all that can happen in an adoption. He is one who must have honest, straightforward answers. When he first came to Tennessee he talked by phone to someone in State Office and was promised a written reply. This did not come but he decided to "give us another chance" by coming to the local office. I explained I would present his

request but would promise him nothing, adding that if Betty was in an adoptive home we would not disrupt a permanent relationship.

He seems to understand court orders are necessary to secure information on adoptions but he assures me if thwarted now he will try again at 21 to find Betty.

AG:mg
Cc: Mr. Hurston C. Burkhart

TCHS
7779

March 29, 1962

Mr. George Latham, Director Hamilton County

Att: Mrs. Anne Griffitts, Child Welfare Consultant

Miss Sarah C. Justice, Supervisor of Adoption Services

Jeffrey Dean Boyar, b. 10-27-43, adopted name

Marion Richard Delaney, original name

TCHS #7779

We have read with interest the report of your interview with the above-mentioned young man who is seeking information regarding his 15-year-old sister, Betty.

The regrettable feature is that even if he had been adopted in Tennessee, we could not tell him anything without authorization from the court in which his adoption was made final. Nor, could we petition the court for re-access to the record until we would have written authorization from both of his adoptive parents.

Does Jeffrey feel his adoptive parents would consent to the reopening of the adoption record? It might have leads as to the family with whom his sister was placed and whether or not they were residents of Tennessee or another state.

Does he want to write his adoptive parents asking them to send written authorization to this Unit? Would he consent for us to write his adoptive parents at the address he gave for them in California?

Then, too, there is this further obstacle - even if we were authorized by his adoptive parents and the court to reopen the record, and through

## Appendix B – The Adoption Records and Other Documents

leads it might possibly contain, locate the family who adopted Betty, we still could not give out any information without communicating with betty's adoptive parents and securing their authorization to reopen their record and reveal their identity and/or the whereabouts of Betty. It is a complicated process in Tennessee, and may be equally, and more so, in California.

April 2, 1962

Since however, you report he was adopted in California, we suggest that he return to California and see what steps he would have to take to have shared with him information from his closed record. Even if his adoptive parents were willing to have the closed record reopened and reviewed and so stated in a written request, it would still be necessary that we have an order from the court in California where Jeffrey was legally adopted. It would be necessary for him or the adoptive parents to petition the court praying that whatever the closed record retained in the Archives in Tennessee be shared with them and/or Jeffrey.

I recall in another case where the child from TCHS, adopted in another state, had to petition the court in that State in the particular court the adoption was made final.

We hope this will enable you to give Jeffrey some direction should he return to your office.

SCJ: esw

## Albert L. Hill, M.D

Suite 815 California Medical Bldg.
Los Angeles 15, Calif.

April 8, 1950

Mrs. Paul Crippen,
3925 West Adams Blvd.,
Los Angeles Calif.

Dear Mrs. Crippen,

On March 31, 1950 you brought your daughter to me for examination and the following is a report of my findings:

Her weight was 22 ½ pounds, her height 33 ¼ inches, this being distinctly under average for her age of 2 years and 6 months.

Physical Examination:

She has a rather square head, prominent forehead: the eyes were negative, pupils were equal and reacted to light. No nystagnus nor squint. The anterior fontanel is completely closed. She has 20 teeth, a marked overbite, the gums are healthy. The throat is clear and the tonsils are small. The thyroid is not visible nor palpable and there is no enlargement of the cervical glands.

The lungs are negative to inspection and auscultation. There is a marked Harrison's groove but no rosary. There is a moderate flaring of the costal margins.

Abdomen is negative, no evidence of enlargement of the liver or spleen, no palpable masses present. There is some projection of the naval. The feet showed some pronation and eversion: exercises were suggested and proper shoes advised. Her color is fair.

# Appendix B – The Adoption Records and Other Documents

Impression:

Malnutrition: some lack of Vitamins A and D. Marked overbite in teeth: probably mild rickets. Pronation of the feet.

**Conclusion: A patch test for tuberculosis is negative. Test for syphilis Kolmer and Line is negative.**

The blood count showed Red Blood Cells 4,510,000 - Hemoglobin .79 - Color index 87. Leucocytes 9,000. Neutrophiles 30%. Segmented 29. Non segmented 1. Eosinphiles 1.0 Lymphocytes 61.0 Monocytes 8.0 Stained smear: The red blood cells are normal in size, regular in shape and take the stain evenly. No nucleated red blood cells found. Platelets appear normal in number. Urinalysis: negative.

My general impression, aside from the defects mentioned, is that this child is a good prospect. With proper nutrition and loving care she will develop into a fine girl.

*Albert L. Hill, M.D.*
Albert. L. Hill, M.D.

Encl/1
ALH:mr

Delaney, Mary Elizabeth

STATE OF TENNESSEE

**DEPARTMENT OF PUBLIC WELFARE**

STATE OFFICE BUILDING
NASHVILLE 3

**12 July 1951**

J.O. McMAHAN
　COMMISSIONER

**Mr. and Mrs. Paul Crippin
3981 Ridgley Drive
Los Angeles 56, Calif.**

My Dear **Mr. And Mrs. Crippin:**

I am glad to be able to inform you that the Board of the Tennessee Children's home Society is now reorganized and has met the requirements for a temporary conditional, license, which was issued by this Department on June 30, 1951. When all requirements for the consummation of pending adoptions have been met this license enables the Tennessee Children's Home Society to give legal consent to the adoption of children already legally received into their guardianship. It does not authorize the acceptance of new applications to adopt Tennessee children by residents of other states.

The agreement worked out cooperatively between this Department and the California Department of Social Welfare in April 1951 was officially approved by the Board of the Tennessee Children's Home Society on June 28, 1951. According to

## APPENDIX B – The Adoption Records and Other Documents 251

this agreement both the Tennessee Children's Home Society and this Department recognizes the California Department of Social Welfare as the official agency in California to make the study required by California law relative to the development and adjustment of the child placed in your home for adoption and the stability of the adoptive relationship.

Such studies will be made upon referral from this Department. After the report of the study is received from the California Department of Social Welfare and review is made of all the facts in each pending adoption, the legal consent will be executed by the Tennessee Children's Home Society and approved by this Department when the adoption is found to be in the best interests of the child. The necessary legal documents will be forwarded by this Department to the California Department of Social Welfare. The California Department of Social Welfare will advise you concerning the filing of the petition for adoption in the California Court and will prepare the necessary report to the Court in accordance with California law.

**All communications concerning children whose adoptions have not been legally consummated should be directed to this Department, attention Mrs. Vallie S. Miller, Supervisor of Adoptions.**

Any communications concerning children whose adoptions already been decreed should be directed to Miss Lena Martin, State Superintendent, Tennessee Children's Home Society, 901 Acklen Avenue, Nashville 4, Tennessee.

We regret the long delay in clarifying procedures for you regarding the service you may expect looking toward assistance in settling permanently the status of the child in your home. This has been due to many complexities arising from the disregard of both Tennessee and California laws in the extensive inter-state placement of children by the Shelby County Branch of the

Tennessee Children's Home Society which, as you know, is now closed and enjoined by court order from further operations.

We hope your child is progressing satisfactorily under your care. It will take some time yet to clear all the pending adoptions because of the large volume but we wanted you to know that the necessary steps are being taken to insure the legality of adoptions pending with the view of giving security to all the parties concerned.

      Very sincerely yours,

      *J O McMahan*

      J. O. McMahan
      Commissioner

JOM/dmc

In reply direct attention to:
(Mrs.) Vallie S. Miller, Director
Division of Field Service Consultants

June 26, 1952

Dr. Charles I. Schottland, Director
Department of Social Welfare
616 K. Street
Sacramento 14, California

Attention: Miss Lucille Kennedy, Chief, Division of Child Welfare

Re: DELANEY, Mary Elizabeth, born 9-18-47 Chattanooga, Tennessee; Court Order transferring guardianship to Tennessee Children's Home Society of March 23, 1950: Placed March 28, 1950 by Shelby County Branch of Tennessee Children's Home Society in the adoptive home of Paul R. and Janet Allen Crippen, 3941 Ridgeley Drive, Los Angeles 56, California

Dear Mr. Schottland:

We are referring for social study the available social date relative to the placement of Mary Elizabeth Delaney by the Shelby County Branch of the Tennessee Children's Home Society in the adoptive home of Mr. And Mrs. Paul R. Crippen, 3941 Ridgeley Drive, Los Angeles 56, California. The attached summary gives the facts in this case situation documented by the photostatic copy of the original birth certificate for the child and a certified copy of the decree of the Circuit Court Judge of Hamilton County awarding guardianship to the Tennessee Children's Home Society.

You will observe that on the foster parents' application form Mr. and Mrs. Crippen reported that prior to the placement of Mary Elizabeth in their home they had adopted a child through the California Department of Social Welfare.

We shall be especially interested in the report of the information obtained by the Adoptions Worker regarding the foster parent's handling of the emotional adjustment of Mary Elizabeth whom the mother described as being emotionally upset especially in view of the fact that she was placed in the adoptive home only five days following transfer of guardianship to the agency.

Reference is made to the summary concerning all that is known about the placements, which this child had experienced prior to the present one. The results of medical and psychological examinations will also be of special interest as indicated by the medical report of April 8, 1950 from Dr. Albert Hill.

We shall appreciate this cooperative service.

      Yours very truly,

      J.O. McMahan
      Commissioner

JOM/dmc
Cc: Miss Lena Martin

Enclosures:

 1. Summary of information contained in the records of the Hamilton County and Shelby County Branches of Tennessee Children's Home Society.

 2. Certified Photostatic copy of original birth certificate No. 66154

 3. Child's history sheet and record of child's own family.

4. Foster parent's application for a child, foster home study, report of placement and supervision.
5. Copy of letter from Dr. E.J. Cook of August 18, 1949 regarding Mrs. Crippen.
6. Copy of letter from Dr. Albert L. Hill of April 8, 1950 reporting on physical examination of child.
7. Certified copy of Decree of Judge L. D. Miller, Circuit Court of Hamilton County, entered March 23, 1950.

August 10, 1951

Honorable L.D. Miller, Judge
Circuit Court
Hamilton County
Chattanooga, Tennessee

RE: Mary Elizabeth Delaney
    Marion Richard Delaney
Dear Judge Miller:    Court Order #83617

    We are assisting in giving service necessary to the completion of adoptions of children placed by the Shelby County Branch of the Tennessee Children's Home Society. In order to complete adoption procedure, we need your help in obtaining a certified, signed and dated copy of the Court Order No. 83617 in the Circuit Court of Hamilton County, Tennessee: Imogene Mathis (Imogene Delaney) vs. Marion H. Delaney; which removed the custody of Marion Richard Delaney, age 7 and Mary Elizabeth Delaney, age 2, from Imogene Mathis and gave custody to the Tennessee Children's Home Society, and authorized that agency to place the children for adoption. The Tennessee Children's Home Society records do not contain a signed copy of this order of March 23, 1950.

    Could you send four certified signed copies, together with the surrender if one was signed, as it will be necessary to file one order with each adoption petition and we need to keep one copy for our files.

    Thank you very much for your cooperation in this matter,

    Very sincerely yours,

    (Mrs.) Vallie S. Miller
    Supervisor of Child Welfare

VSM:gm

In reply direction attention to     (Mrs. Vallie S. Miller, Director
                                    Division of Field Service Consultants

July 1, 1952

Mr. Ralph L. Goff, Area Director
Department of Social Welfare
145 South Spring Street, Los Angeles 12, California

Attention: Mrs. Glady Johns

Re: DELANEY, Mary Elizabeth, born 9-13-47
    Chattanooga, Tennessee; Court Order transferring
    guardianship to Tennessee Children's Home Society
    on March 23, 1950: Placed 3-28-50 by Shelby County
    Branch of Tennessee Children's Home Society in
    adoptive home of Paul R. And Janet Allan Crippen
    3941 Ridgeley Drive, Los Angeles 56, Calif.

Dear Mr. Goff:

We have received a communication from Mrs. Janet Crippen in which she is planning to enter Paula in school. Registration started the week of June 23. Mrs. Crippen stated that it was necessary that she have a birth certificate or some other means of establishing the child's age.

Enclosed is a copy of our letter of reply together with a copy of our letter to Mr. and Mrs. Crippen of June 26, also enclosed is a copy of our letter of referral of June 26 to the Department of Social Welfare in Sacramento.

I thought perhaps Mrs. Crippen might be calling your office for information on this procedure before it would be possible for the case to be assigned to the adoptions worker and this information would enable you to handle this inquiry. The birth date of Mary Elizabeth verified by the Division of Vital Statistics is September 18, 1947.

                        Very truly yours,
                        J.O. McMahan, Commissioner
Encls.
JOM/dmc
Cc: Mr. Charles I Schottland
Attn: Miss Lucille Kennedy

STATE OF TENNESSEE

**DEPARTMENT OF PUBLIC WELFARE**

STATE OFFICE BUILDING
NASHVILLE 3

**June 26, 1952**
J.O. McMAHAN
COMMISSIONER

Miss Lena Martin, State Superintendent
Tennessee Children's Home Society
901 Acklen Avenue
Nashville 4, Tennessee

                Re: DELANEY, Mary Elizabeth, born 9-13-47 Chattanooga, Tennessee Placed for adoption by Shelby County Branch of Tennessee Children's Home Society in the adoptive home of Paul R. And Janet Allan Crippen 3941 Ridgeley Drive, Los Angeles 56, Calif.

Dear Miss Martin:

    We are transferring the complete case record from the Shelby County Branch of the Tennessee Children's Home Society pertaining to the placement of Mary Elizabeth Delaney in the home of Mr. And Mrs. Paul R. Crippen, Los Angeles, California.

# Appendix B – The Adoption Records and Other Documents 259

Please refer to the letter of transmittal of this date to the California Department of Social Welfare. It appears that there are no irregularities in the birth registration for this child and that the parents were before the court at the time Judge Miller, Circuit Judge of Hamilton County, terminated parental rights and transferred guardianship to the Tennessee Children's Home Society. Since the certified copy, which we obtained directly from the court bears only the signature of the clerk and not of the Judge, it may be that we will receive a request for a copy bearing the Judge's signature. However, I have been advised that a certification such as that given by the clerk of the court is acceptable as a legally authenticated copy of the original order. It appears that the service on this case is complete until a report is received from the California Department of Social Welfare.

This record contains the following:

1. A surrender signed by the parents but not witnessed or notarized.
2. A copy of the original court order #83617, copy of petition to modify decree and a certified copy of the Court Order #83617 entered on March 23, 1950.
3. Certified copy of Form 108 verifying age and guardianship on birth registration #66154 (47).
4. Summary of records of Hamilton County and Shelby County Branches of Tennessee Children's Home Society.
5. Child's History Sheet, record of child's own family prepared by Miss Margaret Hall 3-29-50, nursery and medical reports.

6. Foster parents' application for a child, foster home study, report of placement and supervision.
7. Medical and financial reports on the adoptive parents.
8. Certified copy of Marriage certificate verifying marriage of Paul Allen Crippen and Janet E. Allan on August 17, 1941 in Los Angeles, California.
9. Favorable letters of reference and correspondence.

    Yours very truly,

**Valli S. Miller**
(Mrs.) Vallie S. Miller, Director
Division of Field Service Consultants

Encls.
VSM/dmc

November 11, 1952

Mrs. Zelma Sherrill
Clark and Master
Hamilton County Circuit Court
Chattanooga, Tennessee

Dear Mrs. Sherrill:
                Re: Docket No. 83617
                Record Book 32, Page 463

Thank you for your letter of November 6, however, we apparently did not make it clear in our letter of November 3, that the petition referred to as the petition filed by Imogene Mathes, formerly known as Imogene C. Delaney, who appeared before the Court on the 23rd day of March, 1950. We have a certified copy of the Order handed down as of March 23, 1950, but what we need are 2 copies (certified) of the petition that was filed with lead to this hearing and decree. We should also like to know if you have a record showing that Marion G. Delaney surrendered Marion Richard Delaney and Mary Elizabeth Delaney to the Tennessee Children's Home Society for adoption. The certified order in the above mentioned cause divests the mother, Imogene Mathes (Imogene C. Delaney) of her parental rights but does not mention whether the father was divested of his parental rights.

Our need for the copies of the petition described is urgent. We shall have to decide, after study of this petition, whether this agency's guardianship and right to consent to adoption may or may not be valid. We shall appreciate it if you can send the above documents by return mail and bill us for costs. We are enclosing an Air Mail Special Delivery envelope for your

convenience and appreciate your usual cooperation
and promptness.

      Yours very sincerely,

**(Miss) Lena Martin, State. Supt.**
**TENNESSEE CHILDREN'S HOME SOCIETY**

LM/MGM/al

Enc.

# Appendix C – Photograph Album

*Imogene and Marion Delaney*

APPENDIX C – *Photograph Album*

*Marion Richard (Dickie, later Jeff) and Marion Henry Delaney*

Dickie Delaney (later to be Jeff Boyar)
looks rather like a very happy child.

Imogene, Jeff, Marion, Elizabeth, Olivia, Annalee, Emmagene,
Stephen, and Floyd, by contrast, do not appear to be
all that happy as a family.

## Appendix C – Photograph Album

Paula and Jane Crippen,
April 1, 1950

Paula, age 6

Paula and Paul Crippen,
April, 1961

Paula and Marion Delaney,
May, 1990

John – elementary school days

John and Lynna Ruth,
March 28, 1970

John – medical school days

John and Lynna Ruth,
December 3, 2006

## Appendix C – Photograph Album

Paula emailed me this comparison of me
and our birth father, Marion Henry Delaney.
At least she didn't say, "Boy, look at those noses!"

More Resemblances

*John and Paula at Cumberland Falls State Park on the first day they met, January, 1996*

*Paula and John at Cumberland Falls*

*and Lynna Ruth and John – It was cold out.*

*Paula and John – Beth, Jacob, Paula, and Larry
– in Knoxville, Tennessee, in 1996*

*My sister Paula Cope*     *My brother Jeff Boyer*

## The First Reunion of The Delaney Kids

Paula, Larry, Lynna Ruth, Jeff, and John at the first reunion of the Delaney kids

Lynna Ruth, Brenda, Jeff, and Larry at the Chattanoogan during our reunion

Jeff giving John some pointers on how to run the table at the Chattanoogan

Brenda and Jeff with the munchies at the Chattanoogan during our first reunion

APPENDIX C – *Photograph Album* 273

Brenda, Jeff, Paula, and Larry waiting the call to breakfast at the Cracker Barrel before we spend our first day together as a family

Jeff (sticking his tongue out), Paula, and Larry at the fountains in Coolidge Park

John, Larry, Aaron, and Jeff at the Chattanooga Choo Choo

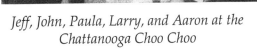

Jeff, John, Paula, Larry, and Aaron at the Chattanooga Choo Choo

Paula and John in Cincinnati during a 2005 visit

Jeff and John in Chattanooga during a 2006 visit

Larry and Paula – and John and Paula –
in the Great Smokey Mountain National Park,
October, 24, 2006 – the day before she died

APPENDIX C – *Photograph Album*  275

John, Lynna Ruth, Paula, and Larry
in the Great Smokey Mountain National Park

Paula, Larry, John, and Lynna Ruth acting silly in an
"old time photograph" in Gatlinburg, Tennessee,
the day before Paula died – the last photograph of the four of us

# Appendix D – Genealogy

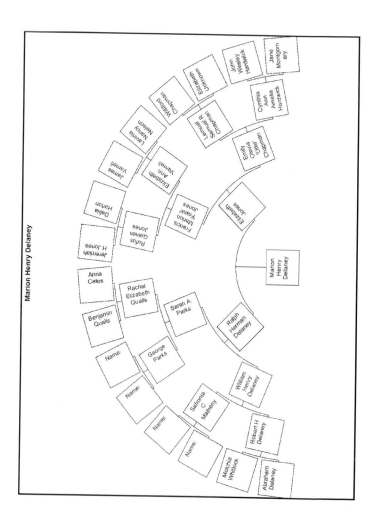

APPENDIX D – *Genealogy* 279

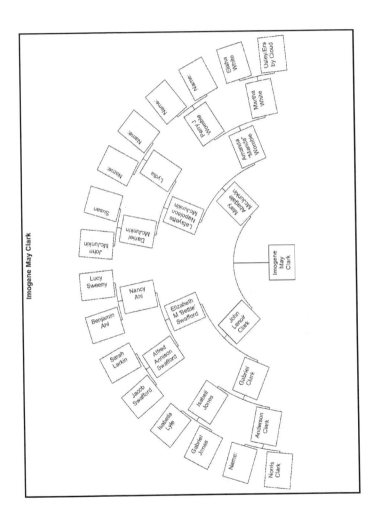

# Descendants of Abraham Delaney

## Generation 1

1. Abraham Delaney [2, 3, 4, 5] was born on Feb 24, 1815 in KY or Ohio [2, 3, 4]. He died on May 02, 1889 in Roane, Tennessee. He married Melchia Whitlock before 1839, daughter of Robert Whitlock and Martha Nance. She was born on Feb 27, 1820 in Tennessee. She died on Jul 13, 1887 in Roane, Tennessee.

Notes for Abraham Delaney:
1880 Census: Roane County TN, District 11, ED #225, Sheet 342A

from http://www.ancestry.com

| | | | | | | |
|---|---|---|---|---|---|---|
| 84 | 85 | Moore, Robert | Age 29 | | | |
| | | Moore, Mary | Age 29 | | | |
| | | Rosa | 8 | | | |
| | | Adda | 7 | | | |
| | | Maggie | 5 | | | |
| | | Benjamin | 3 | | | |
| | | Authur | 1 | | | |
| 85 | 86 | Delany Abraham | Age 67 | Born KY | | Parents born KY |
| | | Milchie | 63 | TN | | NC |
| | | William | 20 | | | |
| | | Dicia | 18 | | | |
| 86 | 87 | Delany Erbe | 31 | | | |
| | | Martha | 26 | | | |
| | | Mary | 5 | | | |
| | | Belle | 2 | | | |
| | | Alice | 1 | | | |

1870 Census: Hamilton County TN, District 3, Subdivision 13
From http://www.ancestry.com:

| | | | |
|---|---|---|---|
| Delano, Abraham | Age 55 | Farmer | Born KY |
| Milchia | 50 | NC | |
| William C | 10 | TN | |
| Dicey | 8 | TN | |
| Mary J | 21 | GA | |
| Malinda C | 14 | TN | |

They appear to have been missed in the 1850 and 1860 censuses.

From www.ancestry.com:

1840 Census, Roane, TN

Name: Delany, Abraham

1 male under 5; 1 male age 20-30; 1 female 15-20

# Appendix D – Genealogy

Children of Abraham Delaney and Melchia Whitlock are:

2. i. John Jackson Delaney, born Nov 12, 1839 in Tennessee [6, 7, 8, 9], died Feb 23, 1920 in Roane, Tennessee.
3. ii. Nancy Ann Delaney, born Oct 08, 1840 in Tennessee, died Apr 15, 1884 in Tennessee.
4. iii. Robert H Delaney, born Dec 10, 1843 in Tennessee [10, 11], died Sep 14, 1909 in Chattanooga, Hamilton, Tennessee.
5. iv. Thomas Madison Delaney, born Oct 29, 1845 in Tennessee [12, 13, 14, 15], died Mar 25, 1913.
6. v. Sherwood Preston "Erb" Delaney, born Oct 13, 1847 in Tennessee, died Sep 05, 1898 in Roane, Tennessee [6].
7. vi. Mary Sarah Jane Delaney, born Dec 26, 1848 in Georgia, died Sep 03, 1929 in Roane, Tennessee.
8. vii. Arminta A Delaney, born Jan 07, 1853 in Tennessee [17], died Oct 19, 1891 in Roane, Tennessee.
9. viii. Malinda Caroline Delaney, born Nov 01, 1855 in Tennessee, died Dec 11, 1924 in Roane, Tennessee.
10. ix. William C Delaney, born Dec 1859 in Tennessee [18, 19, 20], died 1952 in Roane, Tennessee.
11. x. Dicie C Delaney, born Mar 1861 in Tennessee [21], died before 1910 in Roane, Tennessee.

## Generation 2

2. John Jackson Delaney (Abraham Delaney-1) [6, 7, 8, 9, 22] was born on Nov 12, 1839 in Tennessee [6, 7, 8, 9]. He died on Feb 23, 1920 in Roane, Tennessee. He married Mary Ann Davidson on Apr 04, 1859 in Monroe, Tennessee. She was born on Jun 15, 1843 in Tennessee. She died on Oct 15, 1905 in Monroe, Tennessee. He married Mary Ann Davidson on Apr 04, 1859 in Monroe, Tennessee. She was born on Jun 15, 1843 in Tennessee. She died on Oct 15, 1905 in Monroe, Tennessee.

Notes for John Jackson Delaney:

1890 Veterans' census: Roane County TN 9th & 10th Civil Districts Compiled by Robert L. Bailey DELANEY, John J. Pvt. Co. A, 2 TN Inf. Post Office: Kingston.

Death Certificates Index at Roane County Heritage Commission web site
LAST NAME    FIRST NAME    AGE    DOD    COUNTY    RECORD
DELANEY      John Jackson  81     1920   Roane     #196

In the Civil War records of Calvin Neal Wallis (wife Nancy Ann Delaney daughter of Abraham) a statement is made that Calvin Neal Wallis was captured along with his brother-in-law John J. Delaney in Roane Co. in the fall of 1863. Calvin Neal Wallis died in a Confederate Prison in Danville, VA. I don't know if John J. Delaney was imprisoned there also.- (Source: http://genforum.genealogy.com/delaney/messages/598.html)

Children of John Jackson Delaney and Mary Ann Davidson are:

i. Elizabeth Delaney, born 1862, married J. J. Chapman on Dec 02, 1882 in Roane, Tennessee.
ii. Paralee Delaney, born 1867, died 1868.

## The Delaney Kids~ Bought and Paid For

  iii. Frank Delaney, born 1869, died 1870.
  iv. Flutilla Delaney, born 1871, married a Jenkins on Sep 14, 1890 in Roane, Tennessee.
  v. Alice Delaney, born 1873, married Frank Oran on Dec 18, 1892 in Roane, Tennessee.
  vi. Belle Delaney, born 1875, no other information.
  vii. James Willis Delaney, born Feb 1877.
  viii. Ulysses Arthur Delaney, born 1883, no other information.
  ix. Arthur Toad Delaney, born Jul 1883.

3. Nancy Ann Delaney (Abraham Delaney-1) was born on Oct 08, 1840 in Tennessee. She died on Apr 15, 1884 in Tennessee. She married Calvin Neal Wallace on May 13, 1859 in Monroe, Tennessee. He was born on 1840 in Tennessee. He died on Feb 15, 1864 in the Confederate Prison at Danville VA. She married Elisha Rose on Feb 20, 1867 in Roane, Tennessee. He was born on Mar 30, 1825 in Roane, Tennessee, and died on Jul 08, 1910 in Roane, Tennessee.

Notes for Calvin Neal Wallace:
from www.ancestry.com
1860 Census, McMinn County Tennessee, First District, P.O. Fountain Hill

  49  47  Calvin N Wallace    Age 20 B TN
         Nancy    Age 17 B TN
         Martha E   Age 7/12

In the Civil War records of Calvin Neal Wallis, a statement is made that Calvin Neal Wallis was captured along with his brother-in-law John J. Delaney in Roane County in the fall of 1863. Calvin Neal Wallis died in the Confederate Prison, but I do not know if John J. Delaney was imprisoned there also. (Source: http://genforum.genealogy.com/delaney/messages/598.html)

Child of Nancy Ann Delaney and Calvin Neal Wallace is:
  11.  i. Margaret Elizabeth Wallace, born Jul 24, 1863 in Tennessee, died May 03, 1937 in Harriman, Roane, Tennessee.

4. Robert H Delaney (Abraham Delaney-1)[10, 11, 23, 24, 25] was born on Dec 10, 1843 in Tennessee [10, 11]. He died on Sep 14, 1909 in Chattanooga, Hamilton, Tennessee. He married Safronia C Matheny on May 21, 1865 in Nashville, Davidson, Tennessee. She was born around 1845 [26]. She died on May 25, 1917 in Chattanooga, Hamilton, Tennessee.

Notes for Robert H Delaney:
from www.ancestry.com
1900 Census, Hamilton County Tennessee, 17th Dist, ED 72
(mostly unreadable due to staining)
Delaney, Robert H  Age 56
Sophronia C unreadable
children unreadable

1890 Union Veterans Census - Roane County Tennessee 9th & 10th Civil Districts Compiled by Robert L. Bailey

DELANY, Robt. H. PvtCo. A, 5 TN Inf. Post Office: Kingston.1880 Census, Roane County Tennessee, 17th District, ED 223
Robert H. DELANEY Self M Male W 36 Farmer TN / KY / TN

## APPENDIX D – Genealogy 283

Sophronia C. DELANEY Wife M Female W 28 Keeping House TN / TN / TN
William H. DELANEY Son S Male W 10 TN TN TN
Leonides H. DELANEY Son S Male W 9 TN TN TN
Robert H. DELANEY Son S Male W 4 TN TN TN
Florence R. DELANEY Dau S Female W 3 TN TN TN
Mary E. DELANEY Dau S Female W 1 TN TN TN
Census Place District 17, Roane, Tennessee
Source1: www.familysearch.org Family History Library Film 1255275
NA Film Number T9-1275
Page Number 309A
Source2: www.ancestry.com

From www.ancestry.com
1870 Census
Home in 1870: Hamilton County TN, District 3, Subdivision 13
Name: Delano, Robert H  Age 26  Farmer Born TN
       Sophronia            28      GA
       William           10/12      TN

From http://www.tngenweb.org/civilwar/usainf/usa5inf.html: 5TH TENNESSEE VOLUNTEER INFANTRY REGIMENT, U.S.A.

Also called 5th East Tennessee Infantry Regiment

Organized at Barbourville, Kentucky, with six companies, March 28, 1862; mustered out at Nashville, March 29 through June 30, 1865.

FIELD OFFICERS Colonel-James T. Shelley

Lieutenant Colonels-Fremontin Young, Charles C. McCaleb, Nathaniel Witt
Majors-Charles C. McCaleb, Joseph D. Turner, David G. Bowers

CAPTAINS-David C. Bowers, Samuel P. Evans, Co. "A". Enrolled at Kingston, Roane County, February 25; mustered in March 28, 1863; mustered out April 4, 1865

The regiment was placed in Brigadier General J. C. Spears' 25th Brigade, of Brigadier General George W. Morgan's 7th Division, Army of the Ohio. Other members of the brigade were the 3rd, 4th and 6th Tennessee Infantry. The regiment remained in this brigade until the latter part of November 1862. On May 10, the 5th and 6th Tennessee Regiments were at Archer's, near Big Creek Gap. In June, Spear's Brigade forced a passage through Big Creek Gap, and General Spears spoke of Captain Clingan as a brave and gallant officer in his report of an engagement there on June 12. The brigade then went on to occupy Cumberland Gap on June 18, and remained in that area until the evacuation of the Gap by General Morgan on September 17, 1862.

The regiment accompanied General Morgan on his withdrawal from the Gap to the Ohio River in September; and on October 12, at Portland, Ohio, General Morgan, in reporting on his forces, listed the 5th Tennessee with an aggregate of 727. On October 31, Spears' Brigade was reported as the 1st Brigade, District of western Virginia, under General Morgan.

On November 13 the 3rd, 5th and 6th Tennessee were ordered to Cincinnati, Ohio, thence via Bowling Green, Kentucky, to report to Major General William S. Rosecrans, Department of the Cumberland. On November 17, General Spears, at Louisville, reported to General Rosecrans: "I am here with the residue of my command, the 5th Tennessee, and the 1st and 2nd Tennessee Cavalry." On December 4, part of the 5th was reported as still at Louisville, awaiting transportation.

It eventually reached Nashville, where General Spears was assigned to command the 1st Brigade, of Brigadier General J. S Negley's 2nd Division. The brigade consisted of the 1st, 2nd, 3rd, 5th, and 6th Tennessee Regiments, but General Spears made no mention of the 5th being engaged with the rest of the brigade in its operations on January 2 and 3, 1863, in the Stone's River Campaign. The regiment remained at Nashville until April 1863, and then was stationed for a while at Carthage.

On June 8, 1863, the 3rd, 5th, and 6th East Tennessee Regiments were placed in the 3rd Brigade, 3rd Division, Reserve Corps, Department of the Cumberland. On June 30, the same regiments, under Colonel Cooper, of the 6th Tennessee, were reported as the 3rd Brigade, 3rd Division, XXIII Corps, Department of the Ohio; and on July 2, Major General A. E. Burnside, at Cincinnati, at the time of Confederate General John Hunt Morgan's raid, wrote: "I am anxiously awaiting reports from the 8th and 5th Tennessee Regiments." There seems to have been some mix-up as to assignments, for there is no other record of the regiment, or the brigade, having been in Kentucky at this time.

On July 31, Colonel William B. Stokes was reported in command of the brigade, still in the Reserve Corps, Department of the Cumberland. The 5th was at Carthage, and a detachment under Captain Clingan was manning the artillery. On August 31, Brigadier General Spears assumed command of the brigade, with headquarters at Alexandria, Tennessee. On the same date, Major General Gordon Granger ordered Colonel Shelley to move his command to McMinnville. Colonel Shelley, at the time in temporary command of the 3rd and 6th Regiments, plus a detachment of Stokes' 5th Tennessee Cavalry, moved with these units to McMinnville, leaving the 5th Infantry, under Lieutenant Colonel McCaleb, at Carthage.

General Spears, commanding the brigade, moved from McMinnville on September 13 towards Chattanooga, leaving two companies of the 5th Tennessee at Carthage. He arrived at Chattanooga on September 21, just after the battle of Chickamauga, September 19-20, and was directed to place his command at the bridge across Chattanooga Creek, to halt and reform the Federal troops streaming into Chattanooga. He placed Colonel Shelley, with his regiment, at the crossroads. on the point of Lookout Mountain on the south side. On the 22nd, three companies from the regiment were placed upon the river along the railroad, and the 6th Regiment, under Colonel Cooper, joined the remaining five companies of the 5th in line of battle at the crossroads. About noon, they were attacked by Confederate forces, and after an engagement of about an hour and a half, fell back to a more favorable position on the first bench of the point of the mountain. They remained here until early in the morning, September 24, when the whole brigade withdrew into Chattanooga.

## Appendix D – Genealogy

On October 9, 1863, the brigade, under Brigadier General John S. Beatty, was transferred from the Reserve Corps to the XIV Corps, as the 2nd Brigade, 3rd Division. However, on October 22, General Spears was back in command, and the brigade was reported as the 2nd Brigade, 2nd Division, XIV Corps. Headquarters of the brigade were at Sale Creek, and the brigade did duty along the Tennessee River between Chattanooga and Knoxville for the remainder of the year. On December 3, the regiment, with the brigade, was at Kingston, Tennessee; on December 6, at Loudon; on January 1, 1864, at Massengale House, near the Holston River, 30 miles northeast of Knoxville; on January 16 at Flat Creek Bridge. At this time, the 5th Tennessee was detached and ordered to Loudon, and Company "G". under Captain Clingan, was detached as artillery.

On January 21, 1864, the brigade was transferred from the XIV to XXIII Corps, where it was reported as the 1st East Tennessee Brigade, 3rd Division. Orders were issued on February 1, 1864, that the 5th Tennessee be left at Loudon, to garrison the post.

On April 10, 1864, the XXIII Corps was reorganized, and the 5th Tennessee was assigned to Brigadier General M. D. Manson's 2nd Brigade, of Brigadier General Jacob D. Cox's 3rd Division. On April 20, General Cox advised that the 5th Tennessee had not yet reported, and it was presumably still at Loudon, Tennessee. However, it did join the brigade in time for the start of the Atlanta Campaign, and took part in skirmishing at Buzzard Roost and Potato Hill on May 9, and was heavily engaged at Resaca, on May 14. In this engagement, the regiment, under Colonel Shelley, took part in a charge which captured the first line of the Confederate rifle pits, but at heavy loss. Colonel Shelley reported six officers wounded, 16 men killed, 92 wounded and 14 missing.

On June 5, the regiment was transferred to Brigadier General N. C. McLean's 3rd Brigade, of which brigade Colonel Byrd, 1st Tennessee Infantry, took command on June 17. Colonel Shelley resigned on July 22, and Major Bowers was in command of the regiment from that time until after the battle of Nashville. On August 11, 1864, in the field near Atlanta, the XXIII Corps was again reorganized, the 1st Division discontinued, and the regiment remained in the 3rd Brigade, 3rd Division. However, the regiment was reported at the time as detached at Marietta, Georgia.

The regiment arrived at Nashville on November 15, and was sent to join Major General John M. Schofield at Pulaski. With Schofield, it left Pulaski November 22, withdrew through Columbia and Spring Hill, and arrived at Franklin on the morning of November 30, 1864. In the battle of Franklin, the 5th Regiment was in the second line of Colonel Casement's 2nd Brigade, in the center of the Federal lines, between the Columbia and Lewisburg Pikes. Major Bowers reported only six casualties.

In the battle of Nashville, December 15-16, 1864, the regiment was not engaged on the 15th; on the 16th, it was in line of battle on the Hillsboro Pike, and came under musketry fire, but did no serious fighting, and had only one man wounded.

On December 31, Lieutenant Colonel Nathaniel Witt was in command of the regiment, still in the 2nd Brigade, 3rd Division, XXIII Corps. With the division, it moved to North Carolina, arriving at Cape Fear February 8-9-10,

1865, and took part in the campaign which resulted in the occupation of Wilmington, on February 22, 1865.

On March 5, the regiment was relieved from duty in North Carolina, and ordered to proceed to Nashville, to be mustered out of service. On April 30, still under Lieutenant Colonel Witt, it was reported unbrigaded at Nashville, and was mustered out June 30, 1865.

Relationship Notes for Safronia C Matheny and Robert H Delaney:
From http://wendy.library.nashville.org:82
Title Marriage
Section/pg 100
Bride Mathena, Sophronia
Groom Delaney, R. H. Date
21 May 1865 Marriagebk 5

Children of Robert H Delaney and Safronia C Matheny are:

12.   i. William Henry Delaney, born Jul 07, 1869 in Chattanooga, Hamilton, Tennessee, on South Broad Street[27, 28, 29], died Feb 23, 1951 in Chattanooga, Hamilton, Tennessee; 1824 Foust St, Chattanooga Tennessee.
13.   ii. Leonides Houston "Lon" Delaney, born Feb 02, 1871 in Tennessee [30, 31], died Oct 18, 1937 in Tennessee.
     iii. Robert H Delaney, born Jan 10, 1875 in Tennessee, died Nov 22, 1897 in Tennessee.
     iv. Florence Rilla Delaney, born Dec 26, 1876 in Tennessee, died Mar 05, 1896 in Tennessee.
     v. Mary E Delaney, born Nov 09, 1878 in Tennessee, died Apr 26, 1945 in Georgia.
14.   vi. Samuel C Delaney, born Sep 13, 1880 in Tennessee [32], died Dec 26, 1922 in Tennessee.
15.   vii. Ardell P Delaney, born May 22, 1887 in Tennessee [33], died Jul 18, 1925 in Tennessee.
16.   viii. David D Delaney, born Mar 22, 1889 in Rockwood, Roane, Tennessee [34, 35], died Jun 14, 1948 in Jefferson, Kentucky [34].
17.   ix. Sarah C A Delaney, born Jul 07, 1891 in Tennessee, died Feb 01, 1962 in Tennessee.

5. Thomas Madison Delaney (Abraham Delaney-1)[12, 13, 14, 15, 36] was born on Oct 29, 1845 in Tennessee [12, 13, 14, 15]. He died on Mar 25, 1913. He married Elizabeth Chumley on Sep 16, 1865 in Roane, Tennessee. She was born on Jun 18, 1839, and died in 1880. He married Mary Elizabeth Cook Collins on Dec 30, 1893 in Roane, Tennessee. She was born on Mar 20, 1870 in Tennessee.

Children of Thomas Madison Delaney and Elizabeth Chumley are:

     i. James Harvey Delaney, born Nov 07, 1869 in Roane, Tennessee. He married Amanda Pierce on Nov 30, 1895, in Roane, Tennessee.
     ii. Edgar G Delaney, born Nov 04, 1871 in Roane, Tennessee, died 1872.

## APPENDIX D – Genealogy

   iii. Samuel Henry Delaney, born Nov 08, 1874 in Roane, Tennessee, died 1875.
   iv. Laura Delaney, born Sep 08, 1876 in Roane, Tennessee. She married an Elliott on Sep 02, 1896 in Roane, Tennessee.
   v. Eliza Mathena Delaney, born Jun 09, 1878 in Roane, Tennessee, died Sep 06, 1962 in Kingston, Roane, Tennessee. She married Calvin Davis on Mar 16, 1895 in Roane, Tennessee.

6. Sherwood Preston "Erb" Delaney (Abraham Delaney-1)[16, 37, 38] was born on Oct 13, 1847 in Tennessee and died on Sep 05, 1898 in Roane, Tennessee. He married Martha Cook on May 16, 1869 in Roane, Tennessee [16]. She was born on Jun 06, 1853 and died on Aug 14, 1900 in Roane, Tennessee.

   Children of Sherwood Preston "Erb" Delaney and Martha Cook are:
   i. Mary Delaney, born 1875 in Tennessee.
   ii. Belle Delaney, born 1877 in Tennessee.
   iii. Safronia Bell Delaney, born Nov 10, 1874 in Tennessee, died Feb 13, 1958 in Harriman, Roane, Tennessee.
   iv. Nancy Isabell Delaney, born Jul 30, 1878, died Jun 04, 1908.
   v. Alice Delaney, born 1880 and died in 1958 in Roane, Tennessee.
   vi. Gustus Delaney, born Jun 02, 1884, died Apr 27, 1935.
   vii. Susie Merit Delaney, born Jul 12, 1887, died Sep 08, 1889.
   viii. Birdanner Sam Delaney, born Sep 10, 1888.

7. Mary Sarah Jane Delaney (Abraham Delaney-1)[39] was born on Dec 26, 1848 in Georgia. She died on Sep 03, 1929 in Roane, Tennessee. She married Robert Moore on Jul 31, 1870 in Roane, Tennessee. He was born on May 16, 1850 in North Carolina. He died on Oct 1935 in Roane, Tennessee.

   Notes for Mary Sarah Jane Delaney:
   from www.ancestry.com: 1880 Census, Roane County, TN, indicates Mary Jane bore 10 children and 8 were still living

   Children of Mary Sarah Jane Delaney and Robert Moore are:
   i. Rosa Moore, born 1872 in Tennessee, died 1900.
   ii. Addie Moore, born 1873 in Tennessee.
   iii. Benjamin Moore, born Aug 15, 1876 in Tennessee, died Feb 21, 1952.
   iv. Maggie Moore, born Sep 15, 1873, died Mar 23, 1926, married Julian Gunter on May 01, 1892.
   v. Arthur Lee Moore, born Feb 01, 1877 in Roane, Tennessee, died Dec 13, 1960 in Rockwood, Roane, Tennessee.
   vi. Duley Rebecca Moore, born Jan 14, 1882 in Roane, Tennessee, died Oct 14, 1968 in Harriman, Roane, Tennessee.
   vii. Robert L Moore, born Apr 1883 in Tennessee, died 1942.
   viii. Charles Absy Moore, born Oct 05, 1885 in Tennessee, died Oct 27, 1974.

ix. Norah Moore, born Oct 18, 1889 in Roane, Tennessee, died Apr 08, 1956.
x. Samuel A Moore, born Apr 11, 1891, died Sep 16, 1967.
xi. Ernest Moore, born 1893 in Tennessee.

8. Arminta A Delaney (Abraham Delaney-1)[17, 40] was born on Jan 07, 1853 in Tennessee [17]. She died on Oct 19, 1891 in Roane, Tennessee. She married John W A Moore on Nov 10, 1869 in Roane, Tennessee. He was born on Dec 26, 1846 in North Carolina. He died on Aug 03, 1936 in Roane, Tennessee.

Children of Arminta A Delaney and John W A Moore are:
i. Samuel C Moore, born about 1873 in Tennessee, died 1904.
ii. Ida May Moore, born Jul 30, 1874, died Mar 11, 1941 in Knoxville, Knox, Tennessee.
iii. Millard S Moore, born about 1878 in Tennessee, died 1880.
iv. Orissie Martha Moore, born Apr 28, 1880 in Pikeville, Bledsoe, Tennessee, died Mar 20, 1920 in Fackler, Jackson, Alabama.
v. Arabella Isabella Moore, born Nov 1882.
vi. Elba Calli Moore, born Jan 1880, died 1894.
vii. Unknown Moore, born Aug 17, 1884, died 1887.
viii. Dempsey L Moore, born Apr 23, 1888 in Tennessee, died Dec 10, 1951.
ix. J A Moore, born Jul 10, 1886, died 1887.

9. William C Delaney (Abraham Delaney-1)[18, 19, 20, 41] was born on Dec 1859 in Tennessee [18, 19, 20]. He died on 1952 in Roane, Tennessee. He married Betty Adeline James on Feb 12, 1882 in Roane, Tennessee. She was born on Jun 02, 1867 in Virginia and died on Oct 19, 1910 in Harriman, Roane, Tennessee.

Notes for William C Delaney:
1930 Census, living with son-in-law Fred Offenberger (Ava), Roane County TN, ED 73-1, Sheet 8B
1920 Census, living with brother Thomas Delaney in Roane County TN, ED 158, Sheet 14A
1910 Census, Marion County TN, Dist 7, ED 132, Sheet 5A, HH 85, "Delany, William C"
1900 Census, Roane County TN, Dist 6, ED 117, Sheet 6, HH 96: "Deloney, William"

Children of William C Delaney and Betty Adeline James are:
i. Luther V Delaney, born Oct 02, 1884 in Tennessee, died Jul 1967 in Blount, Tennessee.
ii. Mollie Delaney, born Apr 1887 in Tennessee.
iii. Henry Delaney, born Sep 1889 in Tennessee.
18. iv. Ava Delaney, born May 09, 1892 in Tennessee [42, 43, 44], died Jan 1982 in Knoxville, Knox, Tennessee [44].
v. George Delaney, born Sep 1894 in Tennessee.
vi. Jack Delaney, born May 1897 in Tennessee.
vii. Zella May Delaney, born 1902 in Tennessee.

# APPENDIX D – Genealogy

10. Dicie C Delaney (Abraham Delaney-1)[21] was born on Mar 1861 in Tennessee [21]. She died before 1910 in Roane, Tennessee. She married Frank Collins on Oct 09, 1885 in Roane, Tennessee. He was born on Dec 03, 1854. He died on Feb 28, 1914 in Roane, Tennessee.

    Notes for Frank Collins:
    1910 Census, Hamilton County Tennessee, Chattanooga Ward 4, ED 53, Sheet 3B, line 81, 112
    Fulton St
    Collins Frank   Age 54   TN Widowed
            Edward  18
            Alice            16
            Tom     13
            Ethel   10

    1900 Census, Roane County TN, District 16, ED 124
    Collins Frank   Age 45   TN   Married 14 Yrs
            Dicey   39       TN   Bore 7 children, 7 living
            Millie E 18      Tennessee
            Letty   13       Tennessee
            James   12       Tennessee
            Liuie   10       TN
            Edgar   9        TN
            Bertha  6        TN
            Thomas  4        TN
            Ethel   8/12     TN

    Children of Dicie C Delaney and Frank Collins are:
    i. Millie E Collins, born 1882 in Tennessee.
    ii. Letty Collins, born Sep 1886 in Tennessee.
    iii. James Collins, born 1888 in Tennessee.
    iv. Louie Collins, born Mar 1890 in Tennessee.
    v. Edgar L Collins, born Jan 1891 in Tennessee.
    vi. Bertha A Collins, born Nov 1893 in Tennessee.
    vii. Thomas H Collins, born Aug 1896 in Tennessee.
    viii. Ethel L Collins, born Oct 1899 in Tennessee.

## Generation 3

11. Margaret Elizabeth Wallace (Nancy Ann Delaney-2, Abraham Delaney-1) was born on Jul 24, 1863 in Tennessee. She died on May 03, 1937 in Harriman, Roane, Tennessee. She married Levi Mays Peters on Aug 08, 1880 in Roane, Tennessee. He was born on Aug 14, 1855, and died on Oct 18, 1948 in Harriman, Roane, Tennessee.

    Children of Margaret Elizabeth Wallace and Levi Mays Peters are:
    i. Thomas Peters, born Sep 1883 in Tennessee.
    ii. Bertha Peters, born Mar 1885 in Tennessee.
    iii. Delta Peters, born Apr 10, 1887 in Tennessee.
    iv. Myrtie Peters, born 1890 in Tennessee.

v. Zettie Peters, born 1895 in Tennessee.

12. William Henry Delaney (Robert H Delaney-2, Abraham Delaney-1)[27, 28, 29, 45] birth on Jul 07, 1869 in Chattanooga, Hamilton, Tennessee, on South Broad Street [27, 28, 29]. His death occurred on Feb 23, 1951 in Chattanooga, Hamilton, Tennessee, at his home at 1824 Foust Street. William Henry married Sarah A. Parks on Jul 26, 1891 in Roane, Tennessee [47]. We believe Sarah was the daughter of George Parks and Rachel Elizabeth Qualls, and was born on May 09, 1875 in Roane, Tennessee [48, 49, 50]. She died on Apr 19, 1913. After Sarah's death, William Henry married Mollie McCall on Feb 11, 1914 in Rossville, Walker, Georgia. Mollie, the daughter of William McCall and Mary Morgan, was born on Feb 16, 1889 in Georgia [46]. She died on Apr 02, 1978 in Chattanooga, Hamilton, Tennessee.

Notes for William Henry Delaney:

WILLIAM DELANEY DIES; BUSINESSMAN
Native Was 81 -Last of Alton Park Baptist's Charter Members

William Henry Delaney, 81, retired Chattanooga businessman and member of the Chattanooga Half Century Club, died yesterday afternoon in a local hospital. Mr. Delaney was the last Charter member of the Alton Park Baptist Church.

Mr. Delaney is survived by his wife, the former Miss Mollie McCall; three daughters, Mrs. Grace L. Smith, Chattanooga; Mrs. T. H. Strawn, Holland, Ga., and Mrs. W. E. Boyd, Compton, Calif.; three sons, Claud H. Delaney, Ralph H. Delaney and Floyd C. Delaney, all of Chattanooga; a sister, Mrs. Ralph Curtis, Chattanooga; 11 grandchildren and 13 great-grandchildren.

William Henry Delaney was born July 7, 1869, on old Whiteside Street, now South Broad, about yards from the creek, he wrote on his application for membership in the Half Century Club several years ago. His father was Robert H. Delaney and his mother Mrs. Sophronia Matheny Delaney.

Farm on River

He also wrote that, 'When I was 3 weeks old my father moved to the Caldwell farm, a part of which is now Lupton City. In 1875 my father cultivated the river bottom land north of the river below the Market Street and Walnut Street bridges. In June of 1875 my father took the family to Roane County on account of an epidemic here of cholera. We remained in Roane County until Jan. 15, 1899, when we returned to Chattanooga, and I went to work at the Southern Railway freight station. I worked there four years and then seven years for the Chattanooga Transfer Company. Later I sold life insurance for more than eight years.' Mr. Delaney was a member of the Junior Order of United American Mechanics. He had been a member of the Baptist Church 63 years and a deacon 58 years.

Funeral services will be held Sunday at 2:30 p.m. at the Alton Park Baptist Church, with the Revs. Robert Evans, W. C. Tallent and A. M. Stansel officiating. Burial will be in Chattanooga Memorial Park. The body is at the home, 1824 Foust Street.

(Source: Chattanooga Times, Feb. 24, 1951, page 9.)

## APPENDIX D – Genealogy

From www.ancestry.com
1930 Census, Hamilton County Tennessee, ED 13

| 3721 | 140 | | | | |
|---|---|---|---|---|---|
| | 143 | Delaney, William H | Age 60 | Agent, Life & Accident Insurance |
| | | Mollie E | 41 | Hooker, Hosiery Mill |
| | | Florence L | 26 | Inspector, Hosiery Mill |
| | | Floyd C | 25 | Clerk, National Bank |
| | | Helen G | 22 | Collector, Magazine Agency |

1920 Census, Hamilton County TN, First District, ED 196, 1508 Hawthorne Street

| 215 | 237 | Delaney, Will H | Age 50 | Insurance Agent |
|---|---|---|---|---|
| | | Mollie | 30 | |
| | | Ralph | 18 | |
| | | Florence | 16 | |
| | | Floid | 14 | |
| | | Helen | 11 | |

1910 Census, Hamilton County TN, 4th District, ED 85, Sheet 16A

| 310 | 318 | Delaney, William H | Age 40 | Age at first marriage: 19 |
|---|---|---|---|---|
| | | Sara A | 36 | No. children born: 11; No. living: 8 |
| | | Grace L | 18 | |
| | | John F. | 16 | |
| | | Claude H | 12 | |
| | | Ralph H | 9 | |
| | | Florence | 7 | |
| | | Floyd | 5 | |
| | | Helen | 2 | |
| | | Infant (no name) | 2/12 | |

1900 Census, Hamilton County TN, 3rd District, ED 42, Sheet 10, HH 189

| | Delaney, WH | Born July 1870 | |
|---|---|---|---|
| | Sarah | May 1875 | Bore 5 children, 3 living |
| | Gracie | July 1892 | |
| | John | Apr 1894 | |
| | Claude | Oct 1897 | |

Notes for Sarah A. Parks:
A very scant obituary in the Chattanooga Times, April 21, 1913

Children of William Henry Delaney and Sarah A. Parks are:

19. i. Grace L Delaney, born Jul 27, 1892 in Tennessee [50], died Dec 1968.
20. ii. John Franklin Delaney, born Apr 20, 1894[51], died after 1923.
    iii. George R Delaney, born Jun 30, 1896, died before 1900.
21. iv. Claude Hurley Delaney, born Oct 29, 1897 in Tennessee [52, 53, 54, 55, 56], died Jan 16, 1958.
    v. Ray H Delaney, born Aug 14, 1899; 9/30/1899, died Sep 30, 1899.
22. vi. Ralph Herman Delaney, born Apr 16, 1901 in Chattanooga, Hamilton, Tennessee [57, 58], died Nov 25, 1958.

       vii. Florence L Delaney, born May 14, 1903 in Tennessee [59], died Jan 20, 1995. She married Harold Strawn on Mar 10, 1934.
23.  viii. Floyd C Delaney, born Mar 30, 1905 in Tennessee [60], died Feb 02, 1982.
       ix. Mabel E Delaney, born Jan 10, 1907, died Jun 1907.
24.  x. Helen Gertrude Delaney, born Feb 01, 1908 in Tennessee [61, 62], died Aug 05, 2006.
       xi. Jennie Ruth Delaney, born Mar 02, 1910, died Jun 20, 1910.

13. Leonides Houston "Lon" Delaney (Robert H Delaney-2, Abraham Delaney-1) [30, 31, 64] was born on Feb 02, 1871 [30, 31] and died on Oct 18, 1937. He married Laura Shields on Mar 05, 1899 in Roane, Tennessee. She was born on Mar 04, 1881. She died in Feb 1955. They are somewhat difficult to track in the census:

    1930 Hamilton County Tennessee "Lon H Delaney"
    1920 Hamilton County Tennessee "Lonzo H Deloney"
    1910 Hamilton County Tennessee "Lou H Delancy", mostly unreadable

    Children of Leonides Houston "Lon" Delaney and Laura Shields are:

    i. Clyde Delaney, born about 1900
    ii. Earl Delaney, born about 1904
    iii. Gladys Delaney, born about 1906
    iv. Lois L Delaney, born between 1910-1911.

14. Samuel C Delaney (Robert H Delaney-2, Abraham Delaney-1)[32, 65] was born on Sep 13, 1880 in Tennessee [32]. He died on Dec 26, 1922 in Tennessee. He married Mable, last name unknown, presumably around 1905.

    Notes for Samuel C Delaney:
    1910 Census, Hamilton County Tennessee, ED 85, Sheet 24B, HH 494, Washington St

    Children of Samuel C Delaney and Mable are:

    i. Ruth Delaney, born about 1912 in Tennessee.
    ii. Raymond Delaney, born about 1915 in Tennessee.
    iii. Carlisle Delaney, born about 1917 in Tennessee.
    iv. Josephine Delaney, born about 1920 in Tennessee.

15. P Delaney (Robert H Delaney-2, Abraham Delaney-1)[33] was born on May 22, 1887 [33] and died on Jul 18, 1925 in Tennessee. He married Annie, last name unknown, presumably around 1908.

    Notes for Ardell P Delaney:
    1920 Census, Hamilton County TN, "Artle P Delany"
    1910 Census, Hamilton County TN, "Artle P Delaney"

    Child of Ardell P Delaney and Annie is:

    i. Pauline Delaney, born about 1909 in Tennessee.

16. David D Delaney (Robert H Delaney-2, Abraham Delaney-1)[34, 35] was born on Mar 22, 1889 in Rockwood, Roane, Tennessee [34, 35]. He died on Jun 14, 1948 in Jefferson, Kentucky [34]. He married a Myrtle, last name

## APPENDIX D – Genealogy

unknown. She was born on around 1883 in Arkansas, according to census information.

Notes for David D Delaney:
1920 Census, Hamilton County TN, "Dane Delaney"

Children of David D Delaney and Myrtle are:

    i. Mac Delaney, born about 1911 in Tennessee.
    ii. Doris or Iris Delaney, born between 1919-1920 in Tennessee.

17. Sarah C A Delaney (Robert H Delaney-2, Abraham Delaney-1) [66] was born on Jul 07, 1891 in Tennessee. She died on Feb 01, 1962 in Tennessee. She married Ralph Curtis around 1907 (Married at age 16). He was born around 1885 and died on Jan 11, 1958.

Notes for Sarah C A Delaney:
1930 Census, Hamilton County Tennessee, ED 33-43, Sheet 6B, HH 124, 1814 E 26th St

| Curtis, | Ralph | 44 | |
|---|---|---|---|
| | Sarah | 39 | married at age 16 |
| | Roy R | 21 | son and daughter-in-law, Anna E, and granddau, Anna B, 1 3/12 |
| | Wilbur | 17 | |
| | Louise | 13 | |
| | Christina | 10 | |
| | Jean E | 7 | |
| | Clara | 6 | |
| | Ralph Jr | 5 | |

Children of Sarah C A Delaney and Ralph Curtis, based on the 1930 census, are:

    i. Roy R Curtis, born about 1909 in Tennessee.
    ii. Wilbur Curtis, born about 1913 in Tennessee.
    iii. Louise Curtis, born about 1917 in Tennessee.
    iv. Christina Curtis, born about 1920 in Tennessee.
    v. Jean E Curtis, born about 1923 in Tennessee.
    vi. Clara Curtis, born about 1924 in Tennessee.
    vii. Ralph Curtis Jr, born about 1925 in Tennessee.

18. Ava Delaney (William C Delaney-2, Abraham Delaney-1)[42, 43, 44, 67] was born on May 09, 1892 in Tennessee [42, 43, 44]. She died on Jan 1982 in Knoxville, Knox, Tennessee [44]. She first married William Suddath in 1909. He was born on Mar 06, 1886 in Roane, Tennessee, and died on Feb 08, 1914 at Emory Gap, Roane, Tennessee. She married Fred Helfenberger on July 3, 1920 in Roane, Tennessee. He was born on Aug 08, 1890 in Ohio [68]. He died on Nov 05, 1978 in Knox, Tennessee [68].

Children of Ava Delaney and William Suddath are:

    i. James Clifford Suddath, born Sep 30, 1909 in Harriman, Roane, Tennessee, died Jul 20, 1955 in Bremerton, Kitsap, Washington.
    ii. Cleo Suddath, born Mar 05, 1910 in Harriman, Roane, Tennessee, died Jan 22, 1994 in Harriman, Roane, Tennessee.

Children of Ava Delaney and Fred Helfenberger are:
  i. Eula Helfenberger
  ii. Freddie Helfenberger
  iii. Mary E Helfenberger
  iv. Albert Rudolph Helfenberger, born Apr 12, 1925 in Knoxville, Knox, Tennessee [69], died May 27, 1995 in Knoxville, Knox, Tennessee [69].

## Generation 4

19. Grace L Delaney (William Henry Delaney-3, Robert H Delaney-2, Abraham Delaney-1)[50] was born on Jul 27, 1892 in Tennessee [50]. She died in Dec 1968 in Tennessee. She married Walter A Smith on Apr 22, 1917. He was born on Nov 13, 1891. He died on Nov 26, 1921 in Tennessee.

    Children of Grace L Delaney and Walter A Smith are:
    25.  i.  Lamar Smith, born Feb 09, 1918, died Jul 09, 1980.
    26.  ii. Clara A Smith, born Aug 10, 1920, died Oct 23, 1982.

20. John Franklin Delaney (William Henry Delaney-3, Robert H Delaney-2, Abraham Delaney-1)[51, 69] was born on Apr 20, 1894[51]. He died on after 1923. He married Annie Marshall on Jul 1919.

    Notes for John Franklin Delaney:
    Left home March 8, 1923, and was 'never seen again'
    WWII Draft Registration shows residence in Peru, IN, with spouse Nolia

    Child of John Franklin Delaney and Annie Marshall is:
      i. John F. Delaney Jr., born May 1921.

21. Claude Hurley Delaney (William Henry Delaney-3, Robert H Delaney-2, Abraham Delaney-1)[52, 53, 54, 55, 56] was born on Oct 29, 1897 in Tennessee [52, 53, 54, 55, 56]. He died on Jan 16, 1958 in Tennessee. He married Bertha Ashley on Sep 15, 1915. She was born on Nov 27, 1897 in Tennessee [70]. She died on Feb 17, 1990 in Tennessee [70].

    Children of Claude Hurley Delaney and Bertha Ashley are:
    27.  i.   William C Delaney, born Apr 08, 1917 in Tennessee, died Feb 16, 1970.
    28.  ii.  Francis Delaney, born Private.
         iii. Hurley A Delaney, born Private.

22. Ralph Herman Delaney (William Henry Delaney-3, Robert H Delaney-2, Abraham Delaney-1)[57, 58, 71] was born on Apr 16, 1901 in Chattanooga, Hamilton, Tennessee [57, 58]. He died on Nov 25, 1958 in Chattanooga, Hamilton, Tennessee. He married Elizabeth Jones on Nov 11, 1921, daughter of Francis Marion 'Frank' Jones and Emily Olevia 'Ollie' Chapman. Elizabeth was born on Aug 22, 1901 in James County (now either Bradley or Hamilton County), Tennessee [72, 73]. She died on Oct 23, 1985 in Chattanooga, Hamilton, Tennessee [72].

## Appendix D – Genealogy

Frank Jones was the son of Rufus Gaines Jones and Elizabeth Ann Varnell. Rufus Jones was deputy clerk and master from 1855 to 1860, then was clerk and master at the start of the Civil War. During the war, he served under Col. J.E. MacGowan on the Union side as a bookkeeper. In 1880, he was elected city auditor of Chattanooga. Rufus was the son of Jeremiah Jones, one of Hamilton County's "original 765 settlers", according John Wilson[79]. Ollie Chapman Jones was the daughter of Lemuel Chapman and Cynthia Ann Amelia Hardwick of Bradley County, Tennessee. Cynthia Hardwick's parents were John Wesley Hardwick, son of Garland Hardwick and Susan Venable, and Jane Montgomery, daughter of Hugh Lawson Montgomery and Margaret Barkley (or Barclay). John Wesley and Jane Montgomery Hardwick ran a hotel in Cleveland, Bradley County, Tennessee, until 1843, after which time they migrated to Arkansas. John Wesley Hardwick's great-great-great-grandfather, James Hardwick was originally from England. Margaret Barkley's father John was from Antrim, Ireland, and her mother Agnes was a Pinckney from South Carolina. Hugh Lawson Montgomery was an agent for the Cherokee Nation, and his father James was from Down, Ireland.

Notes for Ralph Herman Delaney:
Obituary: R. H. DELANEY, 57, DIES IN HOSPITAL
Former Merchant Assisted in Equipping Playground on Georgia Avenue

Ralph H. Delaney, 57, former merchant and more recently connected with the Interstate Life & Accident Insurance Co., died Tuesday afternoon at a local hospital following an illness of several months. Prior to joining the insurance company, Mr. Delaney had operated the 'Midget Store,' a soft drink and food store at 304 Georgia Ave. Over a period of years, he took a keen interest in the playground adjoining the store and assisted in obtaining equipment for the lot. He also entertained the children of the neighborhood with a party on the ground twice each year.

Mr. Delaney was born in Chattanooga April 16, 1901, the son of the Mr. And Mrs. Will H. Delaney. He was educated in local schools and was a member of the Highland Park Baptist Church. His home was at 500 Battery Place. He is survived by his wife; a son, Marion Delaney, stationed at the Great Lakes Naval Training Station; two daughters, Mrs. Floyd Osborne, Rossville and Mrs. Anna Lee Blackburn, Chattanooga; stepdaughter, Katherine K. Clark, Chattanooga; stepmother, Mrs. Mollie Delaney, Chattanooga; brother, Floyd C. Delaney, Chattanooga, and three sisters, Mrs. Grace L. Smith, Rossville and Mrs. Florence Strawn and Mrs. W. E. Boyd of Los Angeles.

The body is at National Funeral Home. Funeral arrangements will be announced later. (Note: Burial in Chattanooga Memorial Park)
Source: Chattanooga Times, Nov 26, 1958, Page 9

Children of Ralph Herman Delaney and Elizabeth Jones are:

29. i. Emma Gene Delaney, born Mar 23, 1927, died Feb 11, 2009 in Chattanooga, Hamilton, Tennessee.
30. ii. Anna Lee Delaney, born Private.
31. iii. Marion Henry Delaney, born Sep 23, 1922 in Chattanooga, Hamilton, Tennessee [74, 75], died Oct 09, 1991 in Chattanooga, Hamilton, Tennessee.

23. Floyd C Delaney (William Henry Delaney-3, Robert H Delaney-2, Abraham Delaney-1)[60] was born on Mar 30, 1905 in Tennessee [60]. He died on Feb 02, 1982. He married Blanche Elrod on Sep 02, 1930. She was born on Oct 11, 1906. She died on Oct 24, 1999.

Child of Floyd C Delaney and Blanche Elrod is:

32.    i.   Charles Whitney Delaney, born Private.

24. Helen Gertrude Delaney (William Henry Delaney-3, Robert H Delaney-2, Abraham Delaney-1)[61, 62] was born on Feb 01, 1908 in Tennessee [61, 62]. She died on Aug 05, 2006 in Chattanooga, Hamilton, Tennessee [61]. She married William E Boyd on Mar 25, 1936. He was born on Sep 08, 1903. He died on Dec 21, 1977.

Notes for Helen Gertrude Delaney:
From The Chattanoogan.com

Helen Gertrude Delaney Boyd, 98, of Chattanooga, died on Saturday, August 5, 2006 in a local health care facility.

She was born February 1, 1908 to the late William Henry Delaney and Sarah Parks Delaney of Chattanooga. In 1936, she married the late William Earl Boyd and became a Navy wife and homemaker. They eventually retired in Lakewood, Ca., and in 1981, Mrs. Boyd moved back to Chattanooga to be with family and friends, and especially her brother, Floyd and sister Florence.

In addition to her husband, she was preceded in death by her daughter, Edna Earle Horton, grandson, Russell Alan Bartlett, ten brothers and sisters.

She is survived by her grandson, Jeff Bartlett (Marian) and great-granddaughter, Sarah Helen of Anaheim, Ca.; grandson, Ken Williams; great-grandsons, Nick, Chris, and Dillon, all of Anchorage, Al.; nieces, Anna Lee Deitch, Chattanooga, and Emma Gene Osborne, Rossville.

Graveside services will be held Thursday at 11 a.m. at the Chattanooga National Cemetery with Rev. Ron Ragon officiating.

Child of Helen Gertrude Delaney and William E Boyd is:

33.    i.   Edna Earle Boyd, born Mar 23, 1938, died Nov 01, 1988 in California.

25. Lamar Smith (Grace L Delaney-4, William Henry Delaney-3, Robert H Delaney-2, Abraham Delaney-1) was born on Feb 09, 1918. He died on Jul 09, 1980. He married Mary Clarkson on Jul 03, 1938. She was born on Mar 03, 1918. She died on Oct 1981.

Child of Lamar Smith and Mary Clarkson is:

     i.   David Lamar Smith, born Dec 08, 1940, died Sep 08, 1981, married Mar 16, 1963.

26. Clara A Smith (Grace L Delaney-4, William Henry Delaney-3, Robert H Delaney-2, Abraham Delaney-1) was born on Aug 10, 1920. She died on

APPENDIX D – Genealogy   297

Oct 23, 1982. She married Joseph Fred Tuell on Jun 05, 1937. He was born on Feb 26, 1917. He died on Aug 23, 1985.

## Generation 5

Children of Clara A Smith and Joseph Fred Tuell are:
  i. Patricia Ann Tuell, born Private.
  ii. Joseph Fredrick Tuell, born Private.
  iii. Alma Joe Tuell, born Private.

27. William C Delaney (Claude Hurley Delaney-4, William Henry Delaney-3, Robert H Delaney-2, Abraham Delaney-1) was born on Apr 08, 1917 in Tennessee. He died on Feb 16, 1970. He married Gloria Walker on Jun 10, 1938. She was born on Oct 10, 1918.

    Child of William C Delaney and Gloria Walker is:
      i. Claudia Delaney, born Private.

28. Francis Delaney (Claude Hurley Delaney-4, William Henry Delaney-3, Robert H Delaney-2, Abraham Delaney-1) married Hubert Lee Fisher on Apr 13, 1940.

    Child of Francis Delaney and Hubert Lee Fisher is:
      i. Charlotte Lee Fisher, born Private.

29. Emma Gene Delaney (Ralph Herman Delaney-4, William Henry Delaney-3, Robert H Delaney-2, Abraham Delaney-1) was born on Mar 23, 1927. She died on Feb 11, 2009 in Chattanooga, Hamilton, Tennessee. She married Floyd Wilburn Osborne on Oct 30, 1943. He was born on Mar 07, 1923, and died on Jun 08, 1977.

    Children of Emma Gene Delaney and Floyd Wilburn Osborne are:
      i. Stephen Michael Osborne, born Private.
      ii. Phillip Lee Osborne, born Private.
    34. iii. Glenda Sharon Osborne, born Private.

30. Anna Lee Delaney (Ralph Herman Delaney-4, William Henry Delaney-3, Robert H Delaney-2, Abraham Delaney-1) first married James Louis Blackburn on Mar 23, 1951. He was born on Apr 16, 1930. He died on Dec 11, 1993. She married Ike Deitch on Jul 30, 1960. He was born on Sep 18, 1925, and died on Jul 04, 1992 in Chattanooga, Hamilton, Tennessee.

    Child of Anna Lee Delaney and James Louis Blackburn is:
    35. i. Renee Blackburn, born Private.

31. Marion Henry Delaney (Ralph Herman Delaney-4, William Henry Delaney-3, Robert H Delaney-2, Abraham Delaney-1)[76] was born on Sep 23, 1922

in Chattanooga, Hamilton, Tennessee [74, 75]. He died on Oct 09, 1991 in Chattanooga, Hamilton, Tennessee.

He was married twice to Imogene May Clark, the first time on Nov 24, 1941 in Ringgold, Catoosa, Georgia. Imogene was the daughter of John Lenoir Clark and Mary Abagale McJunkin. She was born on Feb 19, 1922 in Chattanooga, Hamilton, Tennessee, and died on Aug 21, 2009 in Chattanooga. Marion Henry next married Mary Joy Ridge. She was born about 1918, and died on Aug 24, 1950. His third wife was Mildred King. They divorced in Orange County, California, in 1967. He then married Louise Thrailkil on Nov 14, 1981. She died on Jun 11, 1997, but they may have divorced prior to her death. Marion Henry lastly married Billie DeFriese.

Notes for Marion Henry Delaney:
Obituary: DELANEY, MARION H., 69, of East Ridge died Tuesday at his home. He retired from the U. S. Navy after 28 years. He was preceded in death by his parents, Ralph H. and Elizabeth Jones Delaney. Survivors include his wife, Billie DeFriese Delaney; daughter, Paula Cope, Cincinnati; son, Marion Richard Delaney, Chattanooga; two stepdaughters, Billie Jean Saterfield and Nancy Todd; stepson, Henry Wall; two sisters, Emma Gene Osborne, Rossville, and Anna Lee Deitch, Chattanooga; one granddaughter, two stepgrandchildren. Funeral services will be 1 p.m. Thursday in the East Chapel of Chattanooga Funeral Home with the Rev. John B. Stone officiating. Burial will be in National Cemetery. The family will receive friends from 2-4 p.m. and 7-9 p.m. Wednesday in the East Chapel. Arrangements are by Chattanooga Funeral Home.
- - Source: Chattanooga Times, Oct. 9, 1991, Page A8

Children of Marion Henry Delaney and Imogene May Clark are:

    i. Marion Richard Delaney, born Oct 27, 1942 in Chattanooga, Hamilton, Tennessee, died Sep 05, 2006 in Centre, Cherokee, Alabama.
Notes for Marion Richard Delaney:

CENTRE - - Jeffrey Dean Boyar, 63, passed away Tuesday, Sept. 5, 2006, at a local Centre hospital. Survivors include his wife, Brenda Boyar; his stepson Howard Duke; Howard's fiance, Tracey Wozniak; and Brenda's mother Margaret French; one sister, Paula Cope, of Cincinnati; and a brother, John Standridge, of Chattanooga.

Jeff was a longtime resident of Centre, where he was well known as "J.B." and for his DJ and karaoke performances. Jeff was well known also for his kind and generous nature and his ready sense of humor.

Memorial services will be held at Clear View Worship Center at a date to be determined with Paul Clark presiding. Perry Funeral Home, directing.

36. ii. Mary Elizabeth Delaney, born Sep 18, 1947 in Chattanooga, Hamilton, Tennessee, died Oct 25, 2006 in Sevier, Tennessee.
37. iii. Jerri Wayne Delaney, born Private.

APPENDIX D – *Genealogy* 299

32. Charles Whitney Delaney (Floyd C Delaney-4, William Henry Delaney-3, Robert H Delaney-2, Abraham Delaney-1) married Barbara Ann Osmundson.

    Child of Charles Whitney Delaney and Barbara Ann Osmundson is:
    i. Holly Christine Delaney, born Private.

33. Edna Earle Boyd (Helen Gertrude Delaney-4, William Henry Delaney-3, Robert H Delaney-2, Abraham Delaney-1) was born on Mar 23, 1938. She died on Nov 01, 1988 in California. She married William Timothy Bartlett. He also died in California.

    Children of Edna Earle Boyd and William Timothy Bartlett are:
    38. i. Jeffrey Dean Bartlett, born Private.
        Russell Bartlett, born Private.
        Kenneth R. Bartlett, born Private.

## Generation 6

34. Glenda Sharon Osborne (Emma Gene Delaney-5, Ralph Herman Delaney-4, William Henry Delaney-3, Robert H Delaney-2, Abraham Delaney-1) married Gary Delano Blevins on Oct 23, 1969. He was born on Jun 06, 1937, in Walker County, Georgia and died on Feb 27, 2008, in Lookout Mountain, Walker, Georgia.

    Child of Glenda Sharon Osborne and Gary Delano Blevins is:
    i. Gary Preston Blevins, born Private.

35. Renee Blackburn (Anna Lee Delaney-5, Ralph Herman Delaney-4, William Henry Delaney-3, Robert H Delaney-2, Abraham Delaney-1) married Robert Jeffrey Rogers on Oct 14, 1972.

    Children of Renee Blackburn and Robert Jeffrey Rogers are:
    i. Robert Carlton Rogers, born Private.
    ii. Kristopher Ike Rogers, born Private.

36. Mary Elizabeth Delaney (Marion Henry Delaney-5, Ralph Herman Delaney-4, William Henry Delaney-3, Robert H Delaney-2, Abraham Delaney-1)[77] was born on Sep 18, 1947 in Chattanooga, Hamilton, Tennessee, and died on Oct 25, 2006 in Pigeon Forge, Sevier, Tennessee. She married Jack Dempsey Fortney Jr. on Apr 01, 1967 in Las Vegas, Clark, Nevada. He was born on Jul 22, 1943 in Berea, Madison, Kentucky. He died on Dec 14, 1986 in Dayton, Greene, Ohio. She later married Larry Cope.

    Notes for Mary Elizabeth Delaney:
    From The Cincinnati Enquirer, October 27, 2006:
    Paula A. Cope (nee Crippen), beloved wife of Larry E. Cope; devoted mother of Betha A. (Paul) Bollman and the late James Fortney; dear sister of John (Lynna Ruth) Standridge, Craig (Cheryl) Crippen, and the late Jeffrey (Brenda) Boyar; loving grandmother of Jacob, Benjamin, and Mary

Bollman, also survived by 13 step-grandchildren and 1 great-grandchild. Oct. 25, 2006. Age 59 years. Residence Anderson Twp. Service at T. P. White & Sons Funeral Home, 2050 Beechmont Ave., Mt. Washington on Sat. Oct. 28, at 1 PM. Friends may visit on Sat. from 12-1 PM. Memorials to American Heart Association. Paula worked for Anthem Blue Cross for 33 years and was a proud member of the Red Hat Society.

Children of Mary Elizabeth Delaney and Jack Dempsey Fortney Jr. are:

39.   i.  Beth Andrea Fortney, born Private.
      ii.  James Dana Fortney, born Dec 15, 1969 in Xenia, Greene, Ohio, died Jul 13, 1987 in Dayton, Greene, Ohio.

37.  Jerri Wayne Delaney (Marion Henry Delaney-5, Ralph Herman Delaney-4, William Henry Delaney-3, Robert H Delaney-2, Abraham Delaney-1) was born in Chattanooga, Hamilton, Tennessee. He married Lynna Ruth Webb on Mar 28, 1970 in Knoxville, Knox, Tennessee.

Children of Jerri Wayne Delaney and Lynna Ruth Webb are:

40.   i.  Adam Brendle Standridge, born Private
      ii.  Aaron Gabriel Standridge, born Private

38.  Jeffrey Dean Bartlett (Edna Earle Boyd-5, Helen Gertrude Delaney-4, William Henry Delaney-3, Robert H Delaney-2, Abraham Delaney-1) married Marian Miller on Jul 31, 1982.

Child of Jeffrey Dean Bartlett and Marian Miller is:

      i.  Sarah Helen Bartlett, born Private.

---

## Generation 7

39.  Beth Andrea Fortney (Mary Elizabeth Delaney-6, Marion Henry Delaney-5, Ralph Herman Delaney-4, William Henry Delaney-3, Robert H Delaney-2, Abraham Delaney-1)[78] was born in Los Angeles, California, and married Paul Daniel Bollman on Sep 01, 1990 in Cincinnati, Clermont, Ohio.

Children of Beth Andrea Fortney and Paul Daniel Bollman are:

    i.    155.    Jacob Daniel Bollman, born Private.
    ii.   156.    Benjamin Paul Bollman, born Private.
    iii.  157.    Mary Josephine Bollman, born Private.

40.  Adam Brendle Standridge (Jerri Wayne Delaney-6, Marion Henry Delaney-5, Ralph Herman Delaney-4, William Henry Delaney-3, Robert H Delaney-2, Abraham Delaney-1) was born in Knox County, Tennessee. He married Betty Jane Tittle from Sullivan County, Tennessee.

Children of Adam Brendle Standridge and Betty Jane Tittle are:

    i.    158.    Addison Brendle Standridge, born Private.
    ii.   159.    Arianna Elizabeth Standridge, born Private.

APPENDIX D – *Genealogy*

## Descendants of Abraham Delaney

### Sources

1. Ancestry.com, 1860 United States Federal Census (Online publication - Provo, UT, USA: The Generations Network, Inc., 2004.Original data - United States of America, Bureau of the Census. Eighth Census of the United States, 1860. Washington, D.C.: National Archives and Records Administration, 1860. M653, 1), Year: 1860; Census Place: District 7, Roane, Tennessee; Roll: M653_1269; Page: 167; Image: 341. Birth date: abt 1815Birth place: Ohio Residence date: 1860Residence place: District 7, Roane, Tennessee.

2. Ancestry.com, 1870 United States Federal Census (Online publication - Provo, UT, USA: The Generations Network, Inc., 2003.Original data - 1870. United States. Ninth Census of the United States, 1870. Washington, D.C. National Archives and Records Administration. M593, RG29, 1, 761 rolls. Minnesota. Minnes), Year: 1870; Census Place: , ; Roll: M593. Birth date: abt 1815 Birth place: Residence date: 1870Residence place: District 3 Subdivision 13, Hamilton, Tennessee.

3. Ancestry.com and The Church of Jesus Christ of Latter-day Saints, 1880 United States Federal Census (Online publication - Provo, UT, USA: The Generations Network, Inc., 2005. 1880 U.S. Census Index provided by The Church of Jesus Christ of Latter-day Saints © Copyright 1999 Intellectual Reserve, Inc. All rights reserved. All use is subject to the limite), Year: 1880; Census Place: District 11, Roane, Tennessee; Roll: T9_1275; Family History Film: 1255275; Page: 342.1000; Enumeration District: 225; Image:. Birth date: abt 1813Birth place: Kentucky Residence date: 1880Residence place: District 11, Roane, Tennessee, United States.

4. Ancestry Family Trees (Online publication - Provo, UT, USA: The Generations Network. Original data: Family Tree files submitted by Ancestry members.), Ancestry Family Trees. http://trees.ancestry.com/pt/AMTCitationRedir.aspx ?tid=10817194&pid=-564630222.

5. Ancestry.com, 1920 United States Federal Census (Online publication - Provo, UT, USA: The Generations Network, Inc., 2005. For details on the contents of the film numbers, visit the following NARA web page: NARA. Note: Enumeration Districts 819-839 on roll 323 (Chicago City.Original data - United States), Year: 1920; Census Place: Civil District 10, Knox, Tennessee; Roll: T625_1750; Page: 8A; Enumeration District: 132; Image: 931. Birth date: abt 1842Birth place: Tennessee Residence date: 1920 Residence place: Civil District 10, Knox, Tennessee.

6. Ancestry.com, 1920 United States Federal Census (Online publication - Provo, UT, USA: The Generations Network, Inc., 2005. For details on the contents of the film numbers, visit the following NARA web page: NARA. Note: Enumeration Districts 819-839 on roll 323 (Chicago City.Original data - United States), Year: 1920; Census Place: Civil District 1, Roane, Tennessee; Roll: T625_1760; Page: 11B; Enumeration District: 156; Image: 645. Birth date: abt 1839Birth place: Tennessee Residence date: 1920Residence place: Civil District 1, Roane, Tennessee.

7. Ancestry.com, 1910 United States Federal Census (Online publication - Provo, UT, USA: The Generations Network, Inc., 2006. For details on the contents of the film numbers, visit the following NARA web page: NARA. Original data - United States of America, Bureau of the Census. Thirteenth Census of the Unit), Year: 1910; Census Place: Civil District 1, Roane, Tennessee; Roll: T624_1517; Page: 15A; Enumeration District: 144; Image: 31. Birth date: abt 1839Birth place: Tennessee Residence date: 1910Residence place: Civil District 1, Roane, Tennessee.

8. Ancestry.com, 1900 United States Federal Census (Online publication - Provo, UT, USA: The Generations Network, Inc., 2004.Original data - United States of America, Bureau of the Census. Twelfth Census of the United States, 1900. Washington, D.C.: National Archives and Records Administration, 1900. T623, ), Year: 1900; Census Place: Civil District 5, Roane, Tennessee; Roll: ; Page: ; Enumeration District:. Birth date: Nov 1838Birth place: Tennessee Marriage date: 1860 Marriage place: Residence date: 1900 Residence place: Kingston Town, Roane, Tennessee.

9. Ancestry.com and The Church of Jesus Christ of Latter-day Saints, 1880 United States Federal Census (Online publication - Provo, UT, USA: The Generations Network, Inc., 2005. 1880 U.S. Census Index provided by The Church of Jesus Christ of Latter-day Saints © Copyright 1999 Intellectual Reserve, Inc. All rights reserved. All use is subject to the limite), Year: 1880; Census Place: District 17, Roane, Tennessee; Roll: T9_1275; Family History Film: 1255275; Page: 309.1000; Enumeration District: 223; Image:. Birth date: abt 1844 Birth place: Tennessee Residence date: 1880 Residence place: District 17, Roane, Tennessee, United States.

10. Ancestry.com, 1900 United States Federal Census (Online publication - Provo, UT, USA: The Generations Network, Inc., 2004.Original data - United States of America, Bureau of the Census. Twelfth Census of the United States, 1900. Washington, D.C.: National Archives and Records Administration, 1900. T623, ), Year: 1900; Census Place: Civil District 17, Hamilton, Tennessee; Roll: ; Page: ; Enumeration District:. Birth date: Dec 1843Birth place: Tennessee Marriage date: 1865 Marriage place: Residence date: 1900 Residence place: Civil Districts 17, 20, Hamilton, Tennessee.

11. Ancestry.com, 1930 United States Federal Census (Online publication - Provo, UT, USA: The Generations Network, Inc., 2002.Original data - United States of America, Bureau of the Census. Fifteenth Census of the United States, 1930. Washington, D.C.: National Archives and Records Administration, 1930. T626), Year: 1930; Census Place: Rockwood, Roane, Tennessee; Roll: 2269; Page: 3B; Enumeration District: 14; Image: 976.0. Birth date: abt 1846 Birth place: Tennessee Residence date: 1930 Residence place: Rockwood, Roane, Tennessee.

12. Ancestry.com, 1920 United States Federal Census (Online publication - Provo, UT, USA: The Generations Network, Inc., 2005. For details on the contents of the film numbers, visit the following NARA web page: NARA. Note: Enumeration Districts 819-839 on roll 323 (Chicago City.Original data - United States), Year: 1920; Census Place: Harriman, Roane, Tennessee; Roll: T625_1760; Page: 14A; Enumeration District: 158; Image: 742. Birth date: abt 1846 Birth place: Tennessee Residence date: 1920 Residence place: Harriman, Roane, Tennessee.

APPENDIX D – Genealogy                                              303

13. Ancestry.com, 1910 United States Federal Census (Online publication - Provo, UT, USA: The Generations Network, Inc., 2006. For details on the contents of the film numbers, visit the following NARA web page: NARA. Original data - United States of America, Bureau of the Census. Thirteenth Census of the Unit), Year: 1910; Census Place: Civil District 1, Roane, Tennessee; Roll: T624_1517; Page: 9B; Enumeration District: 144; Image: 20. Birth date: abt 1846 Birth place: Tennessee Residence date: 1910 Residence place: Civil District 1, Roane, Tennessee.

14. Ancestry.com, 1870 United States Federal Census (Online publication - Provo, UT, USA: The Generations Network, Inc., 2003.Original data - 1870. United States. Ninth Census of the United States, 1870. Washington, D.C. National Archives and Records Administration. M593, RG29, 1, 761 rolls. Minnesota. Minnes), Year: 1870; Census Place: , ; Roll: M593. Birth date: abt 1846 Birth place: Tennessee Residence date: 1870 Residence place: District 11, Roane, Tennessee.

15. Ancestry.com, Tennessee State Marriages, 1780-2002 (Online publication - Provo, UT, USA: The Generations Network, Inc., 2008.Original data - Tennessee State Marriages, 1780-2002. Nashville, TN, USA: Tennessee State Library and Archives. Microfilm.Original data: Tennessee State Marriages, 1780-2002. Nashvill), Marriage date: 16 May 1869 Marriage place: Roane Residence date: Residence place: Tennessee.

16. Ancestry.com and The Church of Jesus Christ of Latter-day Saints, 1880 United States Federal Census (Online publication - Provo, UT, USA: The Generations Network, Inc., 2005. 1880 U.S. Census Index provided by The Church of Jesus Christ of Latter-day Saints © Copyright 1999 Intellectual Reserve, Inc. All rights reserved. All use is subject to the limite), Year: 1880; Census Place: District 9, Roane, Tennessee; Roll: T9_1275; Family History Film: 1255275; Page: 335.3000; Enumeration District: 224; Image:. Birth date: abt 1853 Birth place: Tennessee Residence date: 1880 Residence place: District 9, Roane, Tennessee, United States.

17. Ancestry.com, 1920 United States Federal Census (Online publication - Provo, UT, USA: The Generations Network, Inc., 2005. For details on the contents of the film numbers, visit the following NARA web page: NARA. Note: Enumeration Districts 819-839 on roll 323 (Chicago City.Original data - United States), Year: 1920; Census Place: Harriman, Roane, Tennessee; Roll: T625_1760; Page: 14A; Enumeration District: 158; Image: 742. Birth date: abt 1860 Birth place: Tennessee Residence date: 1920 Residence place: Harriman, Roane, Tennessee.

18. Ancestry.com, 1900 United States Federal Census (Online publication - Provo, UT, USA: The Generations Network, Inc., 2004.Original data - United States of America, Bureau of the Census. Twelfth Census of the United States, 1900. Washington, D.C.: National Archives and Records Administration, 1900. T623, ), Year: 1900; Census Place: Civil District 6, Roane, Tennessee; Roll: ; Page: ; Enumeration District:. Birth date: Dec 1859 Birth place: Tennessee Marriage date: 1882 Marriage place: Residence date: 1900 Residence place: Civil Districts 6, 11, Roane, Tennessee.

19. Ancestry.com, 1930 United States Federal Census (Online publication - Provo, UT, USA: The Generations Network, Inc., 2002.Original data - United States of America, Bureau of the Census. Fifteenth Census of the

# The Delaney Kids~ Bought and Paid For

United States, 1930. Washington, D.C.: National Archives and Records Administration, 1930. T626), Year: 1930; Census Place: Harriman, Roane, Tennessee; Roll: 2269; Page: 8B; Enumeration District: 1; Image: 574.0. Birth date: abt 1860 Birth place: Tennessee Residence date: 1930 Residence place: Harriman, Roane, Tennessee.

20. Ancestry.com, 1900 United States Federal Census (Online publication - Provo, UT, USA: The Generations Network, Inc., 2004.Original data - United States of America, Bureau of the Census. Twelfth Census of the United States, 1900. Washington, D.C.: National Archives and Records Administration, 1900. T623, ), Year: 1900; Census Place: Civil District 16, Roane, Tennessee; Roll: ; Page: ; Enumeration District:. Birth date: Mar 1861 Birth place: Tennessee Marriage date: 1886 Marriage place: Residence date: 1900 Residence place: Civil District 16 (Excl. Harriman Town), Roane, Tennessee.

21. Ancestry Family Trees (Online publication - Provo, UT, USA: The Generations Network. Original data: Family Tree files submitted by Ancestry members.), Ancestry Family Trees. http://trees.ancestry.com/pt/AMTCitationRedir.aspx ?tid=10817194&pid=-564628089.

22. National Park Service, U.S. Civil War Soldiers, 1861-1865 (Online publication - Provo, UT, USA: The Generations Network, Inc., 2007.Original data - National Park Service, Civil War Soldiers and Sailors System, online &lt;http://www.itd.nps.gov/cwss/&gt;, acquired 2007.Original data: National Park Service, Civil Wa).

23. National Archives and Records Administration, Civil War Pension Index: General Index to Pension Files, 1861-1934 (Online publication - Provo, UT, USA: The Generations Network, Inc., 2000.Original data - General Index to Pension Files, 1861-1934. Washington, D.C.: National Archives and Records Administration. T288, 544 rolls. Original data: General Index to Pension File).

24. Ancestry Family Trees (Online publication - Provo, UT, USA: The Generations Network. Original data: Family Tree files submitted by Ancestry members.), Ancestry Family Trees. http://trees.ancestry.com/pt/AMTCitationRedir.aspx ?tid=10817194&pid=-573222888.

25. Ancestry.com, 1900 United States Federal Census (Online publication - Provo, UT, USA: The Generations Network, Inc., 2004.Original data - United States of America, Bureau of the Census. Twelfth Census of the United States, 1900. Washington, D.C.: National Archives and Records Administration, 1900. T623, ), Year: 1900; Census Place: Civil District 17, Hamilton, Tennessee; Roll: ; Page: ; Enumeration District:. Birth date: Nov 1851 Birth place: Marriage date: 1865 Marriage place: Residence date: 1900 Residence place: Civil Districts 17, 20, Hamilton, Tennessee.

26. Ancestry.com, 1930 United States Federal Census (Online publication - Provo, UT, USA: The Generations Network, Inc., 2002.Original data - United States of America, Bureau of the Census. Fifteenth Census of the United States, 1930. Washington, D.C.: National Archives and Records Administration, 1930. T626), Year: 1930; Census Place: Chattanooga, Hamilton, Tennessee; Roll: 2252; Page: 7A; Enumeration District: 47; Image:

## Appendix D – Genealogy 305

129.0. Birth date: abt 1870 Birth place: Tennessee Residence date: 1930 Residence place: Chattanooga, Hamilton, Tennessee.

27. Ancestry.com, 1910 United States Federal Census (Online publication - Provo, UT, USA: The Generations Network, Inc., 2006. For details on the contents of the film numbers, visit the following NARA web page: NARA. Original data - United States of America, Bureau of the Census. Thirteenth Census of the Unit), Year: 1910; Census Place: Civil District 4, Hamilton, Tennessee; Roll: T624_1501; Page: 16A; Enumeration District: 85; Image: 1360. Birth date: abt 1870 Birth place: Tennessee Residence date: 1910 Residence place: Civil District 4, Hamilton, Tennessee. Ancestry.com and The Church of Jesus Christ of Latter-day Saints, 1880 United States Federal Census (Online publication - Provo, UT, USA: The Generations Network, Inc., 2005. 1880 U.S. Census Index provided by The Church of Jesus Christ of Latter-day Saints © Copyright 1999 Intellectual Reserve, Inc. All rights reserved. All use is subject to the limite), Year: 1880; Census Place: District 17, Roane, Tennessee; Roll: T9_1275; Family History Film: 1255275; Page: 309.1000; Enumeration District: 223; Image:. Birth date: abt 1870 Birth place: Tennessee Residence date: 1880 Residence place: District 17, Roane, Tennessee, United States.

28. Ancestry.com, Tennessee State Marriages, 1780-2002 (Online publication - Provo, UT, USA: The Generations Network, Inc., 2008.Original data - Tennessee State Marriages, 1780-2002. Nashville, TN, USA: Tennessee State Library and Archives. Microfilm. Original data: Tennessee State Marriages, 1780-2002. Nashville), Marriage date: 25 Jul 1891 Marriage place: Roane Residence date: Residence place: Tennessee.

29. Ancestry.com, 1900 United States Federal Census (Online publication - Provo, UT, USA: The Generations Network, Inc., 2004.Original data - United States of America, Bureau of the Census. Twelfth Census of the United States, 1900. Washington, D.C.: National Archives and Records Administration, 1900. T623, ), Year: 1900; Census Place: Civil District 3, Hamilton, Tennessee; Roll: ; Page: ; Enumeration District:. Birth date: Feb 1871 Birth place: Tennessee Marriage date: 1899 Marriage place: Residence date: 1900 Residence place: Civil District 3, Hamilton, Tennessee.

30. Ancestry.com, 1930 United States Federal Census (Online publication - Provo, UT, USA: The Generations Network, Inc., 2002.Original data - United States of America, Bureau of the Census. Fifteenth Census of the United States, 1930. Washington, D.C.: National Archives and Records Administration, 1930. T626), Year: 1930; Census Place: Chattanooga, Hamilton, Tennessee; Roll: 2252; Page: 13B; Enumeration District: 64; Image: 820.0. Birth date: abt 1872 Birth place: Tennessee Residence date: 1930 Residence place: Chattanooga, Hamilton, Tennessee.

31. Ancestry.com, 1910 United States Federal Census (Online publication - Provo, UT, USA: The Generations Network, Inc., 2006. For details on the contents of the film numbers, visit the following NARA web page: NARA. Original data - United States of America, Bureau of the Census. Thirteenth Census of the Unit), Year: 1910; Census Place: Civil District 4, Hamilton, Tennessee; Roll: T624_1501; Page: 24B; Enumeration District: 85; Image: 1377. Birth date: abt 1881 Birth place: Tennessee Residence date: 1910 Residence place: Civil District 4, Hamilton, Tennessee.

32. Ancestry.com, 1910 United States Federal Census (Online publication - Provo, UT, USA: The Generations Network, Inc., 2006. For details on the contents of the film numbers, visit the following NARA web page: NARA. Original data - United States of America, Bureau of the Census. Thirteenth Census of the Unit), Year: 1910; Census Place: Civil District 4, Hamilton, Tennessee; Roll: T624_1501; Page: 24B; Enumeration District: 85; Image: 1377. Birth date: abt 1886 Birth place: Tennessee Residence date: 1910 Residence place: Civil District 4, Hamilton, Tennessee.

33. Ancestry.com, Kentucky Death Records, 1852-1953 (Online publication - Provo, UT, USA: The Generations Network, Inc., 2007.Original data - Kentucky. Kentucky Birth, Marriage and Death Records - Microfilm (1852-1910). Microfilm rolls #994027-994058. Kentucky Department for Libraries and Archives, Frankfort), Birth date: 22 Mar 1888 Birth place: Rockwood, Tennessee Death date: 14 Jun 1948 Death place: Jefferson, Kentucky Residence date: Residence place: Kentucky.

34. Ancestry.com, 1910 United States Federal Census (Online publication - Provo, UT, USA: The Generations Network, Inc., 2006. For details on the contents of the film numbers, visit the following NARA web page: NARA. Original data - United States of America, Bureau of the Census. Thirteenth Census of the Unit), Year: 1910; Census Place: Civil District 4, Hamilton, Tennessee; Roll: T624_1501; Page: 25A; Enumeration District: 85; Image: 1378. Birth date: abt 1888 Birth place: Tennessee Residence date: 1910 Residence place: Civil District 4, Hamilton, Tennessee.

35. Ancestry Family Trees (Online publication - Provo, UT, USA: The Generations Network. Original data: Family Tree files submitted by Ancestry members.), Ancestry Family Trees. http://trees.ancestry.com/pt/AMTCitationRedir.aspx ?tid=10817194&pid=-564627443.

36. Ancestry.com, 1890 Veterans Schedules (Online publication - Provo, UT, USA: The Generations Network, Inc., 2005.Original data - United States of America, Bureau of the Census. Special Schedules of the Eleventh Census (1890) Enumerating Union Veterans and Widows of Union Veterans of the Civil War), Year: 1890; Census Place: Districts 6 and 11, Roane, Tennessee; Roll: 95; Page: 2; Enumeration District: 205. Residence date: June 1890 Residence place: Roane, Tennessee, United States.

37. Ancestry Family Trees (Online publication - Provo, UT, USA: The Generations Network. Original data: Family Tree files submitted by Ancestry members.), Ancestry Family Trees. http://trees.ancestry.com/pt/AMTCitationRedir.aspx ?tid=10817194&pid=-564626852.

38. Ancestry Family Trees (Online publication - Provo, UT, USA: The Generations Network. Original data: Family Tree files submitted by Ancestry members.), Ancestry Family Trees. http://trees.ancestry.com/pt/AMTCitationRedir.aspx ?tid=10817194&pid=-564626466.

39. Ancestry Family Trees (Online publication - Provo, UT, USA: The Generations Network. Original data: Family Tree files submitted by Ancestry members.), Ancestry Family Trees. http://trees.ancestry.com/pt/AMTCitationRedir.aspx ?tid=10817194&pid=-564626132.

40. Ancestry Family Trees (Online publication - Provo, UT, USA: The Generations Network. Original data: Family Tree files submitted by Ancestry members.),

# Appendix D – Genealogy

Ancestry Family Trees. http://trees.ancestry.com/pt/AMTCitationRedir.aspx ?tid=10817194&pid=-564624715.

41. Ancestry.com, 1910 United States Federal Census (Online publication - Provo, UT, USA: The Generations Network, Inc., 2006. For details on the contents of the film numbers, visit the following NARA web page: NARA. Original data - United States of America, Bureau of the Census. Thirteenth Census of the Unit), Year: 1910; Census Place: Civil District 1, Roane, Tennessee; Roll: T624_1517; Page: 14B; Enumeration District: 144; Image: 30. Birth date: abt 1893 Birth place: Tennessee Residence date: 1910 Residence place: Civil District 1, Roane, Tennessee.

42. Ancestry.com, 1930 United States Federal Census (Online publication - Provo, UT, USA: The Generations Network, Inc., 2002.Original data - United States of America, Bureau of the Census. Fifteenth Census of the United States, 1930. Washington, D.C.: National Archives and Records Administration, 1930. T626), Year: 1930; Census Place: Harriman, Roane, Tennessee; Roll: 2269; Page: 8B; Enumeration District: 1; Image: 574.0. Birth date: abt 1893 Birth place: Residence date: 1930 Residence place: Harriman, Roane, Tennessee.

43. Ancestry.com, Social Security Death Index (Online publication - Provo, UT, USA: The Generations Network, Inc., 2009.Original data - Social Security Administration. Social Security Death Index, Master File. Social Security Administration.Original data: Social Security Administration. Social Security), Number: 412-08-3525; Issue State: Tennessee; Issue Date: 1973. Birth date: 9 May 1892 Birth place: Death date: Jan 1982 Death place: Knoxville, Knox, Tennessee, United States of America.

44. Ancestry Family Trees (Online publication - Provo, UT, USA: The Generations Network. Original data: Family Tree files submitted by Ancestry members.), Ancestry Family Trees. http://trees.ancestry.com/pt/AMTCitationRedir.aspx ?tid=10817194&pid=-573231009.

45. Ancestry.com, 1900 United States Federal Census (Online publication - Provo, UT, USA: The Generations Network, Inc., 2004.Original data - United States of America, Bureau of the Census. Twelfth Census of the United States, 1900. Washington, D.C.: National Archives and Records Administration, 1900. T623, ), Year: 1900; Census Place: Civil District 3, Hamilton, Tennessee; Roll: ; Page: ; Enumeration District:. Birth date: May 1875 Birth place: Tennessee Marriage date: 1891 Marriage place: Residence date: 1900 Residence place: Civil District 3, Hamilton, Tennessee.

46. Ancestry.com and The Church of Jesus Christ of Latter-day Saints, 1880 United States Federal Census (Online publication - Provo, UT, USA: The Generations Network, Inc., 2005. 1880 U.S. Census Index provided by The Church of Jesus Christ of Latter-day Saints © Copyright 1999 Intellectual Reserve, Inc. All rights reserved. All use is subject to the limite), Year: 1880; Census Place: District 12, Roane, Tennessee; Roll: T9_1275; Family History Film: 1255275; Page: 364.3000; Enumeration District: 226; Image:. Birth date: abt 1875 Birth place: Tennessee Residence date: 1880 Residence place: District 12, Roane, Tennessee, United States.

47. Ancestry.com, 1910 United States Federal Census (Online publication - Provo, UT, USA: The Generations Network, Inc., 2006. For details on the

## The Delaney Kids~ Bought and Paid For

contents of the film numbers, visit the following NARA web page: NARA. Original data - United States of America, Bureau of the Census. Thirteenth Census of the Unit), Year: 1910; Census Place: Civil District 4, Hamilton, Tennessee; Roll: T624_1501; Page: 16A; Enumeration District: 85; Image: 1360. Birth date: abt 1874 Birth place: Tennessee Residence date: 1910 Residence place: Civil District 4, Hamilton, Tennessee.

48. Ancestry.com, Social Security Death Index (Provo, UT, USA, The Generations Network, Inc., 2009), www.ancestry.com, Database online. Record for Mollie Delaney.

49. Ancestry.com, 1920 United States Federal Census (Online publication - Provo, UT, USA: The Generations Network, Inc., 2005. For details on the contents of the film numbers, visit the following NARA web page: NARA. Note: Enumeration Districts 819-839 on roll 323 (Chicago City.Original data - United States), Year: 1920; Census Place: Rossville, Walker, Georgia; Roll: T625_281; Page: 3A; Enumeration District: 188; Image: 534. Birth date: abt 1893 Birth place: Tennessee Residence date: 1920 Residence place: Rossville, Walker, Georgia.

50. Ancestry.com, World War I Draft Registration Cards, 1917-1918 (Provo, UT, USA, The Generations Network, Inc., 2005), www.ancestry.com, Database online. Roll 1852926, DraftBoard 2. Record for John Franklin Delaney.

51. Ancestry.com, 1920 United States Federal Census (Online publication - Provo, UT, USA: The Generations Network, Inc., 2005. For details on the contents of the film numbers, visit the following NARA web page: NARA. Note: Enumeration Districts 819-839 on roll 323 (Chicago City.Original data - United States), Year: 1920; Census Place: Civil District 3, Hamilton, Tennessee; Roll: T625_1744; Page: 2A; Enumeration District: 235; Image: 451. Birth date: abt 1899 Birth place: Tennessee Residence date: 1920 Residence place: Civil District 3, Hamilton, Tennessee.

52. Ancestry.com, 1930 United States Federal Census (Online publication - Provo, UT, USA: The Generations Network, Inc., 2002.Original data - United States of America, Bureau of the Census. Fifteenth Census of the United States, 1930. Washington, D.C.: National Archives and Records Administration, 1930. T626), Year: 1930; Census Place: District 3, Hamilton, Tennessee; Roll: 2253; Page: 16A; Enumeration District: 80; Image: 380.0. Birth date: abt 1899 Birth place: Tennessee Residence date: 1930 Residence place: District 3, Hamilton, Tennessee.

53. Ancestry.com, 1920 United States Federal Census (Online publication - Provo, UT, USA: The Generations Network, Inc., 2005. For details on the contents of the film numbers, visit the following NARA web page: NARA. Note: Enumeration Districts 819-839 on roll 323 (Chicago City.Original data - United States), Year: 1920; Census Place: Petros, Morgan, Tennessee; Roll: T625_1758; Page: 8A; Enumeration District: 48; Image: 53. Birth date: abt 1899 Birth place: Tennessee Residence date: 1920 Residence place: Petros, Morgan, Tennessee.

54. Ancestry.com, 1910 United States Federal Census (Online publication - Provo, UT, USA: The Generations Network, Inc., 2006. For details on the contents of the film numbers, visit the following NARA web page: NARA. Original data - United States of America, Bureau of the Census. Thirteenth

# APPENDIX D – Genealogy 309

Census of the Unit), Year: 1910; Census Place: Civil District 4, Hamilton, Tennessee; Roll: T624_1501; Page: 16A; Enumeration District: 85; Image: 1360. Birth date: abt 1898 Birth place: Tennessee Residence date: 1910 Residence place: Civil District 4, Hamilton, Tennessee.

55. Ancestry.com, 1900 United States Federal Census (Online publication - Provo, UT, USA: The Generations Network, Inc., 2004.Original data - United States of America, Bureau of the Census. Twelfth Census of the United States, 1900. Washington, D.C.: National Archives and Records Administration, 1900. T623, ), Year: 1900; Census Place: Civil District 3, Hamilton, Tennessee; Roll: ; Page: ; Enumeration District:. Birth date: Oct 1897 Birth place: Tennessee Residence date: 1900 Residence place: Civil District 3, Hamilton, Tennessee.

56. Ancestry.com, 1930 United States Federal Census (Online publication - Provo, UT, USA: The Generations Network, Inc., 2002.Original data - United States of America, Bureau of the Census. Fifteenth Census of the United States, 1930. Washington, D.C.: National Archives and Records Administration, 1930. T626), Year: 1930; Census Place: Chattanooga, Hamilton, Tennessee; Roll: 2251; Page: 11B; Enumeration District: 29; Image: 455.0. Birth date: abt 1902 Birth place: Tennessee Residence date: 1930 Residence place: Chattanooga, Hamilton, Tennessee.

57. Ancestry.com, 1910 United States Federal Census (Online publication - Provo, UT, USA: The Generations Network, Inc., 2006. For details on the contents of the film numbers, visit the following NARA web page: NARA. Original data - United States of America, Bureau of the Census. Thirteenth Census of the Unit), Year: 1910; Census Place: Civil District 4, Hamilton, Tennessee; Roll: T624_1501; Page: 16A; Enumeration District: 85; Image: 1360. Birth date: abt 1901 Birth place: Tennessee Residence date: 1910 Residence place: Civil District 4, Hamilton, Tennessee.

58. Ancestry.com, 1910 United States Federal Census (Online publication - Provo, UT, USA: The Generations Network, Inc., 2006. For details on the contents of the film numbers, visit the following NARA web page: NARA. Original data - United States of America, Bureau of the Census. Thirteenth Census of the Unit), Year: 1910; Census Place: Civil District 4, Hamilton, Tennessee; Roll: T624_1501; Page: 16A; Enumeration District: 85; Image: 1360. Birth date: abt 1903 Birth place: Tennessee Residence date: 1910 Residence place: Civil District 4, Hamilton, Tennessee.

59. Ancestry.com, 1910 United States Federal Census (Online publication - Provo, UT, USA: The Generations Network, Inc., 2006. For details on the contents of the film numbers, visit the following NARA web page: NARA. Original data - United States of America, Bureau of the Census. Thirteenth Census of the Unit), Year: 1910; Census Place: Civil District 4, Hamilton, Tennessee; Roll: T624_1501; Page: 16A; Enumeration District: 85; Image: 1360. Birth date: abt 1905 Birth place: Tennessee Residence date: 1910 Residence place: Civil District 4, Hamilton, Tennessee.

60. Ancestry.com, Social Security Death Index (Online publication - Provo, UT, USA: The Generations Network, Inc., 2009.Original data - Social Security Administration. Social Security Death Index, Master File. Social Security Administration.Original data: Social Security Administration. Social Security), Number: 253-09-6966; Issue State: Georgia; Issue Date: Before 1951.

Birth date: 1 Feb 1908 Birth place: Death date: 5 Aug 2006 Death place: Chattanooga, Hamilton, Tennessee.

61. Ancestry.com, 1910 United States Federal Census (Online publication - Provo, UT, USA: The Generations Network, Inc., 2006. For details on the contents of the film numbers, visit the following NARA web page: NARA. Original data - United States of America, Bureau of the Census. Thirteenth Census of the Unit), Year: 1910; Census Place: Civil District 4, Hamilton, Tennessee; Roll: T624_1501; Page: 16A; Enumeration District: 85; Image: 1360. Birth date: abt 1908 Birth place: Tennessee Residence date: 1910 Residence place: Civil District 4, Hamilton, Tennessee.

62. Ancestry Family Trees (Online publication - Provo, UT, USA: The Generations Network. Original data: Family Tree files submitted by Ancestry members.), Ancestry Family Trees. http://trees.ancestry.com/pt/AMTCitationRedir.aspx?tid=10817194&pid=-564623158.

63. Ancestry Family Trees (Online publication - Provo, UT, USA: The Generations Network. Original data: Family Tree files submitted by Ancestry members.), Ancestry Family Trees. http://trees.ancestry.com/pt/AMTCitationRedir.aspx?tid=10817194&pid=-564619714.

64. Ancestry Family Trees (Online publication - Provo, UT, USA: The Generations Network. Original data: Family Tree files submitted by Ancestry members.), Ancestry Family Trees. http://trees.ancestry.com/pt/AMTCitationRedir.aspx?tid=10817194&pid=-564618629.

65. Ancestry Family Trees (Online publication - Provo, UT, USA: The Generations Network. Original data: Family Tree files submitted by Ancestry members.), Ancestry Family Trees. http://trees.ancestry.com/pt/AMTCitationRedir.aspx?tid=10817194&pid=-492717599.

66. Ancestry.com, Social Security Death Index (Online publication - Provo, UT, USA: The Generations Network, Inc., 2009.Original data - Social Security Administration. Social Security Death Index, Master File. Social Security Administration.Original data: Social Security Administration. Social Security), Number: 409-10-4837; Issue State: Tennessee; Issue Date: Before 1951. Birth date: 8 Aug 1890 Birth place: Death date: Nov 1978Death place: Knoxville, Knox, Tennessee, United States of America.

67. Ancestry.com, Social Security Death Index (Online publication - Provo, UT, USA: The Generations Network, Inc., 2009.Original data - Social Security Administration. Social Security Death Index, Master File. Social Security Administration.Original data: Social Security Administration. Social Security), Number: 413-26-6372; Issue State: Tennessee; Issue Date: Before 1951. Birth date: 12 Apr 1925 Birth place: Death date: 27 May 1995 Death place: Knoxville, Knox, Tennessee, United States of America.

68. Ancestry.com, U.S. World War II Draft Registration Cards, 1942 (Provo, UT, USA, The Generations Network, Inc., 2007), www.ancestry.com, Database online. Record for John Franklin Delaney.

69. Ancestry.com, Social Security Death Index (Online publication - Provo, UT, USA: The Generations Network, Inc., 2009.Original data - Social Security Administration. Social Security Death Index, Master File. Social Security Administration.Original data: Social Security Administration. Social Security),

# APPENDIX D – *Genealogy* 311

Number: 408-08-7948; Issue State: Tennessee; Issue Date: 1973. Birth date: 27 Nov 1896 Birth place: Death date: 4 Nov 1990 Death place: Chattanooga, Hamilton, Tennessee, United States of America.

70. Ancestry Family Trees (Online publication - Provo, UT, USA: The Generations Network. Original data: Family Tree files submitted by Ancestry members.), Ancestry Family Trees. http://trees.ancestry.com/pt/AMTCitationRedir.aspx ?tid=10817194&pid=-573234102.

71. Ancestry.com, Social Security Death Index (Online publication - Provo, UT, USA: The Generations Network, Inc., 2009.Original data - Social Security Administration. Social Security Death Index, Master File. Social Security Administration.Original data: Social Security Administration. Social Security), Number: 253-09-7698; Issue State: Georgia; Issue Date: Before 1951. Birth date: 22 Aug 1901 Birth place: Death date: Oct 1985 Death place: Chattanooga, Hamilton, Tennessee, United States of America.

72. Ancestry.com, Social Security Death Index (Provo, UT, USA, The Generations Network, Inc., 2009), www.ancestry.com, Database online. Record for Elizabeth Delaney.

73. National Cemetery Administration, U.S. Veterans Gravesites, ca.1775-2006 (Provo, UT, USA, The Generations Network, Inc., 2006), www.ancestry.com, Database online. Record for Marion H Delaney.

74. Ancestry.com, Social Security Death Index (Provo, UT, USA, The Generations Network, Inc., 2009), www.ancestry.com, Database online. Record for Marion H. Delaney.

75. Ancestry Family Trees (Online publication - Provo, UT, USA: The Generations Network. Original data: Family Tree files submitted by Ancestry members.), Ancestry Family Trees. http://trees.ancestry.com/pt/AMTCitationRedir.aspx ?tid=10817194&pid=-573236917.

76. Ancestry Family Trees (Online publication - Provo, UT, USA: The Generations Network. Original data: Family Tree files submitted by Ancestry members.), Ancestry Family Trees. http://trees.ancestry.com/pt/AMTCitationRedir.aspx ?tid=10817194&pid=-564557673.

77. Ancestry Family Trees (Online publication - Provo, UT, USA: The Generations Network. Original data: Family Tree files submitted by Ancestry members.), Ancestry Family Trees. http://trees.ancestry.com/pt/AMTCitationRedir.aspx ?tid=10817194&pid=-495009394.

78. Wilson, John. HamiltonCounty Pioneers. Self-Published, 1998. Pages 145-46 and 301-302.

## Descendants of Norris Clark

### Generation 1

2. Norris Clark [1] was born about 1758, probably in North Carolina. He died in Bledsoe, Tennessee. [Note: We have not verified that Norris is the father of Anderson and we do not have his wife's name, nor the names of other children.]

    i. Anderson Clark, born Sep 24, 1801 in Stokes, North Carolina [2, 3, 4], died Nov 01, 1879 in McMinn County, Tennessee [2].

### Generation 2

2. Anderson Clark (Norris Clark-1)[2, 3, 4, 5, 6] was born on Sep 24, 1801 in Stokes, North Carolina [2, 3, 4]. He died of consumption on Nov 01, 1879 in McMinn County, Tennessee [2]. He married Isabell Jones on Sep 01, 1820 in Bledsoe, Tennessee, daughter of Gabriel Jones and Isabella Lyle. She was born on Jun 12, 1800 in Stokes, North Carolina [7], and died on Jan 15, 1886 in McMinn County, Tennessee. They are buried at Clear Spring Cumberland Presbyterian Church Cemetery near Bowater Road.

Children of Anderson Clark and Isabella Jones are:

    i. John Clark, born 1822 in Bledsoe, Tennessee; died Aug 29 at 1864; Camp Morgan War Camp, Indiana, United States.
    ii. William Burton Clark, born 1825 in Bledsoe, Tennessee; died Dec 11, 1888 in Bledsoe, Tennessee.
    iii. Hezekiah R Clark, born 1825 in Tennessee; died Sep 24, 1912 in McMinn County, Tennessee.
    iv. Isabella Clark, born Mar 26, 1826 in Bledsoe, Tennessee; died Nov 19, 1890 in McMinn County, Tennessee.
    v. Anderson Clark, born 1828.
    vi. Andrew Jackson Clark, born Sep 07, 1829 in Bledsoe, Tennessee; died Jun 09, 1908 in McMinn County, Tennessee.
    vii. Dorothy Clark, born 1832 in Bledsoe, Tennessee; died 1860 in Texas.
4.  viii. Gabriel Clark, born 1833 in McMinn County, Tennessee [8, 9, 10, 11, 12]; died 1900 in Oklahoma.
    ix. David Cobb Clark, born Apr 22, 1840 in McMinn County, Tennessee; died Apr 01, 1919 in McMinn County, Tennessee.
    x. Joseph P Clark, born Nov 10, 1841 in McMinn County, Tennessee; died Jan 11, 1905 in McMinn County, Tennessee.
    xi. James Clark, born Nov 10, 1841 in McMinn County, Tennessee; died 1879.
    xii. Mary Elizabeth Clark, born Jan 12, 1846 in McMinn County, Tennessee; died Dec 21, 1918 in McMinn County, Tennessee.

# APPENDIX D – Genealogy

## Generation 3

3. Gabriel Clark (Anderson Clark-2, Norris Clark-1)[8, 9, 10, 11, 12, 13] was born on 1833 in McMinn County, Tennessee [8, 9, 10, 11, 12]. He died about 1900 in Oklahoma. He married Elizabeth M 'Bettie' Swafford on Dec 05, 1855 in McMinn County, Tennessee, daughter of Alfred Annison Swafford and Nancy Ahl. Bettie was born on Mar 09, 1840 in McMinn County, Tennessee [14] and died around 1900 in Oklahoma.

Children of Gabriel Clark and Elizabeth M 'Bettie' Swafford are:

    i. Gabriel Wilfred Clark, born Aug 07, 1864 in Athens, McMinn County, Tennessee; died Mar 22, 1922 in Cleveland, Bradley, Tennessee. David C Clark, born 1867 in Tennessee.
    ii. Mary E Clark, born 1869 in Tennessee.
    iii. John Lenoir Clark, born Apr 02, 1871 in McMinn County, Tennessee [15]; died Aug 23, 1922 in Chattanooga, Hamilton, Tennessee.
    iv. Ellen B Clark, born Sep 1874 in Tennessee.
    v. Timothy Clark, born 1876 in Tennessee.
    vi. Faunt McWorter Clark, born Dec 27, 1877 in Tennessee [16, 17, 18]; died Apr 20, 1958 in Oklahoma City, Canadian, Oklahoma.
    vii. Joseph A Clark, born 1881 in Tennessee.
    viii. Sydney J Clark, born Nov 1883 in Tennessee; died Nov 24, 1916 in Wilson, Atoka, Oklahoma.
    ix. Flora G Clark, born Mar 1894 in Tennessee.

## Generation 4

18. John Lenoir Clark (Gabriel Clark-3, Anderson Clark-2, Norris Clark-1) [15, 19, 20, 21] was born on Apr 02, 1871 in McMinn County, Tennessee [15]. He died on Aug 23, 1922 in Chattanooga, Hamilton, Tennessee. According to social history in adoption record, John Clark died 1922 as a result of a hernia operation. John Clark married Mary Abagale McJunkin on Feb 15, 1896 in McMinn County, Tennessee. Mary Abagale was born on Aug 19, 1881 in Polk, Tennessee[22] and was the daughter of Lafayette Napoleon McJunkin and Amanda Womble. She died on Jan 23, 1967 in Chattanooga, Hamilton, Tennessee [23].

Lafayette Napoleon McJunkin, known as 'Nap' or 'Poley', was born in 1858 in Polk County, Tennessee, to Daniel McJunkin and his wife Lydia (last name unknown) from South Carolina. Daniel was the son of John and Susan (last name unknown) McJunkin. Nap McJunkin was minister in Bradley County, Tennessee, and a factory worker in Chattanooga. Amanda was the daughter of Perry Womble and Martha White of Polk County, Tennessee. Martha's parents were Elisha White and Ersby or Ustley Cloud of McMinn County, Tennessee. Amanda Womble McJunkin died young around 1900-1903, after which Nap married Josie Barefield. We can find Nap through the 1920 census in either Polk, Bradley or Hamilton County, but not the 1930 census. Likewise, we are unable to find a death record for him.

Notes for John Lenoir Clark:
1930 Census, Whitfield County, GA; 69 Selvidge St., Dalton, GA

*The Delaney Kids~ Bought and Paid For*

```
32  36  Clark   Mary      Age 47   Widowed        NC / TN / TN
                Willie       26    OK / TN / NC   Knitter, Hosiery Mill
                Hazel        15    TN / TN / NC   Pairer, Hosiery Mill
                Gladys       12    TN / TN / NC
                Imogene       8    TN / TN / NC
1920 Census, Walker County GA: 1102 Spruce St., Rossville
215 255 Clark   John L    Age 40   TN / TN / TN   Cobbler, Shoe Shop
                Mary A       38    TN / TN / TN
                Lizzie M     17    OK / TN / TN
                William J    15    OK / TN / TN
                Annie M      10    TN / OK / TN
                Oda G         8    TN / OK / TN
                Hazel R       5    TN / OK / TN
                Gladys M   2 6/12  TN / OK / TN
```
We are unable to locate them in 1900 or 1910 censuses. They may have resided in Oklahoma

Notes for Mary Abagale McJunkin: Chattanooga Times, Tuesday, January 24, 1967
CLARK - - Mrs. Mary M., 85, of 2459 6th Ave., died Monday morning in a local hospital. Mrs. Clark was the daughter of the late Rev. L. N. and Amanda Womble McJunkin. She was a member of the East 26th Street Baptist Church and her husband was the late John L. Clark. Mrs. Clark is survived by seven daughters, Mrs. Elizabeth Davis, Mrs. Anna Moore, Mrs. John D. Moore, Mrs. Ronald Aslinger, Chattanooga, Mrs. Maggie Melton, Rossville, Mrs. Oda Williams, Knoxville, Tenn.; Mrs. Herman Davis, Morristown, Tenn.; son, W. J. Clark, Gadsden, Ala.; sister, Mrs. John Minyard, Gadsden, Ala.; 20 grandchildren; 20 great-grandchildren; one great-great-grandchild. Funeral services will be held at 1 p.m., Wednesday, in the East Chapel of the Chattanooga Funeral Home, with Rev. Scotty Thomas and Rev. Billy Dean officiating. Interment will be in Forest Hills. Pallbearers will be the grandsons. The body is at the Chattanooga Funeral Home, East Chapel.

Children of John Lenoir Clark and Mary Abagale McJunkin are:

Cordia Clark, born Dec 12, 1896 and died Jul 06, 1898 in Oklahoma.

James Ransome Clark, born Sep 25, 1898 and died Aug 02, 1899 in Oklahoma.

Maggie Henrietta Clark, born Apr 03, 1900 in Oklahoma[24]; died Oct 1992 in Chattanooga, Hamilton, Tennessee[24].

Elizabeth Melvina Clark, born Feb 05, 1902 in Oklahoma[25]; died Jul 1984 in Chattanooga, Hamilton, Tennessee[25]. According to the social history in adoption record, Elizabeth spent time in Silverdale mental institution as a "result of menopause".

5. v. William Joseph "Bill" Clark, born Feb 29, 1904 in Oklahoma[26]; died Nov 12, 1973 in Gadsden, Etowah, Alabama[26].

vi. Callie Mervina Clark, born Nov 17, 1907 in Tennessee; died Sep 25, 1910 in Tennessee.

6. vii. Anna Myrtle Clark, born Dec 31, 1910 in Chattanooga, Hamilton, Tennessee.

APPENDIX D – *Genealogy* 315

    viii. Glennie Oda Clark, born Dec 14, 1911 in Chattanooga, Hamilton, Tennessee.
    ix. Hazel Ruth Clark, born Apr 28, 1914 in Chattanooga, Hamilton, Tennessee.
    x. Gladys Mildred Clark, born Jul 21, 1917 in Chattanooga, Hamilton, Tennessee; died Mar 01, 1990 in Morristown, Hamblen, Tennessee.
    xi. Grant Everette Clark, born Jun 18, 1919 in Chattanooga, Hamilton, Tennessee; died 1919 in Chattanooga, Hamilton, Tennessee.
7.  xii. Imogene May Clark, born Feb 19, 1922 in Chattanooga, Hamilton, Tennessee; died Aug 21, 2009 in Chattanooga, Hamilton, Tennessee.

## Generation 5

5. William Joseph "Bill" Clark (John Lenoir Clark-4, Gabriel Clark-3, Anderson Clark-2, Norris Clark-1) was born on Feb 29, 1904 in Oklahoma [26]. He died on Nov 12, 1973 in Gadsden, Etowah, Alabama [26]. He married Lorine Jones on Jun 30, 1972 in Gadsden, Etowah, Alabama. He married Maudina Elizabeth Harris on Dec 29, 1929 in Rossville, Walker, Georgia. She was born on Apr 08, 1907 in Etowah, McMinn County, Tennessee. She died on May 31, 1971 in Gadsden, Etowah, Alabama. He married Maudina Elizabeth Harris on Dec 29, 1929 in Rossville, Walker, Georgia. She was born on Apr 08, 1907 in Etowah, McMinn County, Tennessee. She died on May 31, 1971 in Gadsden, Etowah, Alabama. Bill worked in an Alabama City, Alabama, steel plant in the 1940's.

Children of William Joseph "Bill" Clark and Maudina Elizabeth Harris are:

    i. Willie Juanita CLARK, born Sep 12, 1933 in Chattanooga, Hamilton, Tennessee; died Jun 30, 2000 in Gadsden, Etowah, Alabama.
    ii. Carolyn Dorothy Clark, born 1936 in Chattanooga, Hamilton, Tennessee; died Jul 20, 1936 in Chattanooga, Hamilton, Tennessee.

6. Anna Myrtle Clark (John Lenoir Clark-4, Gabriel Clark-3, Anderson Clark-2, Norris Clark-1)[27] was born on Dec 31, 1910 in Chattanooga, Hamilton, Tennessee. She married William Leroy Moore. He was born on Aug 15, 1908 in Texas. He died on Mar 28, 1988 in Hamilton, Tennessee.

Children of Anna Myrtle Clark and William Leroy Moore are:

    i. Barbara Jean Moore marred a Spain
    ii. Colleen Moore married a Chauncey
    iii. Karen Moore married a Hooper
    iv. Gary Eugene Moore

7. Imogene May Clark (John Lenoir Clark-4, Gabriel Clark-3, Anderson Clark-2, Norris Clark-1) was born on Feb 19, 1922 in Chattanooga, Hamilton, Tennessee. She died on Aug 21, 2009 in Chattanooga, Hamilton, Tennessee. She married Marion Henry Delaney on Nov 24, 1941 in Ringgold, Catoosa, Georgia, son of Ralph Herman Delaney and Elizabeth Jones. (See the Delaney history for his details.) They divorced and remarried. She later

married a Mathis (first name unknown), then she married Bill Boyd. Her fourth husband was Don Allen, and her fifth husband was Ronald Aslinger.

Notes for Imogene May Clark: Obituary for Imogene Clark Aslinger Posted August 22, 2009, at http://www.chattanoogan.com/articles/article_157318.asp

Imogene Clark Aslinger, 87, of Hixson, Tennessee, died on Friday, Aug. 21, in a local hospital. Mrs. Aslinger was preceded in death by her husband, Ronald C. Aslinger.

She is survived by her children, William C. Aslinger, Donna L. Croft, both of Chattanooga, and Audie R. Aslinger of Ringgold; her grandchildren, Audrey Lacy, Samuel Leon Carr, Timothy R. Aslinger and Christina Aslinger; and four great-grandchildren.

Funeral services will be held at 1 p.m. on Tuesday, Aug. 25, at Heritage Funeral Home Chapel with Rev. Billy Dean officiating. Interment will follow in the Chattanooga National Cemetery. The family will receive friends from 2-4 and 6-8 p.m. on Monday, Aug. 24, at Heritage Funeral Home...

Children of Imogene May Clark and Marion Henry Delaney are:

    i.   Marion Richard Delaney, born Oct 27, 1942 in Chattanooga, Hamilton, Tennessee; died Sep 05, 2006 in Centre, Cherokee, Alabama.

Notes for Marion Richard Delaney:
CENTRE - - Jeffrey Dean Boyar, 63, passed away Tuesday, Sept. 5, 2006, at a local Centre hospital. Survivors include his wife, Brenda Boyar; his stepson Howard Duke; Howard's fiance, Tracey Wozniak; and Brenda's mother Margaret French; one sister, Paula Cope, of Cincinnati; and a brother, John Standridge, of Chattanooga.

Jeff was a longtime resident of Centre, where he was well known as "J.B." and for his DJ and karaoke performances. Jeff was well known also for his kind and generous nature and his ready sense of humor.

Memorial services will be held at Clear View Workship Center at a date to be determined with Paul Clark presiding. Perry Funeral Home, directing.

8.   ii.   Mary Elizabeth Delaney, born Sep 18, 1947 in Chattanooga, Hamilton, Tennessee; died Oct 25, 2006 in Sevier, Tennessee.
9.   iii.   Jerri Wayne Delaney

Child of Imogene May Clark and Bill Boyd is:

    i.   46.    William Aslinger

Child of Imogene May Clark and Don Allen is:

    i.   47.    Donna Allen Aslinger

Child of Imogene May Clark and Ronald Aslinger is:

    i.   48.    Audie Aslinger, born Private.

APPENDIX D – Genealogy 317

## Generation 6

8. Mary Elizabeth Delaney (Imogene May Clark-5, John Lenoir Clark-4, Gabriel Clark-3, Anderson Clark-2, Norris Clark-1)[30] was born on Sep 18, 1947 in Chattanooga, Hamilton, Tennessee. She died suddenly on Oct 25, 2006 in Sevier, Tennessee. She married Jack Dempsey Fortney Jr. on Apr 01, 1967 in Las Vegas, Clark, Nevada. He was born on Jul 22, 1943 in Berea, Madison, Kentucky. He died on Dec 14, 1986 in Dayton, Greene, Ohio. Paula married a second time, to Larry Cope.

    Notes for Mary Elizabeth Delaney:
    From The Cincinnati Enquirer, October 27, 2006:
    Paula A. Cope (nee Crippen), beloved wife of Larry E. Cope; devoted mother of Betha A. (Paul) Bollman and the late James Fortney; dear sister of John (Lynna Ruth) Standridge, Craig (Cheryl) Crippen, and the late Jeffrey (Brenda) Boyar; loving grandmother of Jacob, Benjamin, and Mary Bollman, also survived by 13 step-grandchildren and 1 great-grandchild. Oct. 25, 2006. Age 59 years. Residence Anderson Twp. Service at T. P. White & Sons Funeral Home, 2050 Beechmont Ave., Mt. Washington on Sat. Oct. 28, at 1 PM. Friends may visit on Sat. from 12-1 PM. Memorials to American Heart Association. Paula worked for Anthem Blue Cross for 33 years and was a proud member of the Red Hat Society.

    Children of Mary Elizabeth Delaney and Jack Dempsey Fortney Jr. are:

    i. Beth Andrea Fortney, born Private.

    ii. James Dana Fortney, born Dec 15, 1969 in Xenia, Greene, Ohio; died Jul 13, 1987 in Dayton, Greene, Ohio.

9. Jerri Wayne Delaney (Imogene May Clark-5, John Lenoir Clark-4, Gabriel Clark-3, Anderson Clark-2, Norris Clark-1) was born Private. He married Lynna Ruth Webb in Knoxville, Knox, Tennessee.

    Children of Jerri Wayne Delaney and Lynna Ruth Webb are:

    i. Adam Brendle Standridge, born Private.
    ii. Aaron Gabriel Standridge, born Private.

## Descendants of Norris Clark

### Sources

1. Ancestry Family Trees (Online publication - Provo, UT, USA: The Generations Network. Original data: Family Tree files submitted by Ancestry members.), Ancestry Family Trees. http://trees.ancestry.com/pt/AMTCitationRedir.aspx ?tid=10817194&pid=-487657901.

2. Ancestry.com, U.S. Federal Census Mortality Schedules, 1850-1880 (Online publication - Provo, UT, USA: The Generations Network, Inc., 2007.Original data - State Citation United States. Federal Mortality Census Schedules, 1850-1880 (formerly in the custody of the Daughters of the American Revolution), and Related Indexes, ), Census Place (City, County, State): Calhoun 16 Civil District, McMinn, Tennessee; Roll: T655_29; Page: 106; Enumeration District: 68; Line Number:. Birth date: abt 1802Birth place: North Carolina Death date: Nov 1880Death place: McMinn, Tennessee.

3. Ancestry.com, 1860 United States Federal Census (Online publication - Provo, UT, USA: The Generations Network, Inc., 2004.Original data - United States of America, Bureau of the Census. Eighth Census of the United States, 1860. Washington, D.C.: National Archives and Records Administration, 1860. M653, 1), Year: 1860; Census Place: District 17, McMinn, Tennessee; Roll: M653_1262; Page: 344; Image: 282. Birth date: abt 1799 Birth place: North Carolina Residence date: 1860 Residence place: District 17, McMinn, Tennessee.

4. Ancestry.com, 1850 United States Federal Census (Online publication - Provo, UT, USA: The Generations Network, Inc., 2005.Original data - United States of America, Bureau of the Census. Seventh Census of the United States, 1850. Washington, D.C.: National Archives and Records Administration, 1850. M432, ), Year: 1850; Census Place: Subdivision 23, McMinn, Tennessee; Roll: M432_887; Page: 314; Image: 715. Birth date: abt 1803 Birth place: North Carolina Residence date: 1850 Residence place: Subdivision 23, McMinn, Tennessee.

5. Ancestry Family Trees (Online publication - Provo, UT, USA: The Generations Network. Original data: Family Tree files submitted by Ancestry members.), Ancestry Family Trees. http://trees.ancestry.com/pt/AMTCitationRedir.aspx ?tid=10817194&pid=-491324390.

6. Ancestry.com, U.S. Federal Census Mortality Schedules, 1850-1880 (Provo, UT, USA, The Generations Network, Inc., 2008), www.ancestry. com, Database online. Record for Anderson Clark.

7. Ancestry.com and The Church of Jesus Christ of Latter-day Saints, 1880 United States Federal Census (Online publication - Provo, UT, USA: The Generations Network, Inc., 2005. 1880 U.S. Census Index provided by The Church of Jesus Christ of Latter-day Saints © Copyright 1999 Intellectual Reserve, Inc. All rights reserved. All use is subject to the limite), Year: 1880; Census Place: District 17, Mc Minn, Tennessee; Roll: T9_1268; Family History Film: 1255268; Page: 437.1000; Enumeration District: 68; Image:. Birth date: abt 1804 Birth place: North Carolina Residence date: 1880 Residence place: District 17, Mc Minn, Tennessee, United States.

## Appendix D – Genealogy

8. Ancestry.com, 1900 United States Federal Census (Online publication - Provo, UT, USA: The Generations Network, Inc., 2004.Original data - United States of America, Bureau of the Census. Twelfth Census of the United States, 1900. Washington, D.C.: National Archives and Records Administration, 1900. T623, ), Year: 1900; Census Place: Township 2, Choctaw Nation, Indian Territory; Roll: ; Page: ; Enumeration District:. Birth date: Birth place: Tennessee Residence date: 0Residence place: Township 2, Choctaw Nation, Indian Territory.

9. Ancestry.com, 1850 United States Federal Census (Online publication - Provo, UT, USA: The Generations Network, Inc., 2005.Original data - United States of America, Bureau of the Census. Seventh Census of the United States, 1850. Washington, D.C.: National Archives and Records Administration, 1850. M432, ), Year: 1850; Census Place: Subdivision 23, McMinn, Tennessee; Roll: M432_887; Page: 315; Image: 716. Birth date: abt 1834 Birth place: Tennessee Residence date: 1850 Residence place: Subdivision 23, McMinn, Tennessee.

10. Ancestry.com, 1870 United States Federal Census (Online publication - Provo, UT, USA: The Generations Network, Inc., 2003.Original data - 1870. United States. Ninth Census of the United States, 1870. Washington, D.C. National Archives and Records Administration. M593, RG29, 1, 761 rolls. Minnesota. Minnes), Year: 1870; Census Place: , ; Roll: M593. Birth date: abt 1832 Birth place: Residence date: 1870 Residence place: District 17, McMinn, Tennessee.

11. Ancestry.com and The Church of Jesus Christ of Latter-day Saints, 1880 United States Federal Census (Online publication - Provo, UT, USA: The Generations Network, Inc., 2005. 1880 U.S. Census Index provided by The Church of Jesus Christ of Latter-day Saints © Copyright 1999 Intellectual Reserve, Inc. All rights reserved. All use is subject to the limite), Year: 1880; Census Place: District 17, Mc Minn, Tennessee; Roll: T9_1268; Family History Film: 1255268; Page: 437.1000; Enumeration District: 68; Image:. Birth date: abt 1833 Birth place: Tennessee Residence date: 1880 Residence place: District 17, Mc Minn, Tennessee, United States.

12. Ancestry.com and The Church of Jesus Christ of Latter-day Saints, 1880 United States Federal Census (Provo, UT, USA, The Generations Network, Inc., 2005), www.ancestry.com, Database online. District 17, Mc Minn, Tennessee, ED 68, roll T9_1268, page 437.1000, image. Record for Gabriel Clark.

13. Ancestry Family Trees (Online publication - Provo, UT, USA: The Generations Network. Original data: Family Tree files submitted by Ancestry members.), Ancestry Family Trees. http://trees.ancestry.com/pt/AMTCitationRedir.aspx?tid=10817194&pid=-491328791.

14. Ancestry.com, 1850 United States Federal Census (Provo, UT, USA, The Generations Network, Inc., 2005), www.ancestry.com, Database online. Subdivision 23, McMinn, Tennessee, roll M432_887, page 316, image 719. Record for Elizabeth Swofford.

15. Ancestry.com, 1920 United States Federal Census (Online publication - Provo, UT, USA: The Generations Network, Inc., 2005. For details on the contents of the film numbers, visit the following NARA web page: NARA.

Note: Enumeration Districts 819-839 on roll 323 (Chicago City.Original data - United States), Year: 1920; Census Place: Rossville, Walker, Georgia; Roll: T625_281; Page: 13A; Enumeration District: 188; Image: 554. Birth date: abt 1880 Birth place: Tennessee Residence date: 1920 Residence place: Rossville, Walker, Georgia.

16. Ancestry.com, World War I Draft Registration Cards, 1917-1918 (Online publication - Provo, UT, USA: The Generations Network, Inc., 2005.Original data - United States, Selective Service System. World War I Selective Service System Draft Registration Cards, 1917-1918. Washington, D.C.: National Archives and Records Admi), Registration Location: Atoka County, Oklahoma; Roll: 1851605; Draft Board: 0. Birth date: 27 Dec 1877 Birth place: Residence date: Residence place: Atoka, Oklahoma.

17. Ancestry.com, 1910 United States Federal Census (Online publication - Provo, UT, USA: The Generations Network, Inc., 2006. For details on the contents of the film numbers, visit the following NARA web page: NARA. Original data - United States of America, Bureau of the Census. Thirteenth Census of the Unit), Year: 1910; Census Place: Wilson, Atoka, Oklahoma; Roll: T624_1242; Page: 15B; Enumeration District: 11; Image: 1159. Birth date: abt 1878 Birth place: Tennessee Residence date: 1910 Residence place: Wilson, Atoka, Oklahoma.

18. Ancestry.com, 1920 United States Federal Census (Online publication - Provo, UT, USA: The Generations Network, Inc., 2005. For details on the contents of the film numbers, visit the following NARA web page: NARA. Note: Enumeration Districts 819-839 on roll 323 (Chicago City.Original data - United States), Year: 1920; Census Place: Atoka, Atoka, Oklahoma; Roll: T625_1452; Page: 14A; Enumeration District: 8; Image: 591. Birth date: abt 1873 Birth place: Tennessee Residence date: 1920 Residence place: Atoka, Atoka, Oklahoma.

19. Ancestry.com, Tennessee State Marriages, 1780-2002 (Online publication - Provo, UT, USA: The Generations Network, Inc., 2008.Original data - Tennessee State Marriages, 1780-2002. Nashville, TN, USA: Tennessee State Library and Archives. Microfilm.Original data: Tennessee State Marriages, 1780-2002. Nashville), Marriage date: 15 Feb 1896 Marriage place: McMinn Residence date: Residence place: Tennessee.

20. Ancestry Family Trees (Online publication - Provo, UT, USA: The Generations Network. Original data: Family Tree files submitted by Ancestry members.), Ancestry Family Trees. http://trees.ancestry.com/pt/AMTCitationRedir.aspx ?tid=10817194&pid=-573232844.

21. Ancestry World Tree: DOLLAHITE Family (Alabama Branch); http://awt. ancestry.com/cgi-bin/igm.cgi?op=GET&db=bdollahite2003&id=I47.

22. Ancestry.com, Social Security Death Index (Provo, UT, USA, The Generations Network, Inc., 2009), www.ancestry.com, Database online. Record for Mary Clark.

23. Ancestry.com, Social Security Death Index (Online publication - Provo, UT, USA: The Generations Network, Inc., 2009.Original data - Social Security Administration. Social Security Death Index, Master File. Social Security Administration.Original data: Social Security Administration. Social Security), Number: 413-82-5681; Issue State: Tennessee; Issue Date: 1965. Birth date:

# APPENDIX D – Genealogy 321

19 Aug 1881 Birth place: Death date: Jan 1967 Death place: Chattanooga, Hamilton, Tennessee, United States of America.

24. Ancestry.com, Social Security Death Index (Online publication - Provo, UT, USA: The Generations Network, Inc., 2009.Original data - Social Security Administration. Social Security Death Index, Master File. Social Security Administration.Original data: Social Security Administration. Social Security), Number: 408-24-1090; Issue State: Tennessee; Issue Date: Before 1951. Birth date: 3 Apr 1900 Birth place: Death date: Oct 1992 Death place: Chattanooga, Hamilton, Tennessee, United States of America.

25. Ancestry.com, Social Security Death Index (Online publication - Provo, UT, USA: The Generations Network, Inc., 2009.Original data - Social Security Administration. Social Security Death Index, Master File. Social Security Administration.Original data: Social Security Administration. Social Security), Number: 411-03-2322; Issue State: Tennessee; Issue Date: Before 1951. Birth date: 5 Feb 1902 Birth place: Death date: Jul 1984 Death place: Chattanooga, Hamilton, Tennessee, United States of America.

26. Ancestry.com, Social Security Death Index (Online publication - Provo, UT, USA: The Generations Network, Inc., 2009.Original data - Social Security Administration. Social Security Death Index, Master File. Social Security Administration.Original data: Social Security Administration. Social Security), Number: 411-01-2743; Issue State: Tennessee; Issue Date: Before 1951. Birth date: 29 Feb 1904 Birth place: Death date: Nov 1973 Death place: Gadsden, Etowah, Alabama, United States of America.

27. Ancestry Family Trees (Online publication - Provo, UT, USA: The Generations Network. Original data: Family Tree files submitted by Ancestry members.), Ancestry Family Trees. http://trees.ancestry.com/pt/AMTCitationRedir.aspx ?tid=10817194&pid=-559648004.

28. National Cemetery Administration, U.S. Veterans Gravesites, ca.1775-2006 (Provo, UT, USA, The Generations Network, Inc., 2006), www.ancestry.com, Database online. Record for Marion H Delaney.

29. Ancestry.com, Social Security Death Index (Provo, UT, USA, The Generations Network, Inc., 2009), www.ancestry.com, Database online. Record for Marion H. Delaney.

30. Ancestry Family Trees (Online publication - Provo, UT, USA: The Generations Network. Original data: Family Tree files submitted by Ancestry members.), Ancestry Family Trees. http://trees.ancestry.com/pt/AMTCitationRedir.aspx ?tid=10817194&pid=-564557673.

## L2

### CHATTANOOGA FREE PRESS
### LOCAL COLUMNS
### Sunday May 21, 1995

CHATTANOOGA STORY

Jones Family Pioneers in Rhea, Hamilton

By John Wilson

Benjamin Jones made his way from his native Wales to become a pioneer settler of Rhea and Hamilton counties. Most of his sons moved away, but his daughters married into the neighboring McDonald and Gamble families at Sale Creek. Another prominent Jones pioneer of Rhea and Hamilton was Jeremiah Jones, who was Hamilton County's first register of deeds.

Benjamin Jones was born in 1763, the oldest of six children of Henry Jones and Nancy Anderson. Henry Jones was born in 1734 and Nancy Anderson in 1736. They came to America when Benjamin was seven. The Jones family settled near Baltimore near the Odells at the Plains of Paran. Benjamin Jones married Providence Odell at Baltimore on Dec. 13, 1786. Her parents were John Odell and Providence Baker. John Odell was born in 1737 and died at Baltimore in 1818. His parents were William and Elizabeth Odell.

During the Revolutionary War, Benjamin Jones served with the Maryland Militia. He remained near Baltimore for many years but in 1809 he sold Ellis Jones 483 acres at the Plains of Paran. However, he retained some land that was leased out, including a portion of the area where the city of Baltimore was built. For many years afterwards; some of his Tennessee descendants tried to collect on these leases, but the courts ruled against them.

It was 1814 when Benjamin and Providence Jones moved their family to Sale Creek, which was then within the Rhea County lines. Benjamin Jones lived until June of 1856. He is buried at the Hutchinson cemetery near Coulterville. Providence Odell Jones is buried in the graveyard of the old Hiawassee Garrison.

Their oldest son Henry, lived only a year. The second son, John married Anna Patterson, daughter of the pioneer Robert Patterson. After John Jones did in the 1830s, Anna Patterson Jones married Robert Cozby. He died in the 1840s. One of her sons was Robert Patterson Jones, who married Jenny Ingersoll. A daughter was Mary E. Jones, who married Daniel Hamill.

Thomas A. Jones, a son of Benjamin Jones, moved to Virginia. He had a granddaughter, Ada Jones Lee, who was a Methodist Episcopal missionary to India and was decorated by King George for special service to the people of India. Benjamin Franklin Jones, another son of Benjamin Jones was born in 1799 in Baltimore. He married Jane Lauderdale, the daughter of James Lauderdale Sr. Benjamin F. Jones moved to Bradley County in 1840. Anderson Jones, the youngest son, lived in Rhea County, then moved to Texas. He married Martha Shelton and then Martha Johnson.

The daughters included Nancy who married Soloman Watts and moved to Zanesville, Ohio, and Sally Keturah (Kitty), who was born in 1801, married James McDonald, while Betsy married Robert L. Gamble. Betsy Jones Gamble attended

## APPENDIX D – Genealogy

the first camp meeting held in Rhea County and was a longtime member of the Cumberland Presbyterian Church. James and Kitty McDonald were also devout Cumberland Presbyterians.

The McDonalds named one of their sons Benjamin Jones McDonald, while a daughter was Providence Jane. Another daughter was Kitty McDonald. Benjamin Jones McDonald named one of his son, Franklin Jones McDonald. He was the father of Roy McDonald, founder of the [Chattanooga News] Free Press. [He was also founder of BlueCross BlueShield of Tennessee – J.B.S.]

Jeremiah H. Jones, according to old bible records, was born April 18, 1791. His wife Delilah, was born Aug. 15, 1787. As a young man he moved to Rhea County, where his neighbors about 1812 were listed as Seymore Ketchins, Alexander Watson, Mrs. Carter, George Walker, Allen Murphree, David Beck, Joseph Williams and John A. Smith. They lived by the Tennessee River at Yellow Creek.

Jeremiah Jones took part in the Creek Indian War in 1813. He was one of Hamilton County's "765" original settlers," taking up a large tract of the Soddy area. He was a commissioner for the town of Dallas and served as a justice of the peace. Jeremiah Jones was described as "a scholar of some prominence in his day, and an efficient accountant."

In 1826, he paid only $250 for 100 acres lying by Soddy Creek and extending to the foot of Walden's Ridge. This was part of the huge property owned by Charles McClung and James Cozby. Six years later, Jones was able to get $3, 100 for this tract from John Myers. In 1839 he sold 160 acres to Alexander McDaniel of Jefferson County, Tenn., for $2, 000. The following year, he sold another 160 acres at Soddy to Evan Parker for $800.

Jeremiah Jones died Oct. 27, 1857. Delilah Jones had died Oct. 8, 1848. Their sons included Rufus Gains Jones (born 1823) and Percival H. Jones (born in 1827). Rufus Jones married Elizabeth Ann Varnell in 1849. He was deputy clerk and master from 1855 to 1860, then was a clerk and master at the start of the Civil War. During the war, he served under Col. J.E. MacGowan on the Union side as a bookkeeper. In 1880, he was elected city auditor of Chattanooga. He also was a bookkeeper for the Lookout Water Co. and the W.O. Peeples and Co. He was later an official of the Nashville, Chattanooga and St. Louis Railroad. The Rufus Jones family lived at Tyner. Rufus Jones died in 1888 and he and his wife are buried at the Varnell Cemetery at the Volunteer Army Ammunition Plant. Elizabeth Ann Varnell Jones died in 1908.

Percival H. Jones resided mainly in North Georgia, first living in Whitfield County, then Catoosa County at Graysville. He was living on Missionary Ridge at the time of his brother's death in 1888.

Rufus Jones had an adopted son, John Jefferson Jones, who was a furniture maker. He also had a son, Francis Marion (Frank) Jones, who lived from 1871 to 1939. He married Emily Olivia Chapman. Their children were Aubrey Everet who married Myrtle Hewit, Rufus V. Who married Clara Ledbetter, Anna Belle who married Lavoy Mitchell Howard, Carl Chapman who married Jessie Roberts, Elizabeth Hardwick who married Ralph Delaney, Eugene Lemuel who married Grace Plumlee, and Lloyd Earnest who died when he was five. Architect Edwin Howard is a grandson of Frank Jones and great-great grandson of Jeremiah H. Jones.

# Appendix E –
# Bibliography

## The Delaney Kids~ Bought and Paid For

Stolen Babies

Actors: Lea Thompson, Kathleen Quinlan, Mary Nell Santacroce, Mary Tyler Moore, Brett Rice, See more

Director: Eric Laneuville

US Theatrical Release Date: March 25, 1993

Production Company: Lifetime Television

ASIN: B00004CNL0

The Baby Thief: The Untold Story of Georgia Tann, the Baby Seller Who Corrupted Adoption by Barbara Bisantz Raymond

Publisher: Carroll & Graf (April 28, 2007)

ISBN-10: 0786719443

ISBN-13: 978-0786719440

Ireland: A Novel by Frank Delaney

Publisher: HarperCollins (February 15, 2005)

ISBN-10: 0060563486

ISBN-13: 978-0060563486

How the Irish Saved Civilization (Hinges of History) by Thomas Cahill

Publisher: Nan A. Talese; 1st edition (February 15, 1995)

ISBN: 0385418485

A Short History of Ireland by Sean McMahon

Publisher: Mercier Press (Feb 1997)

ISBN: 1856351378

The Course of Irish History by T. W. Moody and F. X. Martin

Publisher: Court Wayne Press; Rev&Enlrgd edition (March 1995)

ISBN: 1570980152

Mick: The Real Michael Collins by Peter Hart

Publisher: Viking Press (2006)

ISBN: 067003147X

## Appendix E – Bibliography

Your Right to Privacy and Children's Rights/Family Law A Selective Bibliography by Sandra S. Klein
Legal Reference Services Quarterly
Volume: 13 Issue: 4
ISSN: 0270-319X Pub Date: 8/4/1994

The Story of the Irish Race by Seumas MacManus
Publisher: The Devin-Adair Company (1921)
ISBN: 0-517-064081

The Irish Americans: A History, by Jay P. Dolan
Publisher: Bloomsbury Press (2008)
ISBN-13: 978-1-59691-419-3
ISBN-10: 1-59691-419-X

The Fourth Turning, by William Strauss, Neil Howe
Publisher: Bantam Books (1997)
ISBN-13: 9780767900461

A Long Long Way, by Sebastian Barry
Publisher: Penguin Group (USA) (2005)
ISBN-13: 9780143035091

The Hero with a Thousand Faces, by Joseph Campbell
Publisher: New World Library (1949)
ISBN: 978-1577315933

Hamilton County Pioneers, by John Wilson
Self published (1998)

Made in the USA
Lexington, KY
27 April 2012